Praise for *Reimagining Nonprofits and Philanthropy*

"What would it be like to have a friendly, smart and funny unicorn come over and sit next to you and chat for a couple of hours about your life working in nonprofits? Vu Le is that unicorn and his book is full of fun and extremely on-target, pointed essays on grantwriting, budgets, burning bridges, and more."

—Jan Masaoka
Co-chair, Philanthropy Project

"*Reimagining Nonprofits and Philanthropy* by Vu Le provides a vision of what is possible even though the problems facing these sectors seem intractable. Bold, honest, and instructive, this book is essential reading in the current political climate where institutions are incentivized to be risk averse and unimaginative."

—Alice Wong
Author of *Year of the Tiger: An Activist's Life*

"*Reimagining Nonprofits and Philanthropy* delivers a bold, powerful vision for transforming a vital sector, and compelling, relatable stories that bring these ideas to life. Vu Le is a trusted voice and a gifted storyteller, who writes about complex challenges in a way that is accessible and urgent. This book is essential reading, arriving at a pivotal moment when we need nonprofits and philanthropy operating at their best to meet the challenges of our times and build a more just future."

—Dimple Abichandani
Author of *A New Era of Philanthropy: Ten Practices to Transform Wealth into a More Just and Sustainable Future: How We Fund in Times of Crisis and Opportunity*

"Whether you have been in nonprofit for a day, a decade or a lifetime, this will push your thinking, offer new solutions, and remind you why we all love this hard work we do."

—Jane Leu
Founder and Board Member of Smarter Good,
Co-author of *Unicorns Unite: How Nonprofits and Foundations Can Build EPIC Partnership*

"To those hoarding wealth and power, Vu Le is Mojo Jojo – a villain relentlessly repeating the obvious: 'Invest in community-led solutions! General operating, multi-year funding NOW!' But to those of us in the nonprofit sector, Vu is our rainbow-hued, values-driven Care Bear, radiating justice, joy, and hummus-fueled truth. Through sharp wit and deep conviction, he reminds us of the WHY in our work, especially when it's hard. There is no doubt that our nonprofit sector is stronger and more equitable because he has the audacity to use his voice. Buy the book and join our fight! (But seriously, he needs more hummus.)"
—**Nonoko Sato**
President and CEO, Minnesota Council of Nonprofits

"With his signature blend of sharp analysis and irreverent humor, delivers the wake-up call our sector desperately needs, challenging us to shed outdated practices and embrace the audacious vision required to create real change. This isn't just another nonprofit how-to book—it's a revolutionary roadmap for transforming our sector into the resilient justice-driven force it was meant to be. "
—**Beth Kanter**
Speaker, Trainer, and Author, *The Smart Nonprofit: Staying Human-Centered in an Automated World*

"Vu Le, the ultimate nonprofit nerd and a true visionary, brings his trademark heart, authenticity, and laugh-out-loud humor to his new book, making it an essential read for anyone navigating the nonprofit world."
—**Kevin Dean**
President and CEO, Tennessee Nonprofit Network

"A book that says what so many of us have been thinking. Bold, brilliant, hilarious, and unapologetically honest."
—**Nichole June Maher**
President and CEO, Inatai Foundation

"With wit, sharp cultural references, and a healthy dose of tough love, *Reimagining Nonprofits and Philanthropy: Unlocking the Full Potential of a Vital and Complex Sector* offers both strategic insight and a timely call to action. Vu Le's manifesto stitches together years of wisdom from Nonprofit AF with progressive, equity-centered practices, challenging the sector to finally get our *ish* together. Equal parts analysis and rallying cry, this book invites nonprofit professionals to reimagine our work as a path toward collective liberation — all while keeping our humanity and humor intact."

—**Carly Hare**
(Pawnee/Yankton) Philathroelder,
Equity Auntie, and CEO at Headwaters Foundation

"For the many fans of Vu Le's blog Nonprofit AF, we finally have his witty and searing observations in binge-able form. *Reimagining Nonprofits and Philanthropy* demonstrates how much the nonprofit sector needs Vu's voice, especially during these turbulent times. He has proven to be our inspirational coach, nonprofit therapist, industry Greek chorus, all-seeing court jester, and the kid who yells that the emperor is (*gasp*) naked. He is asking us to raise our standards so let us buy this book in bulk and at full price, read it in community, hold each other accountable to changing at least three behaviors, and buy him massage sessions. He's given us a blueprint, so let the man rest: It's our collective turn now to do more and better."

—**Angie Kim**
President and CEO, Center for Cultural Innovation

"This book masterfully examines the philanthropic sector and offers lived and learned lessons on how we can reshape not only the sector, but an equitable world. It is a must-read for the sector, which is in transition."

—**Monique Curry-Mims, MBA, MSEd, CAP®**
Founder, Civic Capital Consulting and
Co-Host of Beyond Philanthropy

"Irrepressibly charming and searingly honest, Vu Le's comprehensive look at the nonprofit sector is a critical addition to the study of what goes right - and what could be done better - in the world of philanthropy. His love and passion for the people and causes that make up the nonprofit arena is palpable, even as he dispenses solutions to so many of the challenges of the sector. From boards to fundraising, philanthropists to democracy, Le's book is a must-read for anyone who cares about making our world more beautiful, peaceful, healthy, and just."

—**Maria Kolby-Wolfe**
President and CEO, Washington Women's Foundation

"With love and humor, Vu Le offers us a way forward."

—**Crystal Hayling**
Philanthropy Guide and Mentor

"You know that kid in the Emperor's Clothes – the one who shouts, 'He's naked!'? In the nonprofit sector, that truth-teller is Vu Le, calling BS on the sacred cows that make nonprofit work so frustrating. Aiming his trademark wit, passion, and insight at the systems that keep changemakers stuck, Vu shows a path to what is possible. Whether you work in a nonprofit, a foundation, or you provide capacity building, you owe it to your community to read every word of this book and put it to work."

—**Hildy Gottlieb**
Co-founder, Creating the Future

"Vu has penned a blueprint for funders that is as practical as it is irreverent, as fiery as it is funny, and as critical as a parachute when we've fallen off a cliff. Which we have. In a time where nonsense and misinformation reigns supreme, Vu gives us the opposite: sense, clarity, and a vision for how to turn falling into flying."

—**Pia Infante**
Co-executive Director, Trust-Based Philanthropy Project

Reimagining Nonprofits *and* Philanthropy

Vu Le

Reimagining Nonprofits *and* Philanthropy

UNLOCKING THE FULL POTENTIAL OF A VITAL AND COMPLEX SECTOR

WILEY

Copyright © 2026 by Vu Le. All rights reserved.

Published by John Wiley & Sons, Inc., Hoboken, New Jersey.
Published simultaneously in Canada.

The manufacturer's authorized representative according to the EU General Product Safety Regulation is Wiley-VCH GmbH, Boschstr. 12, 69469 Weinheim, Germany, e-mail: Product_Safety@wiley.com.

No part of this publication may be reproduced, stored in a retrieval system, or transmitted in any form or by any means, electronic, mechanical, photocopying, recording, scanning, or otherwise, except as permitted under Section 107 or 108 of the 1976 United States Copyright Act, without either the prior written permission of the Publisher, or authorization through payment of the appropriate per-copy fee to the Copyright Clearance Center, Inc., 222 Rosewood Drive, Danvers, MA 01923, (978) 750-8400, fax (978) 750-4470, or on the web at www.copyright.com. Requests to the Publisher for permission should be addressed to the Permissions Department, John Wiley & Sons, Inc., 111 River Street, Hoboken, NJ 07030, (201) 748-6011, fax (201) 748-6008, or online at http://www.wiley.com/go/permission.

Trademarks: Wiley and the Wiley logo are trademarks or registered trademarks of John Wiley & Sons, Inc. and/or its affiliates in the United States and other countries and may not be used without written permission. All other trademarks are the property of their respective owners. John Wiley & Sons, Inc. is not associated with any product or vendor mentioned in this book.

Limit of Liability/Disclaimer of Warranty: While the publisher and author have used their best efforts in preparing this book, they make no representations or warranties with respect to the accuracy or completeness of the contents of this book and specifically disclaim any implied warranties of merchantability or fitness for a particular purpose. No warranty may be created or extended by sales representatives or written sales materials. The advice and strategies contained herein may not be suitable for your situation. You should consult with a professional where appropriate. Further, readers should be aware that websites listed in this work may have changed or disappeared between when this work was written and when it is read. Neither the publisher nor authors shall be liable for any loss of profit or any other commercial damages, including but not limited to special, incidental, consequential, or other damages.

For general information on our other products and services or for technical support, please contact our Customer Care Department within the United States at (800) 762-2974, outside the United States at (317) 572-3993 or fax (317) 572-4002.

Wiley also publishes its books in a variety of electronic formats. Some content that appears in print may not be available in electronic formats. For more information about Wiley products, visit our web site at www.wiley.com.

Library of Congress Cataloging-in-Publication Data is Available:

ISBN: 9781394313129 (Cloth)
ISBN: 9781394313136 (ePub)
ISBN: 9781394313143 (ePDF)

Cover Design: Paul McCarthy
Cover Art: © Shuttershock | Avector

SKY10124759_082625

Contents

	Introduction	1
Chapter 1	A Love Letter to Nonprofit and Philanthropy	9
Chapter 2	The Nine Horsemen of Nonprofit and Philanthropic Ineffectiveness	25
Chapter 3	Reimagining Fundraising and Donor Engagement	43
Chapter 4	Governance and Boards	63
Chapter 5	Reimagining Leadership and Leadership Structures	83
Chapter 6	Building Nonprofit Capacity to Fight Fascism	99
Chapter 7	Advocacy, Community Organizing, and the Levers of Power for Systems Change	117
Chapter 8	Reimagining Philanthropy, Foundations, and Funder–Nonprofit Dynamics	133
Chapter 9	Reimagining Hiring Practices	155

Chapter 10 Reimagining Work Culture	171
Chapter 11 Don't Bring Spreadsheets to a Knife Fight: Using Data to Effectively Advance Justice	187
Chapter 12 Diversity, Equity, and Inclusion (DEI)	203
Chapter 13 The Barriers Holding Back Change and What to Do About Them	219
Appendix A Principles of Community-Centric Fundraising	*231*
Appendix B White Moderation Checklist	*237*
Notes	*241*
Acknowledgements	*255*
About the Author	*259*
Index	*261*

Introduction

When life itself seems lunatic, who knows where madness lies?
To surrender dreams, this may be madness...
Too much sanity may be madness!
But maddest of all is to see life as it is and not as it should be.
—Don Quixote

When my family and I arrived in the United States, I was an eight-year-old boy with a terrible haircut, thanks to my father, who had fought against North Vietnam and had been put into reeducation camp. Despite all the challenges he had gone through, Dad still retained unproven confidence in his haircutting skills and still managed to carry his rusty pair of scissors past the refugee camps in the Philippines, across the Pacific Ocean, and through multiple states. He was saving our family desperately needed money.

The result, however, was that every month, at least those first few years, my brothers and I had to sit and endure the butchering of our locks, watching in horror as he transformed our acceptably aloof—dare I say even cool—just-got-out-of-bed looks into monstrosities that had me mocked and ridiculed at school. At least, I think it was mockery and ridicule. I didn't understand English back then. But the pointing and laughing were easy clues.

I dreaded going to school. Each morning, I watched *Care Bears*, finding comfort in the fluffy, colorful bears, who each had their own personality and unique skills. They lived in a village high above in the sky, in the clouds. When their community faced great danger—from a group of villains that included a furry pig/potato hybrid named Beastly—they did the "Care Bear Stare," where they lined up in a row, activated the clover or sunshine or other symbol on their stomachs, and produced a powerful rainbow in unison that drove away the bad guys and sometimes healed or fixed whatever had been broken.

I guess that may have been the seed of my nonprofit career. A seed that was watered by other experiences during those first few months in the United States. I think of the morning my mother, trying to motivate me to go to school despite the constant teasing, sent me off with two quarters so I could buy a treat for myself. When I stopped at the convenience store and realized the snacks I wanted would cost more than fifty cents, I broke down, cursing the heavens and weeping in despair. Then I got up, raised my fist defiantly, and vowed to get my mom to double the amount she would give me the next day. And that is my fundraiser origin story.

Jokes aside, it was the kindness shown to my family by the various organizations that would nudge me down this path. They rallied people to bring us pots and pans, forks and spoons, and warm clothing to protect us from a cold we had never imagined, let alone experienced before in our village in the mountains of Vietnam. They helped my parents find jobs and enroll me and my two brothers in school. They hooked us up with a sponsor family who took us for the first time for pizza and to see *The Nutcracker*, a night we'll always remember for how out of place the five of us felt amidst the unfamiliar colors and sounds and warm cheesy gooeyness.

The kindness my family received had a profound impact on me. These people we didn't know and could barely communicate with, organized by nonprofit organizations we had never heard of, funded by donors and funders we had never met, through their generosity and warmth, restored hope and community to my small family who had left everyone we knew and loved behind. I wanted to pay it forward.

So I went to college, studied psychology, and got a master's in social work, focusing on socioeconomic development, community organizing, and advocacy. I was ready to join the nonprofit sector, put into practice everything I had learned in grad school, and make the world a better place. Though I sometimes strayed from the path, I always knew this sector was where I was meant to be. I wanted to help people the way so many had helped my family. I wanted to build a community. I wanted to be a Care Bear.

I landed a position working at a small organization called the Vietnamese Friendship Association (VFA, now Kandelia), which focused on helping Vietnamese and other recent immigrant kids succeed academically, as well as helping their parents navigate the school system. It had a budget of $14,000, an office the size of a walk-in closet, and several hamburger wrappers someone had put in the solitary filing cabinet.

And I was the only full-time staff member. I had been dropped there by an AmeriCorps-funded program in DC that placed young up-and-coming leaders into various Vietnamese-focused nonprofits across the United States to help them run their programs and strengthen their infrastructure and effectiveness, with the concurrent goal of having many of these young leaders rise through the ranks in the sector. The program drew idealistic kids who defied their families' hopes and dreams that they would end up a doctor or lawyer or engineer, idealists who wanted to make the world better and who were okay with subsisting on spaghetti and bánh mìs several meals a week.

The reality of the nonprofit sector, however, was very different than the academically challenging but comfortable bubble that was my grad school experience. Some of the foundational skills I had learned were very helpful: active listening, empathy, facilitating meetings, crashing various events for free food. But much of the more technical stuff—board governance, fundraising, leadership, and so on—I found was not always applicable in the ways I had been trained.

I remember the first time I wrote a grant proposal. Being an ESL kid who was constantly made fun of for not fully understanding English, I was determined to conquer this weakness, and I worked hard at it by reading all the time, and I prided myself on being a competent writer and always got good grades on term papers and others written assignments. It was a jolt to my ego to get the draft of my first grant proposal back from my mentor. "Vu," he said, "this is a grant proposal.

You have to use grant language. Basically, stop being so flowery and just get to the point." On reflection, maybe including several references to *Don Quixote* by Miguel Cervantes was too much.

There would be so many more experiences like this, where my lack of skills and experience, combined with my naiveté about how this sector worked, made me doubt myself and whether I had chosen the right path. I had envisioned, for example, that nonprofits would be supportive of and collaborative with one another, but that didn't always prove to be true. During what I thought was a friendly one-on-one with the executive director of an organization with a similar mission, I could feel palpable disdain.

"How long are you going to stick around?" she asked, "We've seen enough people parachute into our community and then leave when things get difficult." I reassured her that I was not going anywhere, that I would stay for as long as I was needed. During year two of my placement, I raised enough money that the board hired me on after my program ended and, at the grizzled age of 26, I became the organization's first executive director.

For all the prestige of the title, the ED position came with even more challenges. The Hunger Games were relentless. At an event once, I sat down at a table with a colleague who was a major gifts officer at another organization. She was sitting with a nice elderly couple, who I would realize later were two of her major donors. We had a great conversation where I learned they loved Vietnamese food. "I know a great restaurant," I said, "we should all go sometime." The elderly couple turned to my colleague and said, "That sounds fun! Perhaps you can connect us all over email." She never did. At another event, months later, I ran into her, and she half-jokingly introduced me by saying, "This is Vu, the guy who tried to *poach two of my major donors.*"

Even when funding was going well, there were frustrations. There was the time a staff member and I were in the conference room, figuratively bashing our heads against the wall because a funder wanted to set limits on how much per hour we could pay the tutors in our after-school program, but also refused to pony up for planning hours. And the time my board voted down a policy to provide paid family leave, citing the lack of resources, a risk-averse position I knew to be unfounded, as I was the one writing the budget and leading the fundraising.

The most difficult and eye-opening challenges I encountered involved many of the practices our sector considered standard best practices. Not only did they fail for organizations led by marginalized communities, but they were also often harmful and counterproductive. Foundations, which are mostly led by white leaders, for instance, are more likely to fund white-led organizations. Individual donors, who are also mostly white, often respond better to leaders who understand how to navigate dominant culture, and these leaders tend to be white. Capacity-building strategies, meanwhile, are focused on getting orgs led by communities of color to conform to behave like white-led orgs. All of this has coalesced into a series of entangled dynamics that have left organizations and communities like mine behind.

In 2014, after nine years as the executive director at VFA, I stepped down and became the founding ED of Rainier Valley Corps (RVC, now standing for Rooted in Vibrant Communities), a capacity-building and leadership organization that strives to support leaders of color, strengthen the capacity of organizations led by communities of color, and foster collaboration among marginalized communities. As I continued to navigate the sector, and as I met more brilliant thinkers and became exposed to different ideas and had more time to reflect, I realized several things. Top among them is that our sector is awesome and as vital as air. I love our field and the people in it. I love our passion for making life that much easier, neighborhoods that much more beautiful, existence that much less lonely. I love our idiosyncrasies. Our creativity. Our ability to find humor in bleak times and joy despite heartaches. Our righteous anger at the constant injustices that many of us have dedicated our lives to fighting. Even our proclivity for having hummus at every meeting.

I love that despite relentless challenges with funding and other barriers, we keep going. On some of the disheartening days—of which there were many—I think of leaving the sector and opening a stand at the farmer's market selling homemade vegan jerky or something. But I always get pulled back by the fierce determination of my colleagues and the people we serve, and the gravity of the collective mission we are trying to accomplish together.

I also realized that the existence of our sector, comprising both nonprofit and philanthropy, is problematic. It signifies that our world is deeply flawed and filled with inequity and injustice. In an ideal world, wealthy corporations and individuals would compensate their workers equitably and pay their fair share of taxes, government would represent its people and take care of them, neighbors would look out for one another and vote for what's best for the collective, and the negative effects of capitalism would be mitigated. We would not have all the problems we are seeing in the world, nor the excessively wealthy people and foundations who determine, based on their whims and interests, which issues get attention and who in society is deserving of being helped.

In such a reality, most nonprofits and foundations would have no reason to exist; the only ones operating might be arts and cultural organizations, dedicated to preserving and expanding our humanity. It is a reality we need to dream into being and work toward. But often, like fish unaware of the water they swim in, we fall into a pattern where we forget why we are here in the first place. Fundraisers forget that they raise money to end injustice, not just to meet or exceed year-end goals. Funders forget that nonprofits are partners in an effort to make the world more equitable, not parasites and freeloaders begging for handouts. Board members, EDs, and CEOs forget that their purpose is to achieve a collective vision, not prioritize their org's survival.

To achieve such a reality will take time, dedication, and a willingness to let go of many philosophies and practices that we have been so used to, that have been passed down for hundreds of years. It will require us to dream bigger and be bolder and own our full power. It will also require some difficult and uncomfortable discussions, including about white supremacy and white moderation and how each of us is complicit in perpetuating the injustices we are trying to fight.

Some years ago, I read a study about groups of kids who were asked to draw a fish. One group of kids was shown a drawing of a fish as an example, whereas the other was not shown any drawings at all. The kids who were not exposed to someone else's version of a fish illustration were very creative in their own drawings, while the kids who saw the drawing tended to produce similar versions of that drawing.

(I can't seem to find this study, and I might have hallucinated the whole thing during a stressful fundraising gala season.) The point is that we have fish archetypes passed down over the years: fundraising fish, HR fish, accounting fish, board fish, leadership fish, and so on. It is hard for us to think and do things differently because these archetypes have been ingrained in our minds. For so long, we have been taught—by school, leadership management programs, supervisors, mentors, conference speakers, and so on—that these are the ways to do things. And in some ways, they work, but often not as effectively as our communities need them to, and certainly not always in the best interests of the communities most affected by systemic injustice.

The aim of this book is to encourage us to draw new fish, so to speak, new and better and more equitable fish by examining the old archetypes and discussing some new ways of doing things. We'll talk to people and organizations across the sector who have been radical in their experimentation in different areas. These remarkable people, orgs, foundations, and movements are doing awesome, innovative, and possibly blasphemous stuff. Through them, we'll see that nonprofits can support one another and even raise money for one another; that boards, staff, and CEOs/EDs can share power; and that funders and nonprofits can take courageous stands against injustice.

This book includes many examples of people and organizations drawing new fish. Each chapter focuses on a particular topic, so feel free to hop around to whatever is most relevant to you and your work. Feel free to disagree with anything you read here. Our sector tends to attract very nice people, which means that we often don't feel comfortable with conflict. I encourage constructive disagreement because thinking critically and debating what works and what doesn't, especially with an equity lens, is how we will be able to fully unlock our sector's full power to create a just world.

It's been nearly four decades since I was that eight-year-old boy with a terrible haircut. Now I am a mid-aged man with a terrible haircut. I don't know the names of any of these organizations and their staff, funders, donors, volunteers, and consultants who played such a critical role in my family's survival and well-being those first difficult few years. But I still recall the sense of hope and community that warmed us during some of the coldest nights.

For all its challenges, ours is an amazing sector filled with incredible people. And chances are, if you're reading this book, you are one of them. Thank you for being a Care Bear with me and using all your gifts to make our community better. Grab some hummus, take several deep breaths, and let's dive in. Together, let's own our power, ramp up our ambition, reimagine our sector, draw some new fishes, and work to actualize our sector's vision of a just and equitable world.

1

A Love Letter to Nonprofit and Philanthropy

Another world is not only possible, she is on her way. On a quiet day, I can hear her breathing.

—Arundhati Roy

A FEW YEARS AGO, before the pandemic, I was waiting to board a plane when I heard a voice calling my name. "Mr. Vu!" I turned to see a young man behind an airline counter beaming at me. He looked familiar, but I couldn't place him. Before I could deploy the usual strategy of smiling and faking it, he said, "Do you remember me? Bình. I was one of the students in your afterschool and Saturday morning programs."

For several years, I worked at the Vietnamese Friendship Association (VFA, now Kandelia), a nonprofit focused on helping immigrant and refugee kids and their families who had just arrived in the United States. We had several programs, including some to help kids catch up on their academic and social skills and find jobs, and others to help parents navigate the school system.

Bình arrived as a tall, lanky teenager. A bit awkward, but also bright and gregarious, always cracking jokes, he was a favorite among the staff. Over the years, as his language and social skills developed, he became a great resource for the programs, helping other kids and interpreting for the staff. He was a reliable volunteer every Saturday morning and throughout the week.

By then, I had become the executive director, so I was out attending meetings, wrangling money, writing reports, and occasionally huddling in the fetal position in the supply closet, weeping and beating my chest in despair over cash flow and assorted other issues.

While the work had been fun and meaningful, it was also full of challenges. There was a constant feeling that everything was in crisis mode, and I was failing as a leader. The search for funding was relentless and anxiety-inducing, and any relief that came through a grant or donation was short-lived.

On some days, I wondered if I might have chosen the wrong profession. I had been a pre-med student as an undergrad. I could have been a doctor! And now it was midnight, and I was still in the office, sitting on a rolling chair with a broken wheel, working to edit answers on a grant proposal, while trying to ignore the scratching noises coming from the walls, an indication of the pest issue we were dealing with.

But the students made it all worthwhile.

My team was also amazing. Every person on my staff was brilliant and courageous, coordinating the programs and helping our students with the same level of creativity, thoughtfulness, and determination as they did in handling budget shortfalls, random community members who showed up thinking we were an immigration attorney's office or medical clinic, and the increasingly assertive rodents living in our walls.

"Bình," I said, "it's so good to see you! I'm sorry I didn't recognize you at first. It's been so many years since I last saw you. How have you been?"

"I'm good, Mr. Vu," he said, "Thanks to VFA, I graduated from high school and college, and I got this job with this airline!"

We traded more pleasantries before I boarded the plane, Bình waving and smiling at me as I passed him.

Seeing Bình was a reminder for me of how amazing our sector is and of all the good we do. It was also a reminder that our work creates ripples we may never fully see. The programs my nonprofit ran served so many kids and families over the years. They graduated or left and gradually lost touch, so we were never sure of the long-term impact, if any, we made on them.

It was by chance that I ran into Bình and learned how he was doing and how he thought our programs affected his life. It was nice to see our program participants ending up happy and successful. It was good to have the rare confirmation that my nonprofit and its dedicated, hardworking team had contributed somehow to making life just a bit better for him and his family.

Best of all, I got a free seat upgrade, which is a tangible proof of the ripples we make, even if we seldom see them!

Invisible and Essential as Air

I've always thought nonprofits are like air, whereas other sectors, especially the corporate sector, are like food. People can see food, so they appreciate it; they take pictures of food and call themselves *foodies*. Air is just as essential, if not more so, but because it's invisible, no one appreciates it until they need it. People don't recognize the value of senior centers, for example, until they or their parents start aging. They may not pay much attention to food pantries until they lose their jobs. They don't think much about mental health organizations or suicide hotlines until they are in trouble or know someone who is.

The general public is ignorant about how nonprofits work and contribute to society at large, benefitting all people, not only those they directly serve. I wrote a blog post dispelling some myths people had about nonprofits and received a bunch of comments pushing back. One stood out:

> When we invest in for-profits we do so for the potential of realizing more value (thicker wallet) to us as individuals. When we donate money to nonprofits, we give our money with no hope of self-gain. Therefore those of us who give our hard-earned money have every right to judge a nonprofit any way we want.

This sort of attitude is pervasive, probably because our sector tends to attract nice people who are more focused on helping others than trying to educate clueless numpties on the Internet. If people just take a minute to think about it, they will realize that just because they can't hold or see something does not mean they do not benefit from it.

We all benefit from nonprofits' work more than we'll ever know. If people feel safe walking down the street, it's likely due in part to the nonprofits working on neighborhood safety and providing services to those who need help. If they appreciate the free art and music in their neighborhood and city, it's likely because there are nonprofits supporting kick-ass artists and musicians in the community. If they like parks and clean air, it's probably because there are nonprofits focused on making sure there are green spaces and recycling services and clean transportation. If people care about democracy, there are nonprofits educating and engaging people around voting and policy-related issues.

For so long, nonprofits have remained invisible and underappreciated even as we are vital to a functioning society. We barely have any shows about us! I sometimes daydream about pitching some ideas to TV executives on shows we could have about nonprofit work. For example:

- *The Amazing Free Supplies Race.* In each episode, a bank or large business moves or shuts down, and they send out a notice about free supplies and furniture, and all these nonprofits assemble into teams and try to be the first to get there and secure that sweet metal filing cabinet that locks. They'll use it for the personnel files!
- *Nonprofit and Afraid,* based on the Discovery Channel's *Naked and Afraid*, which pairs up strangers who must endure the wilderness for three weeks. They each get a survival item, usually a machete and some sort of fire-starting device, and they must find food and shelter. Each episode of *Nonprofit and Afraid* would feature someone who has never worked at a nonprofit being placed at a nonprofit. They must accomplish difficult tasks to help community members. They get a survival item, like a 1993 Honda Accord.
- I'm also thinking of creating *Nonprofit, the Musical* and have thought about what kind of characters it would have. For example,

there's a robot that's also a consultant, and it repeats exactly what the staff says...but the board listens to it! And the development director character is played by a new actor in every scene.

Nonprofits' Role in Society

The nonprofit sector contributes over a trillion dollars every year to the U.S. economy, which is 5.6 percent of GDP.[1] In the United States, nonprofit is the third-largest sector, eclipsing several industries, including construction, finance, and manufacturing, according to the Johns Hopkins Center for Civil Society Studies 2020 Nonprofit Employment Report.[2] The sector employs over 12.5 million workers, behind only retail and trade (15.8 million) and accommodation and food services (13.6 million). That means that one out of every 10 workers in the United States is employed by a nonprofit.

Meanwhile, some of the most important advances and transformations in society have occurred because of nonprofits, including the Civil Rights Act of 1964 and the Voting Rights Act of 1965, marriage equality, the Affordable Care Act, the Clean Air Act, the Clean Water Act, the Paris Climate Accord, and so on. Think of any social transformation in history and our sector has likely been involved in some significant way.

None of these things mean that our sector is perfect; far from it. The fact that we have so many nonprofits and foundations, with many more forming every day, often reflects the failure of other systems. In an ideal world, many nonprofit organizations would not exist because capitalism wouldn't be an all-consuming exploitative force that concentrates wealth in the hands of a few super-rich people while starving the poorest; corporations would compensate their workers with thriving wages; the wealthy would pay their fair share of taxes; and government would not be controlled by a bunch of oligarchs but instead is strong and representative and takes care of its people. Such a world would have many fewer nonprofits because there wouldn't be a need for them.

Unfortunately, that's not our reality. We can work toward it, but until we reach that vision, nonprofits will continue to play a critical role. And it's been super frustrating how taken for granted, ignored, and abused this sector has been by the rest of society. As air, we allow our communities to breathe, providing vital social goods everyone benefits from. But it's time we stop being invisible, own our full power, demand respect, and push back against things that impede our work.

The Crap We Put Up With

Over the past two decades I've been in this sector, I'm constantly amazed by the people in it. Yeah, there are a few assholes, but most people are incredible: hardworking, kind, hilarious, determined, brilliant, and creative. We would have to be all those things to put up with the shenanigans thrown at us every day, stuff that other sectors don't have to deal with, philosophies and practices we've taken at face value that are inane or infuriating. Here are just a few of them.

Overhead: What's Your Hose-to-Water Ratio?

There has been a long-held belief that certain expenses are good, such as books and backpacks for students, and others are bad and should be minimized as much as possible. These "bad" expenses are called "overhead" or "indirect" expenses and include things such as staff salaries, office rent and utilities, insurance, and website hosting. Funders and donors hate paying for these expenses and often limit how much nonprofits can spend on them, often clutching their pearls if overhead rates are above 20 percent, which is ironic, as the average overhead rate for for-profits can be 35 percent or higher.[3] This is one of the biggest, most annoying, and most nonsensical barriers in our work. We've taken it as par for nonprofit work, but imagine if for-profits had to deal with it.

Any funder that still restricts funds or fixates on overhead is basically the equivalent of a climate-change-denying anti-vaxxer of our sector.

Imagine a bakery where a customer walks in and asks for a cake. However, they agree to pay only 20 percent of the cake and ask that other customers help pay for the rest. They also insist that the $20 only be spent on eggs and butter, not any of the other ingredients, because they don't like paying for those, and definitely not for the electricity for the oven, since that's an indirect cost.

Everything has been so urgent, so I've been using a different metaphor, which is that nonprofits are like firefighters working to put out the fires of injustice. We're rushing to a fire and someone stops us and says, "Hey, I want to donate money to help you put out fires, but I only want my money to go to the water, not the hose, because the hose is overhead. What is your hose-to-water ratio?"

The focus on overhead has been distracting and harmful, forcing nonprofits to fight serious societal problems with underpaid staff and inadequate resources. Plus, the more time we spend playing Funding Sudoku, the less time we spend putting out fires. So this "overhead" fixation among funders and donors is not just annoying, it's been harmful, allowing the fires of injustice to spread.

We need to move away from overhead. Don't mention it on your website. Don't brag about how "94 cents of every dollar raised go to programming" or whatever. And funders need to stop asking about it. Considering the vast amount of data that is out there regarding how effective multi-year general operating dollars (MYGOD) are, any funder that still restricts funds or fixates on overhead is basically the equivalent of a climate-change–denying anti-vaxxer in our sector.

The Sustainability Question

A few years ago, I called up a program officer of a foundation to discuss my org's mission to bring leaders of color into the nonprofit field. "That's a great idea," he said, "but what's your sustainability plan? We don't tend to support projects unless we know they will be financially independent in the future."

"Well," I said, "I have a great plan for that. Have you heard of teeth tattoo? Imagine: the Seahawks logo on your incisors! We will open a teeth tattoo parlor, and it will generate millions of dollars in income, enough to fund the project forever!"

All right, I didn't say that. I waffled something that sounded intelligent—"We are building up our base of individual donors, establishing relationships with local businesses, and using the synergistic paradigm action matrix (SPAM) to explore earned revenues"—like a good grant-seeker. Then, I hung up and unwrapped a bar of dark chocolate and ate it, both me and the chocolate 72% bitter.

Sustainability is the idea that nonprofits should be able to be financially self-reliant, and buried in innocent-sounding questions like "how will you sustain this program" is the deeply held belief that nonprofits are a bunch of freeloading parasites. Many funders are terrified nonprofits will be "dependent" on them, like lazy adult children who moved into their parents' basement, eat all their parents' food, and refuse to get a job and be out on their own.

Well, who says nonprofits should be sustainable? Maybe some of us would like to do a good job, solve whatever problems we're working on, close our organizations, and follow our long-deferred dream of opening a vegan butcher stand at the farmer's market to share our joy of plant-based protein. The thinking that every organization should be around for the long term reflects a lack of imagination, which I elaborate more on in the next chapter.

The concept of sustainability is insulting, when nonprofits are filling in the gaps left behind by the rest of society and addressing problems we didn't cause in the first place. Plus, it's impossible to achieve; even large organizations still rely on grants. Also, funders' obsession with this ridiculous concept has paradoxically prevented sustainability. Imagine if all customers of a bakery refused to order cakes from it unless the bakery had a "long-term sustainability plan to avoid being financially dependent on customers."

A bakery's job is to make pastries, and as long as it does a good job at that, customers keep buying from it; that's how it's sustainable. The same goes for nonprofits. Nonprofits' jobs are to run programs and services, and funders' jobs are to fund nonprofits as long as they're doing good work. If funders want nonprofits to be sustainable, it should be the *funders'* jobs to sustain them.

Bizsplaining

One time, I was showing a potential board member our Saturday morning program, which served 150 kids. It was his first visit, and he launched into a lecture about having a business plan. "We have a three-year strategic plan," I said, and before I could elaborate, he interrupted to explain what a business plan was. This man, who had never run a nonprofit before, cut in several more times to explain various *important business concepts* to me as if I had never heard of such things as revenues or returns on investment.

There is a pervasive belief that nonprofits are generally ineffective and should run more like for-profits, and it manifests in what my friend and colleague Allison Carney calls *bizsplaining*:[4]

> Bizsplaining, similar to mansplaining, is when someone from the "business" world talks to a nonprofit employee about their work in a condescending manner ... I understand that since we make less money and "do good," you think that we don't know what we're doing. The truth is, we're in a completely different world than you.

I rarely see nonprofit folks ever assuming the same patronizing attitude toward for-profits. But maybe we should start saying things like "I've never run a restaurant before, but I have eaten at several, and I think you need to consolidate with other restaurants in your neighborhood into one mega-restaurant, to lower overhead costs" and "When I'm retired from my career in youth development, I'd love to open my own corporate law firm. It seems so rewarding!"

I don't know where our corporate friends' arrogance comes from, when they have a leg up in almost everything. As Nancy Long, former executive director of 501 Commons, says, "Business has easy access to capital. Nonprofits are doing much more difficult jobs and producing harder 'products,' if you will—changing lives, without access to working capital."

Even with such an advantage, 49 percent of for-profits fail within their first five years and 65 percent within 10 years, according to the U.S. Bureau of Labor Statistics.[5] Nonprofits are working on some seriously entrenched problems, such as poverty and homelessness, with completely different funding models and dynamics.

There are always things the sectors can learn from one another. For-profit colleagues need to knock it off with the know-it-all attitude, and nonprofit professionals need to stop internalizing this inferiority complex and unproven belief that our sector is somehow less effective and inefficient than any other sector.

The Reality We Face

One of my favorite shows is *Chopped* because it's a great visual analogy for our sector and the creativity of the people in it. *Chopped* features a competition where contestants are given baskets of random ingredients and asked to make delicious meals out of them: "Here's some trout, three slices of fermented beets, and some licorice-flavored marshmallows. Go make a dessert!"

In our sector it's like, "Here's a 12-year-old computer, a printer that only prints when the moon is in Gemini, one half-time underpaid staff member, several people on the Internet who hate you for no reason, and a $5,000 grant you can only spend on paperclips on Tuesdays. Go end poverty!"

And you know what, we still manage to do incredible, life-changing stuff every day. Sure, I am biased because I've mostly worked in this sector, and because I'm so grateful for all the organizations that helped me and my family when we first arrived. But I am always impressed and humbled by the people in this sector and what we manage to achieve despite inadequate funding, unrealistic societal expectations, unfair comparisons to other sectors, and the involuntary twitch in one eye some of us have developed from planning galas.

However, things are horribly dire. Humanity has entered what I call the era of Fascist Extremist Assholes' Reign (FEAR). Democracy, fueled by misinformation and a rise in right-wing extremism, falters as dictators increasingly assume power. As I'm writing this book, Trump and the Republicans have taken control of all three branches of government and have been using their power to exponentially further injustice and inequity. They are dismantling vital institutions, cutting critical services, destroying reproductive and other rights many people before us fought hard for, suppressing free speech, and disappearing people who protest their actions.

Meanwhile, the wealth gap continues to widen, and a handful of billionaires have more money than half the world's poorest population combined. The planet becomes more and more uninhabitable as ocean levels rise and natural disasters intensify. Israel's genocide of Palestinians continues, funded by our tax dollars. Horrific injustices continue against people in Sudan, Congo, Tigray, and other areas of the world. The people and communities all around the world who are already most marginalized by the ongoing effects of capitalism, white supremacy, and patriarchy continue to suffer even further.

Amidst all this, when our sector is most needed to address these rising problems, the U.S. government, corrupted by billionaire oligarchs, goes all in on demonizing nonprofits and eroding the public's trust in us. They dismantled USAID, tried to freeze federal grants that had already been allocated to nonprofits, cut down provisions for the USDA to send to food pantries across the country, tried to pass the bill HR9495 to allow the government to mark any organization it doesn't like as "terrorist-supporting," and took over vital nonprofit organizations like the U.S. Institute for Peace, among other horrific things designed to overwhelm and demoralize us so we don't fight back.

Are We Ready for the Fights Ahead?

As much as I love our sector, I don't think in our current conditions we are prepared for the battles ahead. I've been watching a lot of TV shows and movies, mainly because I am exhausted, and these forms of entertainment give me needed reprieve. The best ones provide a sense of hope and optimism we all desperately need from time to time. In shows and movies where the forces of good are fighting the forces of evil, there is a trope where during the final battle, when all hope is lost, everyone who is on the side of Good shows up at the last minute and mounts a final push to save humanity.

J.R.R. Tolkien's *Lord of the Rings* comes to mind. It parallels what we have now: Evil forces led by one man, moving across the land, destroying everything in their path, blanketing the world with strife and despair. The beings on the side of Good must combine forces and fight back. But if *Lord of the Rings* were set in our sector, here's what it would look like:

The elves, who hold the most power and resources, decide they're only going to give out 5 percent of their riches to fight Sauron, maybe increase it to 6 percent, and keep the rest in their endowments, since they are immortal beings who plan to leave for the Undying Lands of Perpetuity, where none of Sauron's actions really affect them.

Gandalf thinks the best way to fight Sauron is to gather a fellowship of brilliant warriors—so they can spend the next three years researching which communities have been most hurt by Sauron. They release a white paper and hold a summit. The first recommendation in this white paper is. . .to do more research.

Aragorn's Council of Advisors believes it's "mission drift" for him to form an army to fight Sauron, since his focus has been to be a ranger and protect the forests. Fighting Sauron is too "political" and that's just not something they think he should do.

Boromir thinks maybe it would be best to work with Sauron, meet him in the middle; he can't be that bad, and it's good to have diverse perspectives; the important thing is that everyone is civil with one another and with Sauron when they disagree.

Gollum, meanwhile, is a consultant teaching people how to raise money to fight Sauron, using traditional tactics that center the emotions and whims of donors, despite Sam and Frodo saying these tactics strengthen Sauron's power: "Why do they hates the old ways of fundraising, Precious? The old ways works! They raises money, Precious!! They keeps us employed!"

A Time for Righteous Anger

But we don't have to be like that. Our sector has all the potential to fight against an evil as great as the one we're facing now. To do that effectively, we need to shift how we do things. We need to shed our skin of niceness and compliance and adopt one of righteous anger. The kind that Desmond Tutu describes here:

> Righteous anger is usually not about oneself. It is about those whom one sees being harmed and whom one wants to help. In short, righteous anger is a tool of justice, a scythe of compassion, more than a reactive emotion. Although it may have its roots deep in our fight-or-flight desire to protect those in our family or group who are threatened, it is a chosen response and not simply an uncontrollable reaction. And it is not about

one's own besieged self-image, or one's feelings of separation, but of one's collective responsibility, and one's feeling of deep, empowering connection.

We need to be angry at the cruelty of this administration and the horrible things it has been doing. We need to be angry at all the politicians who are aiding in the dismantling of democracy and civil society.

Meanwhile, instead of being compliant, we need to be angry at those who wield money and power in our sector, who waste our time and make our work difficult. We can't continue to be like air, invisible and underappreciated, helping our communities breathe while we ourselves suffocate and burn out. We need to be angry so we can resist and fight and protect the people and communities we care about.

The time to be nice and put up with bullshit—whether from political leaders, funders, corporate partners, donors, society in general, or other nonprofits—is over.

Another World Is on Her Way

Lately, it's been hard not to fall into despair. Or to become numb or avoidant. On several days these past few months, that's where I find myself—in bed, doomscrolling the state of the world, feeling small and futile. I am filled with fear and grief for the people whose lives have been or will be torn apart, dread for the years ahead, and preemptive exhaustion brought on thoughts of the horrors and battles we will be facing every day.

But I am also fired up and determined to fight. On a walk to clear my head, I saw someone had written this quote by writer and activist Arundhati Roy: "*Another world is not only possible, she is on her way. On a quiet day, I can hear her breathing.*"

> We can't continue to be like air, invisible and underappreciated, helping our communities breathe while we ourselves suffocate and burn out.

I appreciate this hopeful vision, not just because it contrasts with the chaos and destruction we're facing, but also because of Roy's courage and conviction. In her unapologetic speech[6] accepting the PEN

Pinter Prize, she condemns the collective imagination that would condone and fund Israel's genocidal campaign against Palestinians:

> An imagination that cannot countenance diversity, cannot countenance the idea of living in a country alongside other people, equally, with equal rights. Like everybody else in the world does. An imagination that cannot afford to acknowledge that Palestinians want to be free, like South Africa is, like India is, like all countries that have thrown off the yoke of colonialism are.

The pushback against Palestine's liberation, as well as DEI, trans people's existence, immigrants, the poor—all of it stems from this narrow, sad imagination of greedy, cowardly people. They know a better, more inclusive world is coming, and they are fighting tooth and nail to stop it. But this reality of a better world is inevitable.

In an article[7] written during the current turmoil, writer and consultant Venkatesh Rao elaborates on the quote by Antonio Gramsci, an Italian philosopher and communist who loudly criticized fascist dictator Mussolini and was imprisoned. Gramsci's words have been translated as *"The old world is dying and the new world struggles to be born. Now is the time of monsters."* Rao calls this period between the old world finally dying and the new world being born as the Gramsci Gap.

It seems we are firmly in that gap right now, a "time of monsters." In many ways, our society may be like a snake shedding its old skin—the yoke of colonialism, imperialism, white supremacy, capitalism. What we are seeing is the resistance to this evolution as white nationalists, misogynists, racists, and xenophobes start to reckon with the fact that they will soon be outnumbered, oligarchs start to realize their time is nearing its end. They will fight desperately to preserve the old order and hierarchy where they have been on top, and they will try to consume the systems, structures, and communities in their way. But like a snake eating its own tail, will destroy themselves.

A snake eating its own tail is the ouroboros, the Egyptian symbol of the cycle of destruction and rebirth. We are in the destruction phase, marked by the prevalence of monsters, ones fueled by bigotry, ignorance, and lack of imagination. Though it may not seem like it now, this period of destruction will be followed by a period of renewal and growth, and a world many of us write about in our vision statements. It may take a while, and I have no illusions it will be easy. But I have faith humanity will get there.

And our sector, filled with amazing, dedicated, kind, thoughtful, talented, brilliant, and obviously very good-looking people despite the graying hair and involuntary eye-twitch thing, has a significant role to play in creating that reality. That is, if we keep hope and imagination alive, hold on to our values, and are ready to shed our own skins, which include many of the philosophies, practices, hang-ups, traditions, and fears that have been holding us back.

I believe in us.

Discussion Questions

1. If you have experience working in the nonprofit sector, how and why did you get into it? If you haven't, what intrigues you about it?
2. What do you think are the strengths of this sector?
3. Think of some key nonprofits in your geographic area. What do they do, and how does it benefit people, both the ones who use their services, as well as those who don't?
4. Why is it that our sector plays such an important role in society and yet remains so invisible and underappreciated?
5. Have you encountered instances of the overhead myth, sustainability question, or bizsplaining?
6. What other forms of BS and shenanigans have we been dealing with?
7. How does our sector push back against these things?
8. What fears do you have with everything happening sociopolitically?
9. What positive things do you hope may come out of this "cycle of destruction and rebirth"?

2

The Nine Horsemen of Nonprofit and Philanthropic Ineffectiveness

The best lack all conviction, while the worst
Are full of passionate intensity.

—W.B. Yeats

When My Family first arrived in the United States, we landed in Philadelphia. Life was rough, but at least we had a fridge. In Vietnam back then, refrigerators were uncommon, owned by wealthy families, and ice was a mark of luxury, so I was super excited that we had our own fridge inside the house, which meant I could make all the ice I wanted.

So every day, before school started, I placed little containers of water in the fridge: bowls, cups, empty plastic tubs, the shelves were filled with them. Each day, I came home, anxious to see if my water had turned into ice. And always I was disappointed. There were sometimes thin crackling layers floating on top of my little containers, but never the solid frozen masses I had envisioned. But I continued my quest, hoping that someday, somehow, magically, I would get the results I desperately wanted.

One day, Mr. Farnon, the patriarch of the kind sponsor family who had been supporting us, came to the house. He had taken us out to see *The Nutcracker* and to have pizza for the first time.

We had tried to choke down as many of the exotic cheesy triangles as we could out of politeness. There was a lot left over, and he insisted we have all of it. He opened the fridge to put the pizza inside and saw my containers of water.

"What are these for?" he asked, staring down at me.

"I make ice," I said.

Mr. Farnon chuckled. "That's not how you make ice. See up here? This is the freezer. You have to put the water up here for it to turn into ice." I had been too short and too narrowly focused on what was going on in the fridge to see the separate compartment for frozen stuff. He moved some of my containers of water up to the freezer to make room for the boxes of pizza.

After that day, I made so much ice, all the time. The months were cold, and everything was uncertain, and I dreaded school, and somehow we would have to finish the leftover pizza because my parents were not going to let us waste food when we barely had any. But with unlimited frozen water (and eventually fruit juices), I started to feel that maybe life here was not so bad after all.

The Nonprofit Rut

For all the good it does and for all the brilliance of the professionals doing this work, our sector seems to be stuck in a rut, where the issues we've been working on have often not gotten better, but oftentimes have gotten worse. With our world facing some of the most pressing challenges as right-wing forces destroy long-held vital institutions, shatter democracy, fuel the flames of cruelty and chaos, and lift into power fascist dictators, we need to get ourselves out of this rut.

But maybe we're not putting our water in the right place. Maybe we're so used to working in the fridge that we don't look up and see the freezer.

Our sector can be very set in its way, passing things down through the decades until they become second nature. We normalize philosophies, entrench them in our work, and transfer them from one person to another. Most of the time, we don't even think about them and how they affect us. They are just there, invisible forces undermining everything we do.

While there are many undermining forces, I'm going to focus on a few I'm calling the Nine Horsemen of Nonprofit and Philanthropic Ineffectiveness. These are broad, overarching philosophies influencing everything, and to unlock our sector's full potential to protect democracy, fight tyranny, and actualize a better world, we must have a better understanding of them so we can mitigate for them.

Suppressed Imagination

In 2020, police officer Derek Chauvin murdered George Floyd, sparking worldwide protests. The movement Defund the Police gained momentum, demanding the government decrease its funding of police departments and use those resources instead to bolster community solutions such as mental health programs, housing for homeless people, and social work services. A few voices called for the abolition of the police entirely.

During this time, it was apparent how much imagination our society and sector has lost. The calls to reduce funding for the police were met with significant opposition, including in our own sector. Many people could not imagine a society without a strong police presence, where crimes would be significantly lower because people would have access to healthcare, education, housing, jobs, arts, recreation, and civic engagement.

Martin Luther King Jr. once said, "*A nation that continues year after year to spend more money on military defense than on programs of social uplift is approaching spiritual death.*"

Despite his warning, the United States has accepted a strong police presence as normal. This is why many cities' police budgets are obscene in comparison to other line items.[1] In 2020, for example, Houston's city budget totaled $5.1B. Of that, $934M went to the police while only a tenth of that, $92M, went to public health. In Philadelphia, the city budget was $4.9B. Of that, $740M went to the police, $214M went to education, $159M went to public health, and $87M went to transportation. And yet, even after so much spending on the police, research shows boosting funding for law enforcement has not shown a decrease in crime rates, but often an increase.[2] Meanwhile, according to the University of Illinois Chicago's Law

Enforcement Epidemiology Project,[3] police officers injure about 250,000 civilians and kill over 600 each year.

Defund the Police is just one example of how our sector (and much of society) has lost its imagination. A colleague told me of an event celebrating the 50th year anniversary of the founding of a homelessness-focused organization. One of the speakers went on stage during his speech and made a toast "to 50 more years" to the applause of the crowd, while a few people recognized the irony of celebrating the continuation of homelessness.

Among funders, the lack of imagination manifests in the concept of perpetuity, where foundations aim to exist forever by spending out only the minimum of their assets each year to address problems in society, which allows their endowments to stay at the same level or grow. But this reflects an inability to imagine a future where inequity no longer exists, and thus foundations and nonprofits are no longer needed.

There was a time when many people, even progressive ones, didn't think the abolition of slavery was possible, or women would ever get to vote, or marriage equality would happen in their lifetimes.

People who could imagine such things as the abolition of slavery or women voting were often ridiculed or worse. But they forged ahead, built movement and momentum, and worked until their visions became reality. Our sector must reclaim its sense of imagination, hope, and optimism.

White Moderation

One of the most important concepts we must understand is what Dr. Martin Luther King Jr. calls the "white moderate." From his Letter from a Birmingham Jail,[4] he wrote:

> I have almost reached the regrettable conclusion that the Negro's great stumbling block in his stride toward freedom is not the White Citizen's Council-er or the Ku Klux Klanner, but the white moderate, who is more devoted to "order" than to justice; who prefers a negative peace which is the absence of tension to a positive peace which is the presence of justice; who constantly says:

"I agree with you in the goal you seek, but I cannot agree with your methods of direct action"; who paternalistically believes he can set the timetable for another man's freedom; who lives by a mythical concept of time and who constantly advises the Negro to wait for a "more convenient season." Shallow understanding from people of good will is more frustrating than absolute misunderstanding from people of ill will.

These are people who call for "civility" during heated dialogues about injustice, advocate for folks to see "both sides," play devil's advocates, and encourage pragmatism. During protests against injustice, they proclaim that rioting is not the answer and prioritize the safety of buildings.

Nonprofit and philanthropy have, in many ways, become one giant white moderate sector, a sector of kind and well-meaning people who believe in the ideals of a just world, but often prioritize civility and people getting along rather than supporting courageous actions to address it. We see it in the reluctance to engage in anything "controversial" for fear of alienating donors and funders.

In foundations, it manifests in the reluctance to fund Black, Indigenous, and other communities-of-color–led organizations; insistence on order and bureaucracy through grant applications and budgets and deadlines; dismissal of solutions proposed by marginalized communities in favor of those proposed by educated white elites; and gravitation toward long timelines at the convenience and whims of rich mostly white family members who sit on foundation boards of trustees.

The most damaging aspect of white moderation in our sector is that it prevents us from engaging in political actions and systems change work that are necessary to effectively address the root causes of inequity. Nonprofits are terrified of doing anything political, or even perceived to be political, such as voter engagement. Funders, meanwhile, have a severe disdain for funding advocacy and systems change work, which has let the fires spread unchecked.

You can check out Appendix B for a fuller list of how white moderation manifests. Some of these actions can be so subtle, you may not realize you and your organization have been participating in them.

Overall, white moderation is one of society's and our sector's biggest challenges. It allows people and organizations to uphold white supremacy while genuinely believing they are not doing so. We must break out of it by grounding all aspects of our work in equity and justice. And we must constantly be vigilant and interrogate ourselves and our practices continually to ensure we are not staying on that path.

Neoliberalism

Neoliberalism, at least the way I understand it, is the idea that capitalism is still the best and most effective economic system, even considering all its destructive tendencies. This creates dissonance as we try to solve entrenched societal issues, most of which are caused by capitalism. It's kind of like living inside a house that's full of asbestos, and your family is constantly getting sick from it, but you still think this is the best house and there's no other viable choice, so you try your best to mitigate damages while still refusing to entertain the idea of moving. In the nonprofit sector, we can see neoliberalism's grip in various ways:

- **Unwavering belief in the free market.** There is the belief—among many donors and funders, but also tons of nonprofit leaders—that nonprofits are basically like little for-profits that should compete with one another for resources, with the idea that the "best" nonprofits would thrive, very much like in the business world. We treat donors like customers and adopt business concepts like scalability.
- **Privatization of public services.** Many of the issues nonprofits are addressing, such as hunger, education inequity, healthcare, and so on would ideally be handled by an effective, representative government. But that would be "socialism." And since neoliberals believe capitalism is still the best way to handle social issues, they prefer individuals avoid paying taxes and then get to pick and choose among causes they care about, leading to our sector being a loose collection of individual nonprofits and foundations.

- **Concentration of influence among the wealthy.** Permitting wealthy individuals to avoid paying taxes and instead get to select and support whatever issues they care about gives them great influence and power over what issues society tackles. It is undemocratic, because unlike government officials who can be elected to formal positions and removed based on the will of voters, there are few mechanisms for removing these wealthy, mostly white individuals from power or controlling what issues they support.
- **Overemphasis on narrow, measurable outcomes.** The capitalistic tendency to measure success of businesses through how much money they earn, and how efficient they are at earning it, is seen in our sector's overemphasis on outcomes, metrics, and so on. We have logic models. We talk about return on investments (ROI). We are trained to say things like "every one dollar spent in early learning leads to X dollars in future benefits to society." It perpetuates the viewing of individuals as economic units and often locks us into narrow goals instead of broad societal changes.
- **Avoidance of systemic change.** Built into capitalism is the focus on individual responsibility and the "pull yourself up by the bootstraps" mentality, the philosophy that individuals should be responsible for their own well-being by working hard to lift themselves out of poverty. This means that many donors and funders would rather support programs and services that target individuals—such as workshops to help people develop financial literacy skills—than support efforts to address systemic issues that cause those individuals to be poor in the first place. It also means that many nonprofits themselves are reluctant to engage in this type of work.

Risk Aversion and Incrementalism

Fear is a major guiding force in this field. Fear of offending donors. Fear of getting targeted by politicians. Fear of losing our tax status. Fear of having to let go of staff because of insufficient funding. Fear of not being able to run the critical programs and services so many people depend on. These fears are all valid; funders are not known to be forgiving of nonprofits who fail to meet outcomes, for example.

But over time, these fears lead to pervasive risk-aversion, where nonprofits are terrified to take bold actions. Instead, we embrace incrementalism, comfortable with smaller steps and accomplishments. Over the past few years, I've been on the board of Creating the Future, which is co-founded by Hildy Gottlieb. Hildy and I have had many conversations about nonprofits and the kind of rut the sector has been in. One of the marks of this rut is incremental thinking. I'm paraphrasing Hildy's words a bit here:

> Nonprofits and funders are conditioned to think that success is doing 10 percent better year over year. If this year our budget is $500,000, then next year, we're successful if we increase it to $550,000. If this year we're serving 100 families, then next year, we're on the right track if we serve 110 families, and the following year 121 families, etc. That's incremental.

Incrementalism is not always bad. Sometimes we do need to be practical, and any progress in helping people and solving societal problems should be appreciated. But it's a matter of balance. Too much dreaming and visioning not backed with action would not be good.

Fear is a major guiding force in this field. Fear of offending donors. Fear of getting targeted by politicians. Fear of losing our tax status.

But the pendulum has swung too much toward the practical, at the cost of loftier goals. It's like society is a sinking ship, and we're trained to think of success as bailing out the water. This is still a very vital task; the work so many dedicated nonprofit professionals do daily to mitigate damage is important. But we must simultaneously think of fixing the leak and building new and better boats. Or perhaps even abandoning the boat altogether and traveling by plane.

Toxic Intellectualizing

A while ago I talked to a foundation CEO who asked me to help facilitate a process to get his team to better fund Black and Indigenous communities. It would take about six months, he thought. I told him to just increase the foundation's payout and give multi-year general operating dollars to Black and Indigenous-led organizations. There was no need to pay a consultant and spend six months mired in process and discussion when this process has been done multiple times already over the years. (To their credit, a couple of months later, the foundation did release a fund specifically for organizations led by these communities.)

Another funder, when I told them something similar about increasing funding to communities-of-color–led orgs, said, "Well, we would love to do that, but we are very white and haven't really done our inner work yet to be more diverse, so it would feel hypocritical." They were planning to pause giving out funds the next two years so they could do this "inner work."

Our sector loves white papers, logic models, theories of change, and summits where we put sticky dots on easy paper to vote on various strategies, which are then often ignored. We are often excessively skeptical, planful, and mired in vetting. We are addicted to appearing intelligent and measured, so we overdo it with the outcomes and metrics and proof of concept, and so on. Instead of acting, we discuss. Instead of taking risks, we research. Instead of learning by trying and failing, we waffle and equivocate.

And gradually, over the years, we start to praise ourselves for doing endless researching, planning, and pontificating instead of taking actions, to the point where we now consider this course of inaction to be "best practices."

Toxic intellectualizing is pervasive across our sector. We have deeply internalized it, overusing concepts like "due diligence" and refrains like "the process is just as important as the results" to justify it. We are geared toward planning and thinking because it is safer and less risky to do. The consequences of taking impulsive actions and failing are usually serious in our sector and in society, but we don't want to seem like we're not taking any actions, so the middle ground is to think and talk about stuff, and in doing so we continue to waste so much time and resources while believing we're making progress.

None of this is to say that we should never think or plan or do due diligence and instead just impulsively act all the time. Being deliberate and thoughtful is vital to the success of any organization's work; and the process sometimes is just as important as the results. However, the balance has been off, and we need to start shifting it toward decisive action and accepting that it will come with imperfect data and occasional failures.

Scarcity and Martyrdom

The crappy office chair is a hilarious trope in our sector. Everyone seems to have some sort of story about a terrible chair they've had to sit on, one that's missing a wheel or is duct-taped together. There's my ED friend whose chair was so bad and she was so frugal that her board had to half-jokingly pass a vote to get her to buy a new one.

Many of us in this sector take pride in our ability to accomplish amazing things for our community while having some of the fewest and lowest-quality resources. We take pride in not "wasting" funding, keeping our "overhead" low, and showing donors and funders we are "responsible" stewards of the work. I often hear fellow executive directors complaining, but not without a tiny hint of bragging, how they haven't taken a vacation in several years.

We need to stop this pride in scarcity and sacrifice (PISS) mentality. Scarcity and martyrdom should not be badges of honor. Sure, they make for great comedy, like *The Onion*'s headline[5] "Nonprofit Fights Poverty with Poverty." But this attitude is toxic to the sector's effectiveness and to the well-being of its professionals. Not having adequate resources makes it harder to solve the problems we're working on. It leads people to burn out and punishes people who dedicate their lives to this work, as they fail to receive adequate pay or fund adequate retirement savings. Plus, it stifles imagination and perpetuates uninformed expectations among funders, donors, and the rest of society.

Let's get out of this mindset and into one of abundance. You deserve a decent chair to sit on—and a thriving wage, and plenty of vacation days, and retirement savings—while you change the world.

The Dunning–Kruger Effect

In W.B. Yeats's poem "The Second Coming," published in 1919, he wrote "The best lack all conviction, while the worst/Are full of passionate intensity."

Eighty years later, psychologists David Dunning and Justin Kruger came up with the *Dunning–Kruger effect*, where people with lower skills, knowledge, and expertise tend to overestimate themselves, while those who are more skilled and knowledgeable tend to be more aware of their limitations so, ironically, have less confidence. Some of this is hypothesized to be because incompetent people may be too incompetent to recognize that they are incompetent, while competent people are competent enough to realize they may not yet know everything and still need to learn and improve.

A spin-off from Dunning–Krueger is what I call the *Personal Integrity Paradox*. Basically, those with integrity often feel like crap about themselves because they care about people and feel like they're not doing enough to help, and those without integrity often feel good about themselves and the world because they're too ignorant or bigoted to see reality.

These concepts manifest everywhere. Good parents tend to have anxiety about whether they are good parents; crappy parents generally think they're awesome. Great teachers often feel like they're letting their students down, while terrible teachers are more likely to think they're brilliant. We see it a lot in politics, where some of the most racist, hateful, corrupt politicians are full of confidence, while those who believe in equity and democracy often feel they are not measuring up in the fight against injustice.

This plays out all the time in our field, and other factors, like race, are involved. White, male, nondisabled, formally educated, and neurotypical colleagues, and organizations led by leaders with these identities, tend to be more confident or tend to be perceived to be more confident, despite often being less competent and effective. We joke a lot about having "the confidence of a mediocre white man," but this phenomenon is based in human psychology and reality.

But it also applies to the sector as a whole. As a sector that fights for equity and justice, we collectively have more doubt in our ability, which often translates to inaction or ineffective actions. Meanwhile,

36 Reimagining Nonprofits and Philanthropy

> *Those of us fighting for a better world need to own our awesomeness and be louder and more confident.*

those who work to preserve the status quo of racism, misogyny, patriarchy, and so on, are confident what they're doing is morally right, so they are full steam ahead. We must reverse this.

Inferiority Complex

Bizsplaining, as I talked about in Chapter 1, is certainly annoying, indicative of the superiority complex among many of our colleagues from the corporate sector. And we perpetuate it because our work often relies on corporate support in the form of sponsorships, donors, board members, and volunteers.

However, there is a parallel inferiority complex we've internalized. A lot of the "we should run more like for-profits" mentality comes from people who have been in the nonprofit sector a long time. Even among many nonprofit leaders, there's an assumption that people with corporate backgrounds are somehow more qualified than people with nonprofit experience. We see this in the large number of CEOs/EDs who get hired with little to no nonprofit experience. A report[6] from Center for Effective Philanthropy looks at the leadership of the largest 100 foundations in the United States. It finds:

> Experience as a grantee, if you exclude colleges and universities .... isn't much valued by foundation boards when they're searching for a CEO. In 2012 we identified just 14 foundation CEOs with immediate previous experience at an operating nonprofit that wasn't a college or university. Today, that number is even lower—just 10.

There's also the neoliberal zombie belief that social enterprise, where basically nonprofits open side businesses to generate earned revenues, would be the magic bullet that will solve all nonprofit funding woes. I call it a zombie belief because it has been disproven repeatedly over the years that generating earned revenues would be feasible for most nonprofits, and yet it still lingers. This unaddressed inferiority complex has caused us to elevate leaders who should not be in positions of influence, prioritize strategies with little chance of working, doubt our own power and ability to tackle systemic issues, and stifle creative solutions that may come from outside the trappings and failures of capitalism. We need to understand that the solutions to the entrenched problems we're tackling will not come from the sector whose beliefs and actions have led to many of these problems in the first place.

Self-Interest

On a rainy December day, a few years ago, I walked into a room of 20 or so colleagues who worked in local foundations. I had been invited to discuss how to improve grantmaking. As usual, I mentioned the importance of multiyear general operating funds, the need to allocate more resources to marginalized-community–led organizations, the urgency of funding advocacy, and so on.

"Communities of color are tired," I said, "We've been asking for these things again and again. You've been hearing these ideas for decades. Yet nothing changes. Why? What's the holdup?"

The room went quiet for a few seconds. Then one program officer said, and I paraphrase, "Let's admit it. Most of us have cushy jobs working for foundations. How can we rock the boat when we have well-paying jobs we don't want to lose?"

Andrea Arenas, my friend and one of the co-founders of the Community-Centric Fundraising movement, and a former foundation program officer, describes this phenomenon as wearing "golden handcuffs"[7]:

> The concept of "wearing golden handcuffs" refers to individuals who feel trapped in their jobs due to attractive salaries and benefits, even if they may feel unfulfilled, denied professional growth opportunities, or restricted in their actions and expressions.

While she is mostly talking about foundation staff, a similar conflict affects everyone in the sector to some degree, and probably in ways we may not be aware of. Many of us rely on the existence of inequity for our livelihoods. We get paid to fight it, so we are unconsciously incentivized to ensure that it is never completely eradicated.

Donors and wealthy individuals in general, meanwhile, have a different sort of self-interest. Being better off financially, they do not have the same fear of not being able to pay their mortgage or feed their families. Their self-interest may lie in being perceived as good people and heroes. They may be invested in their legacy, marked by things like a foundation or a building with their family's name emblazoned on it.

Until we're honest enough with ourselves to have these uncomfortable reckoning with how our own self-interests, conscious and unconscious, affect our actions and decisions, we're each at risk of continuing to perpetuate the very injustices we're fighting.

Reclaim Our Vision

These Nine Horsemen have made it very challenging for our sector to do its work effectively. They build upon themselves, the presence of one opening doors for and lending strength to others. It will be hard to overcome decades of this deadly mixture of white moderation, neoliberalism, toxic intellectualizing, and the other entrenched philosophies holding us back. But we can start by reclaiming our collective and individual visions, grounding our work in our values, and having the audacity to dream big and be bold and unapologetic in working toward those visions.

A few years ago, one of the organizations I led brought in a consultant. The board, staff, and I were divided into teams and given large pads of sticky paper. "Imagine it's 20 years in the future," said the consultant, "and your organization has been wildly successful. A large national newspaper is featuring your nonprofit on its front page. What does the headline say? With your group, draw the front page. Use your imagination. Dream big. Be creative."

Creating the Future, which I mentioned earlier in the section on incrementalism, has been advancing a framework called catalytic thinking, which focuses on changing the thinking and assumptions about the issues we are trying to address and how we go about addressing them. It asks us to consider these questions:

- "What is the future we want to create, and what will it take to create that reality?"
- "Who else cares about this? What can we accomplish together that none of us can accomplish on our own?"
- "What resources do we have together that none of us has all of on our own?"

The catalytic thinking framework is especially helpful in combating incrementalism. According to Hildy:

> We should think of the kind of future we want to create, and then work backwards. If we want to eradicate hunger in ten years and then go out of business, for example, then we need to think about what that will take and act on it, and maybe that means next year we increase our budget ten-fold, or we serve 100 families this year but aim to serve 800 families next year and significantly ramp up our policy and advocacy work.

As a sector, we need to be more vision-driven. It means nonprofit leaders reviewing their organizations' visions regularly and assessing if their current strategies still align; cooperating more deeply with other organizations, as many visions are only able to be actualized through partnership among many nonprofits as well as entities from other sectors; engaging in strategies organizations may not have been involved in before, such as advocacy and lobbying; and engaging in the occasional painful soul-searching process that leads to some organizations and foundations realizing their presence may be doing more harm than good and that it may be time to wind down some projects, merge with other organizations, or possibly end their work and fade gracefully into the sunset.

Ground Our Work in Values of Equity, Justice, and Community

Nonprofits all have a set of values. We display them on our website and then often forget they exist. But values should serve as our beacon, and everything we do must be grounded in them. They are an essential tool in avoiding many of the Horsemen of Ineffectiveness.

As one example, after George Floyd's murder by the police, Seattle Works, a nonprofit in Seattle, sent out a statement in support of Black lives and defunding the police. Ben Reuler, the former executive director, says:

> We anchored our work in antiracist values and started being unapologetic with it. It was so powerful. At the end of 2020 I wrote a public letter to our network not mincing words, sharing how we were navigating the moment by following the lead of our BIPOC colleagues, including donating funds to orgs like National Bail Out.

Supporting the defunding of the police movement is still considered very radical even in a progressive city like Seattle. It would have been easier and less controversial to fall in line with our sector's white moderate tendency to maintain peace and civility. Being aligned with its values allowed Seattle Works to do its best and most authentic work.

All nonprofits being grounded in values of equity and justice will help mitigate the effects of the Nine Horsemen. Neoliberalism is not as influential, if we are truly immersed in equity.

White moderation and toxic intellectualizing cannot take such a strong hold if we truly believe in justice. Self-interest can't thrive if we all choose community.

Have the Audacity of Ambition

Finally, strong visions and strong values must be combined with the courage and ambition to actualize our imagination. This is one area we can learn from our colleagues in for-profit, such as the ones behind Juicero, a Wi-Fi-connected juicing machine that came out of Silicon Valley in 2013. It was originally $700, and you had to subscribe to these proprietary packets of pre-cut-and-mixed produce for around $7 each. Each packet, once you placed it into the machine, would yield exactly one glass of juice. The news outlet Bloomberg did an investigation where they took the packets of cut-up fruit and vegetables, squeezed them by hand, and got almost the same amount of juice, but *faster*.

When their damning (yet hilarious) article[8] and related video[9] came out, the machine went down to $400 in price, and when that didn't stop the damage to investor confidence and consumer demand, the company went bankrupt.

But before it did, Juicero had secured over $120 million in investments.[10] It had 50 full-time engineers, 12 PhDs, and 7 food scientists[11] working on it. Juicero is now an example of one of the most insipid and hubris-filled projects that ever came out of Silicon Valley. Or perhaps it was just an idea that was way ahead of its time, who knows.

I bring up Juicero because it is one of the most infuriating stories yet yields some of the most important lessons for those of us in the profession of making the world better. The biggest lesson for us to take away from this fiasco is the *audacity of ambition*. This ridiculous juicer, which no one asked for, which the world didn't need, unapologetically secured *$120 million dollars* in investment. Meanwhile, many nonprofits, haunted by the Horsemen of Inferiority Complex and Stunted Imagination, are like, "Please sir, may we have $10,000 this year to help kids who are homeless?"

Over the past several decades, we've been conditioned to think small, to think incrementally. Not just nonprofits, but also funders and donors. Over time, the whole sector has lost its ability to have audacious dreams and ambitions. Can you imagine what any of us, what any nonprofit, can do with $120 million that would be so much better for the world?

As a sector, we need to get it back, the audacity to dream big. We are working to solve some of the most complex and entrenched problems in society, and we're now facing the global dismantling of democracy and acceptance of fascism. We would do well to take a page from Juicero's book and add a zero or two to our budgets and funding requests, because chances are, whatever our work is, it's likely more important than a Wi-Fi-connected juicing machine.

Discussion Questions

1. Have you had similar "ice-making" experiences in your personal or professional life, where you were so set in your ways, you didn't see an obvious obstacle or better path?

2. Which of the Horsemen of Ineffectiveness do you think is most problematic in our sector?
3. How do you see these Horsemen affecting one another?
4. Are there other underlying philosophies preventing nonprofits from being as effective as they can be?
5. Examine your organization's vision (or your personal vision if you don't work for an organization). How on track are you in achieving it? What would it take to get there?
6. What are your or your organization's values? Are they still the right values to guide your work?
7. If you had $120M, what would you or your organization do?

3

Reimagining Fundraising and Donor Engagement

We are living in the ancestral imagination of others, and we have to imagine something else.

—adrienne maree brown

When I was 11, all the students in the fifth and sixth grades had to write an essay about Veterans' Day and why we should honor our veterans, and the three students with the best essays would have to read their pieces at the school assembly. I had no interest in doing that. Thus began my quest to sabotage my own work by making up outlandish details in my essay about my father and his role fighting North Vietnam. My plan failed, and I found myself standing at the lectern at the assembly. "My father's friends were dodging bombs and bullets," I read, "Body parts flew everywhere! Arms and feet! Intestines! So much blood on the ground and trees and grass. That's why we should appreciate veterans. My father's friend had one ear ripped off."

I read the rest of the short essay and walked off the stage. "That was so moving," said one teacher, her eyes glistening with tears. "Your father and you and your family are so brave."

Why Fundraising Sometimes Perpetuates Harmful Myths

Fast forward several years, and I was at a gala, seated in the audience in my finest button-down shirt and trousers I had bought at Ross Dress for Less, the unofficial clothier of nonprofit professionals in the United States. On stage was a charismatic young man recounting his story of growing up impoverished. The room of mostly white attendees in suits and evening dresses was enraptured, everyone displaying smiles of sympathy while a few eyes misted up. During the "raise the paddle" event, where donors hold up pieces of paper with their assigned numbers to indicate how much they would donate, several gave at the $10,000 level.

I have been to countless fundraising events now and so many fundraising conferences and workshops. I learned about house parties, methods for finding out how wealthy a specific donor is, when to make the formal request for a gift, what to say when they say no, the importance of handwritten thank-you notes, and various psychological techniques that have been proven to move people to give:

> Donors are emotional. They don't care so much about statistics. Make them feel emotions by focusing on a specific individual with a name and a sad story. Show how the donor is the hero of the story. Make sure you use the word *you* as often as possible. "Because of *you*, children are able to go to school," "*You* enabled families to thrive," etc.

At another training, the advice was concise and catchy: "Make them laugh, make them cry, make the ask, say goodbye."

Fundraising, the way we have been taught, has led to many organizations being able to do good work. And fundraisers are some of the most creative and hardworking in our field. Yet fundraising has been frustrating. It is too focused on donors' thoughts and feelings and what pulls at their heart strings. It fosters competition among nonprofits. It promotes poverty porn, maintains power imbalance, and furthers the idea that wealth equals intelligence, which allows donors to meddle in nonprofit work without any qualifications. It sanctions conscience-laundering and charity-washing for individuals and corporations who should just pay more taxes. It excuses racism, sexual harassment, and other forms of inequity due to fear of losing donations.

Traditional fundraising has led to a toxic *retailification of nonprofit work.* This is the pervasive philosophy that, as fundraisers, our job is to connect donors to what they care about, helping them pick and choose among hundreds of equally good causes. Our sector then becomes a giant SkyMall catalog of programs and services, and fundraisers take on the role of donors' personal shoppers of equity and justice, making donors feel relevant and appreciated, and that by doing that we help them realize their goals of making the world better. It sounds fine on the surface, even noble. But what donors care about are often the things that will *least* likely change the systems of injustice that makes nonprofit and philanthropy necessary in the first place. And the expectation that donors be treated as customers whose whims should be catered to is gross and counterproductive to our work.

The traditional fundraising philosophies and tactics we've all learned to use and have been told are best practices are perpetuating the very injustices we're raising money to fight.

Imagine we're in a boat that's rapidly sinking. We need to work together to bail out the water, fix the leaks, and get everyone into life jackets. Now, imagine there are passengers who want to help. They mean well; they're just not used to handling buckets or duct tape or whatever. And they all already have their life jackets on, so they're not in as much danger as everyone else. One says, "Hi, I know you need someone on bucket duty, but that's not what I'm passionate about. My passion is to send flare signals!"

Another says, "I don't mind bailing out the water, but metal buckets make me feel warm and fuzzy because they remind me of my childhood growing up on a farm. You only have plastic ones; let me know if you find a metal bucket."

Yet another one says, "The last time I picked up a bucket, I didn't get a handwritten thank-you note fast enough, so I am still upset and don't want to participate this time."

Our society is one giant boat sinking under the weight of white supremacy and capitalism. It is problematic for fundraisers to believe that our primary goal remains connecting wealthy people to a salad bar of feel-good ingredients, where they can mix and match and choose whatever tugs most at their heartstrings, spurred on by our gratitude and hero worship, shielded from any analysis of systemic injustice and their roles in addressing it.

It is doubly problematic when most of our donors are white. For decades now, we've been conditioning white donors to think they're heroes and saviors of people of color and others on the margin. I have no doubt that most of our donors are wonderful people, for the most part, but we must acknowledge we've trained them to believe their feelings and emotions are of paramount importance, that it is okay for them to ignore how their wealth has been obtained and how their privilege enables the perpetuation of that wealth, that it's perfectly valid for them to avoid paying taxes and instead let their whims and passions dictate which issues get addressed, and that they know more than the people who have directly experienced inequity and injustice.

The traditional fundraising philosophies and tactics we've all learned to use and have been told are best practices are perpetuating the very injustices we're raising money to fight.

And we've conditioned one another to believe that this "Hunger Games," is good and normal. We fight with one another incessantly for donors' attention, and money, telling the best and most moving stories and showing the most gratitude and deference. It's time we evolve this model and line of thinking.

Necessary Shifts in Fundraising

This is not to say there are no redeeming qualities to traditional fundraising approaches. There are. Be transparent and communicative, build relationships, don't treat people like ATMs, ask for feedback, help donors see the role they play and the impact they make, and so on—these are all good things. However, to evolve the current fundraising model to fully align with our sector's values and vision, I propose five key shifts in our philosophy and approach, discussed in the following sections.

The Goal of Fundraising Should Be to Create an Equitable World

Over time, it seems many fundraisers and fundraising experts have forgotten this basic premise that fundraising is not about getting a bunch of money and calling it a day, but about making the world better. As James Hong, one of the founders of the CCF movement, says:

> We rarely talk about race and equity in fundraising. We always talk about race and equity in the context of programs, services, advocacy, etc., ... never fundraising. Right now, this donor-centered model of fundraising isn't designed to build power for people and communities. It's designed to make money. And frankly, you can double the revenues of an organization, increase donations, staff, etc., and still fail horribly at your mission.

Not only have you failed at your mission, but if your organization is perpetuating inequity, your fundraising efforts are pointless or possibly even destructive. If we don't use money raised as the main metric for fundraising success, what should we use then? This is where we can be more creative and grounded by our values of equity. I had an opportunity to interview the leaders of the Community Philanthropy Team at Oregon Food Bank (OFB), C. Nathan Harris (they/them) and Vivien Trinh (she/her). OFB has a unique radical approach. As they write in this article[1]:

> Decentering money is an inherent decentering of whiteness, colonialism, and greed. And in a profession where money reigns supreme, when we decenter money, a massive space opens up for something else. We're filling that space with love. For OFB, our new version of success meant recentering around the true meaning of philanthropy—a love of humankind.
>
> Measuring love for OFB includes such metrics as donors' awareness and understanding of systemic inequities that lead to hunger, donors' ability to identify and engage in actions to end hunger, donors' involvement in civic and political activities in general, and donors' involvement in other food justice organizations.

They also use metrics having to do with staff's happiness and well-being, including whether staff feel that their work is aligned with their values and purpose; how effectively they perceive they're able to engage with donors equitably, including those who don't give as much money or who are experiencing food insecurity themselves; whether they feel safe and supported regarding power differentials when interacting with donors; and the extent to which they believe OFB builds "power with our clients and donors for our collective liberation." You can read more about their approach and get some examples and tools at www.oregonfoodbank.org/lovecentric. To be clear, OFB does not dismiss the importance of financial goals in fundraising; like most nonprofits, they need resources to do their work. "What we said goodbye to were financial goals as a driver of decision-making and as a measurement of staff performance." This new lens of focusing on LOVE provides a much more values-aligned and expansive approach to their fundraising as well as to their work in general.

Justice Should Be a Donor's Main Motivator

Empathy has been the primary vehicle fundraisers use to motivate donors to give. We are trained to employ the "identifiable victim effect"[2] where instead of overwhelming donors with statistics about the hundreds or thousands of people who are suffering, we point out specific individuals—with names and faces and hopes and dreams and personalities—who could be helped if donors pitch in. This explains why we bring people on stage at our fundraising events to tell their stories, why we have pictures of smiling kids in our newsletters and appeals.

I am not against empathy. It is an effective tool. Many important policies are passed because people's sense of empathy is activated, as we have seen from various conservative politicians who change their minds on various issues because their child has a disability or is LGBTQIA+. But there are serious problems with this approach. Many of the issues we are trying to address are difficult if not impossible to generate empathy for, due to racial and other dynamics at play. It is unconsciously easier for our donors to empathize with certain issues and people than others. We, as human beings, are programmed to relate to and help people who are most like us.

While empathy can be helpful, it does steer attention and resources toward certain issues while allowing others to be ignored. Paul Bloom, who wrote the book *Against Empathy: The Case for Rational Compassion*, says in this article[3]:

> A reliance on empathy is part of the reason why people's desire to help abused dogs or oil-drenched penguins often exceeds their interest in suffering millions in other countries or ethnic minorities in their own. It's why governments and individuals often care more about a little girl stuck in a well than about crises that affect so many more.

The shift we as a sector must embrace is to move from empathy to *trust and justice*:

- **Trust** asks us to believe the people who are most affected by an unjust system, to take their words at value, even if it's outside our understanding or ability to relate. It also asks us to accept that the solutions proposed by the most marginalized people and communities would have the best chance of succeeding and to act accordingly.
- **Justice** demands that we support those who are most affected by inequity and oppression, whether or not we understand or feel empathy for them. It demands the recognition that our thoughts and feelings are secondary, if not irrelevant, to the realities facing many people with whom we will never completely empathize.

A few years ago, I was invited to present to a giving circle. This was a group of employees at a large tech companies; they pooled their donations, and the group chose one nonprofit to give the funds to. These were nice young professionals, and they nodded with empathy as I talked about my organization's work.

In contrast, Deborah, a donor to my former organization and now a friend of mine, joined a giving circle organized by Social Justice Fund. In similar veins, they also had to choose among nonprofits to give grants to. What was different was that during the weeks-long program, facilitators asked donors to examine their privilege, family's wealth, and philosophies around systemic injustice. Deborah realized the land her grandparents had bought and farmed and built their wealth on was originally stolen from Indigenous people.

The discovery prompted her resolve to return any money she inherits back to the Native community. "When I reflect on my forthcoming inheritance, my values insist that I make some small reparation. I'm going to give that money, my share of the inheritance, back to the tribe who historically lived on the land my family lives on now."

Justice demands the recognition that our thoughts and feelings are secondary, if not irrelevant, to the realities facing many people with whom we will never completely empathize.

The two giving circles both donated pooled funds to nonprofits. One, however, focused on empathy, while the other one focused on justice. If we rely solely on empathy, we may train donors to feel for the individuals they can relate to and do what they can to help, but we may be training them to only be focused on people and communities they can fully empathize with, and to be less focused on the systemic injustices they may be complicit in maintaining.

Again, I am not against empathy as a tool we use to motivate donors. But we must reexamine the time that we spend trying to get people to understand and empathize as a precondition for them to act. We must figure out how to encourage donors to support the people, communities, and issues that they may never fully or even partially understand.

Donors Should Be Treated as Partners, Not Heroes and Saviors

The idea of catering to donors as a guiding philosophy has been pervasive. It involves centering the happiness, desires, and convenience of donors, especially "major" donors. Over time, it becomes the air that many fundraisers breathe and pass on as best practice. There are many think pieces from fundraising experts telling fundraisers to literally treat donors like heroes. There have been efforts and campaigns such as #DonorLove, which is about constantly showing gratitude to donors.

A major problem with centering donors' emotions and treating them like heroes is the fact that most donors are white, and so much wealth has been built on white supremacy and inequity, and we have an entire field trained to tell mostly white people that they are heroes who should be coddled and catered to. Over time, rich, mostly white people start expecting and demanding to be treated this way. How do we mitigate white supremacy when we keep perpetuating it through our everyday practices?

Donors, as vital as they are to the work, are not any more vital than staff, volunteers, and other elements needed to get stuff done. Donors should be treated with respect and consideration, when warranted, but that same respect and consideration must be equally extended to everyone else, as the work cannot happen with donors alone.

Another problem is that built into this worship of donors is the simultaneous infantilization of them. One colleague on LinkedIn said in defense of donors when I pointed out that many donors treat philanthropy like a hobby (a statement that ignited a firestorm on LinkedIn among donor-centered fundraising experts):

"They share our foibles and failings yet, through philanthropy, discover the 'angels of their better nature.' They are the best of us; they make us all better."

Treating donors as fragile baby birds or Victorian era nobles who would collapse on their fainting couch at the slightest whiff of criticism and feedback does a disservice to donors, many of whom crave meaningful engagement on issues of equity and justice. At my last organization, Jon, a donor, told me once that he didn't need these handwritten thank-you notes we were sending. I asked what he would like instead. He said, "I hear you and the team are attending a two-day workshop on undoing institutional racism. Can I join?" He joined for the full two days. That workshop was known to be challenging for everyone, especially white attendees.

That was years ago. I checked in with Jon a few months back to get his reflections on the experience. "A part of that workshop that stayed with me was when the facilitators asked, 'Why are there poor people?' And one of our colleagues, her answer was pretty succinct: 'So there can be rich people.' That wasn't comfortable for me as a rich person. But it was a moment for me of clarity and truth that I wouldn't otherwise achieve."

He went on to describe how it felt in being there with my team and me:

> There is something in our being together—really being together—in solidarity, that I think brings joy. It doesn't have to feel easy. Being in solidarity is not the easiest. But it's meaningful. Trusting one another to be that authentic was its own reward. That workshop was an opportunity for us to grow together. That was better than a thousand handwritten thank-you notes.

Many of our donors have moved far ahead of fundraisers and wealth advisors in terms of being aligned with equity and progressive values. Austrian heiress Marlene Engelhorn, for example, who inherited $27 million dollars, is determined to allow the public to distribute the wealth. She cofounded Tax Me Now, a movement to mobilize wealthy Europeans to change tax codes to address inequity.[4]

This strong orientation toward justice is where many of our donors are. Fundraising should evolve to help get our other donors there. But we can only achieve that if we stop worshipping and infantilizing our donors and treat them as partners, including inviting them to have these deep and meaningful experiences and reflections.

Fundraisers Should Be Agents of Justice

Traditional fundraising is based on the belief that fundraisers' job is simply to bring in money and that the work of equity and justice is the purview of others at the organization, perhaps senior leadership or program staff. When DEI is mentioned, it has usually been in the context of getting money from donors of different races and ethnicities, or how to make sure fundraising staff of color don't quit. In those purposes, diversity, equity, and inclusion become only tools in service of obtaining funds, and fundraisers simply serve as catalysts for getting resources.

We are underutilizing our fundraisers' skills and brilliance. Fundraisers have been trained to be excellent communicators and relationship builders, which means they often have the strongest opportunities and chance for success in having meaningful conversations with donors and funders. That can have profound changes in how these folks perceive the world and what actions they take to advance equity and justice.

With money being so essential in our line of work, it sends an extremely clear and powerful message when nonprofits and fundraisers use fundraising to communicate their alignment with their values of equity and justice. Detroit Justice Center (DJC), a nonprofit law firm focused on transforming the justice system, creating economic opportunities, and making cities more equitable, received a Yield Giving grant from philanthropist Mackenzie Scott, whose wealth is built through the inequity created by Amazon, which is known for using legal loopholes to avoid paying billions in taxes[5] while exploiting its workers.[6] Here's an excerpt from the organization's press release[7]:

> "We see this donation as an act of wealth reclamation," said DJC's Executive Director Nancy A. Parker, "and we will use it to redistribute wealth stolen from overworked and underemployed Amazon workers and put it toward serving our community, which is disproportionately affected by cycles of incarceration."

Traditional fundraising tells us to constantly be thankful and appreciative, without much analysis of the inequitable systems that allowed wealth to be accumulated. It is courageous for DJC to publicly state that the "gift" they received is actually a form of reparation for injustice. The organization takes this approach with all their donors, as evidenced by the cordial but firm and educational email response from founding Development Director Regina M. Sharma to a donor who was upset that the staff were being paid "too much":

> We are a Black, women-led organization, and our pay structure acknowledges the massive wealth disparities and pay inequities that historically have most affected women of color. The salary for this position is also a fair market rate that takes into account the expertise needed, time spent, and personal sacrifices that our leaders make in order to advance our mission and best serve our clients.

Having conversations with donors—one-on-one, or in groups such as giving circles—about white supremacy, wealth disparity, complicity, reparation, taxes, and more, and pushing back when they're being unreasonable will be much more difficult than what we've been trained to do, which is to just take their money and be thankful. But if fundraisers all embrace it, it will be easier for everyone, and more importantly, it will meaningfully move our sector forward.

Nonprofits Should Be Mutually Supportive

After the police murdered Michael Brown Jr. in 2015 in Ferguson, Missouri, thousands of people rose up in protest. Forward Through Ferguson (FTF) was established as a nonprofit to carry on the work of advancing equity. In 2020, after the murder of George Floyd by the police, FTF received a rapid influx of resources as funders and donors rushed to support racial equity work. The organization was in a situation in which nonprofits rarely find themselves and had to reevaluate its fundraising strategies and tactics. It had a new summer fundraising event that had already been planned, but there was now no immediate need for the revenues from this event. The FTF staff decided to call up four other nonprofits in the area they believed were doing critical work and asked if these organizations would like to receive an equal share of the revenues generated by the event.

We can be more effective as a sector if nonprofits care about and invest in one another's success.

The other organizations were understandably a bit confused at first, possibly somewhat suspicious, wondering if there would be strings attached. FTF's board members, meanwhile, also had doubts; giving money away to other nonprofits was definitely unusual, and they were concerned about the legal ramifications of such an action. However, FTF continued with its plans, and the ripples of this action extend to this day, as the organizations continue to maintain and strengthen their collaborations.

"We didn't need to hoard the money," said Rachel D'Souza of Gladiator Consulting, the former Justice Philanthropy Catalyst of FTF and current Community-Centric Fundraising Global Council member,

"We had the resources. It didn't feel competitive. It didn't feel performative. We're only successful if we are supportive of one another."

At Wayne State University (WSU), a similar decision was made. Michigan State University (MSU) experienced a mass shooting that resulted in the deaths of several students and faculty members. The fundraising team at WSU sent out an email appeal asking donors to support MSU. Encouraging donors to give to a different organization is blasphemous in traditional fundraising.

"We were a bit nervous, not sure how leadership would take it," says Leslie Carmona, WSU's Senior Director of Donor Experience and Individual Giving, "but we thought it was the right thing to do, and if there were consequences, we'd deal with them later. The standard 'ask for forgiveness, not permission!'"

The consequences that came from this thoughtful gesture was that MSU was appreciative, donors were deeply moved, and senior leaders were impressed.

Nonprofits' missions are interrelated, and education, housing, mental health, youth development, early learning, the environment, public safety, arts, and so on, mutually affect one another. We can be more effective as a sector if nonprofits care about and invest in one another's success. The result, as we often see when that happens, is that donors have increased motivation to give, more resources are generated, and our sector's potential to address inequity is greatly advanced.

Community-Centric Fundraising

In 2015, I wrote about a concept I called community-centric fundraising (CCF) that involves many elements covered in this chapter. It resonated with fundraisers who had been equally frustrated with traditional fundraising. Several fundraisers of color and I got together regularly in Seattle to commiserate and brainstorm actions to get our sector to evolve the way it does fundraising. This core group—comprising Andrea Arenas, Erika Chen, James Hong, Rehana Lanewala, Ana Rebecca Lopez, Michelle Muri, Christina Shimizu, Sean Watts, and me—became the Founding Council of the formal Community-Centric Fundraising movement.

After a summit, where we convened nearly 100 fundraisers of color in Seattle, we launched the official CCF movement virtually during the first year of the pandemic. We anticipated maybe two or three hundred people would join. Nearly 2,800 people attended. Since then, CCF has been catching on and spreading across the sector and creating a robust community of practitioners thinking about and experimenting with fundraising in ways that are more aligned with our sector's stated values. You can read more about the movement and get involved at communitycentricfundraising.com.

CCF has 10 principles, outlined in the following parts of this chapter. See Appendix A for a more extensive list of sample actions that align with each principle. These principles were synthesized after years of observation, conversations with other leaders—especially leaders of color and white allies—and various reflections. They have evolved as others in the CCF movement contributed their thoughts and feedback, and will continue to change as we have more conversations.

Principles of Community-Centric Fundraising

Principle 1: We Ground Fundraising in Race, Equity, and Social Justice These elements must be central to everything related to raising funds. They must inform and guide every decision and action taken by fundraisers. Fundraisers should be trained to undo racism. Donors should be asked to reflect on the origins of their wealth.

Principle 2: We Prioritize the Collective Community over Individual Missions Nonprofit missions are interrelated, and the community is best served if we see ourselves as part of a larger ecosystem working collectively to build a just society. Stop doing things that benefit your organization but harm the entire sector, such as boasting about your nonprofit's low overhead.

Principle 3: We Are Generous and Mutually Supportive of Other Missions Nonprofits see and treat one another not as competitors, but as critical partners with the common mission to strengthen the community. This includes sharing funding opportunities, credit, and even declining funding if appropriate.

Principle 4: We Value and Equally Appreciate All Elements That Strengthen Community We respect, appreciate, recognize, and build relationships with our donors equally, no matter their level of giving. We use the same approach with other members of our sector and express equal appreciation for colleagues, board members, volunteers, and clients.

Principle 5: We Value Time and Money Equally Time is the only resource we cannot make more of, and thus the donation of time (from volunteers and from staff who work unpaid hours) must be valued as much as the donation of money.

Principle 6: We Respect Our Donors' Integrity and Treat Them as Partners We have honest, respectful conversations, including strong disagreements as needed, with our donors. We do not hide challenging truths from donors, but instead treat them as adults who are capable of handling difficult conversations and feedback.

Principle 7: We Foster a Sense of Belonging in Our Fundraising Work; We Avoid Treating Anyone as an "Other" We strive to ensure everyone feels a sense of belonging, whether they are donor, volunteers, staff, or clients, and we authentically partner with community members when asking them to be involved in fundraising efforts. For instance, we make sure events are accessible and are thoughtful about using people's stories and images to avoid casting people needing to be "saved."

Principle 8: We Encourage Everyone to Believe We All Benefit from This Work Some call it "enlightened self-interest." It is important to get donors to see they and their families benefit from their donations, that they are not donating only for others' benefits. We avoid training donors to see themselves as heroes and saviors.

Principle 9: We Treat the Work as Holistic, Not as a Collection of Isolated Segments We need to stop simplifying our work and breaking it into misleading parts ("$100 will save 5 kids!") and instead get everyone to see and understand how the entire sector operates. We need to stop using low overhead rates to drive donations and instead encourage the support of core operating expenses.

Principle 10: We Recognize That Healing and Liberation Require a Commitment to Economic Justice This involves fundraisers and donors grappling with and addressing the root causes of inequity, including the destructive effects of capitalism and how we may be complicit in furthering them through our practices. We support progressive policies like increasing taxes on the wealthy and raising the minimum wage.

Does Community-Centric Fundraising Work?

This is the question and criticism that CCF most frequently receives from people who are thoroughly entrenched in traditional fundraising practices. Even fundraisers who are curious about the CCF approach can be fearful that doing things differently may have financial consequences. By "work," people mean *does it bring in money*. I am not arguing that traditional fundraising practices aren't effective at this, but just because something results in money does not mean it is an ethical thing to do. Putting a picture of a starving kid of color into an appeal letter may inspire donors to give, but that does not mean it's not harmful by perpetuating poverty porn and white saviorism. If something results in a ton of money but increases injustice, then it is not working, no matter how much money it generates.

However, if you insist on sticking to the old definition of what "works," there's growing evidence that organizations using CCF-aligned fundraising strategies are raising plenty of money. Sure, they may lose a few donors in the short run, but in the long run, they often attract other, more loyal donors who are compelled by the organizations' strong alignment with its values. In many cases, they raise even more funding than when they were using traditional fundraising tactics.

As one example, mentioned in Chapter 2, after George Floyd's murder by the police, Seattle Works, a nonprofit in Seattle, sent out a statement in support of Black lives and defunding the police. They knew the letter would result in some donors leaving. And indeed, several sent in scathing comments and pulled their support, and a couple of board members were nervous. However, the letter garnered an outpouring of support and a significant bump in donations, and it eventually turned out to be one of the most successful fundraising years for the organization. According to Ben Reuler, the ED at the time:

> For every donor who walked away, 10 new people saw themselves in the organization who hadn't prior. I'll never forget, a wealthy, white donor couple responded to the letter saying "Wow, this is bold, you might turn some people off. How can we help?" I made an audacious ask and they increased their giving by tenfold—to a six-figure, multi-year general operating support gift, the largest in the 30-year history of the organization, BECAUSE we were leading with values. Undoubtedly the most joyful, rewarding, values-led fundraising I've ever been a part of.

Seattle Works and the other examples I discussed are proof that we can successfully raise funds while taking bold, courageous actions to advance a just and equitable world.

If something results in a ton of money but increases injustice, then it is not working, no matter how much money it generates.

A Culture of Philanthropy

Over the past several years, we've been hearing the term "culture of philanthropy" a lot. According to the 2013 report, "Underdeveloped,"[8] by Haas Jr. Fund and Compass Point, the culture of philanthropy incorporates these key elements:

Most people in the organization (across positions) act as ambassadors and engage in relationship-building. Everyone promotes philanthropy and can articulate a case for giving. Fund development is viewed and valued as a mission-aligned program of the organization. Organizational systems are established to support donors. The executive director is committed and personally involved in fundraising.

The culture of philanthropy, the way our sector currently defines and implements it, is really about everyone being involved in building relationships with donors in order to raise as much money as possible for their organization. That's not philanthropy; that's fundraising. Philanthropy and fundraising are two separate things. They may be deeply interrelated, but they're not the same. And as I've discussed, traditional fundraising poses all sorts of problems and, in many ways, has been helping to perpetuate the injustices we're raising money to fight, so to build an entire culture around this is something we must be cautious about.

If we're going to build a culture of philanthropy, then let's do it right, by making sure everyone in our sector is grounded in and prioritizing equity and justice, and that means a deep engagement with undoing racism, white supremacy, and capitalism. Fundraising is about creating a better world; the funds are a means to this important end. We encourage donors to engage meaningfully in some uncomfortable conversations about how their wealth has been obtained and how they may need to do things like making reparations for inequities and paying more taxes. We set justice, not empathy, as the primary guiding force in interacting with donors. Fundraisers embrace their roles as agents of justice. And nonprofits are mutually supportive of one another, prioritizing the community over their own missions, with the collective vision of a just and equitable world.

Fundraising is about creating a better world; the funds are a means to this important end.

It may take some time, practice, and probably a few failures as we experiment with these new strategies, and more importantly, a radical shift in how we think about fundraising and donor engagement, but I have confidence in the brilliance of our fundraising professionals.

Discussion Questions

1. What aspects of traditional fundraising practices do you like?
2. What aspects of traditional fundraising practices have you been concerned about?
3. Which of the shifts in fundraising approaches resonates most with you?
4. Which of the CCF principles resonates most with you?
5. Which one are you most concerned about?
6. What actions can you or your organization take in the short run to make your fundraising practices more equitable? In the long run?
7. What are potential barriers that might prevent you from taking these actions or from these actions being successful?
8. How might you address these barriers?

4

Governance and Boards

To get something done, a committee should consist of no more than three people, two of whom are absent.

—Robert Copeland

IN 2015, I made probably one of the biggest leadership mistakes in my career. I had just founded RVC (Rainier Valley Corps, later Rooted in Vibrant Communities) the year prior under the fiscal sponsorship of another organization. Because the fiscal sponsor had its own formal board, and we were technically a program of it, we did not need our own formal board. We were in start-up mode with me as the only staff member, and I needed help, so I started a community board that met quarterly. Each meeting was an event, complete with dinner from local minority-owned businesses and professional childcare so people could bring their children. Thirty to 80 people attended each time. The gatherings were vibrant, fun, and sometimes chaotic, and the attendees looked like the communities we were serving. During these meetings, we discussed and voted on values, strategies, and even the logo. Eight or so committees were formed that met between meetings. For a couple of years, it was glorious.

The mistake I made was that as RVC raised money, grew, and had to move out of fiscal sponsorship, I decided we needed a traditional board made up of eight or so people who met once a month. That was the model I had been taught, so that's what we created. At first, it was certainly more efficient; we could make decisions much faster. But over time, volunteers who had been actively engaged in the community board suddenly felt left adrift, confused as to what their roles were now; gradually, they dropped out, the committees becoming less and less active.

Meanwhile the official board members became more and more micromanage-y, risk-averse, and occasionally even adversarial. Months before my second baby was born, for instance, I asked the board to create a family leave policy. I encouraged them to consider providing paid leave in alignment with our value of equity, but I referred them to an HR consultant and recused myself due to conflicts of interest. When the baby was born and no leave policy had been approved, I emailed the executive committee to ask how much time I could take off. They responded that, due to our tight budget, I would be getting zero paid family leave, and that the board would get back to me when they've decided how much *unpaid* leave I could take.

These and other words and actions from the board nearly drove me to resign from the organization I had founded. I imagined leaving a snarky note like "I have decided to take 365 days of unpaid family leave this year and all future years to spend time with my new baby. Good luck."

It was confusing and frustrating because this board comprised brilliant, kind, caring individuals I had personally asked to join. What happened? Where were the thoughtful and expansive-thinking colleagues who had been in the trenches with me when we had our community gatherings? Why did they transform into people I barely recognized in this new structure?

Structure or Culture: Why Are So Many Boards Dysfunctional?

Board members are volunteers who contribute time, money, skills, connections, and even the occasional shoulder to cry on during challenging moments. I know how hard boards and board members work, and we owe a lot to the dedicated board members out there who are helping us make the world better every day. And despite the many challenges I have experienced with my own boards and board members across my career, they have been instrumental in my organizations' success.

However, we need to admit that boards in general are seriously problematic. In any given year, boards of directors are the direct cause of 87 percent of migraines for nonprofit leaders, according to statistics I just made up.

After years of observations, I have developed a *Rule of One-Thirds* when it comes to boards. Among all boards in our sector, one-third of them are helpful to their missions, one-third are useless, and one-third are destructive to their missions. It can be argued that among most boards, the same rule applies to the members themselves.

This means that, in general, two-thirds of nonprofit boards and board members are useless or harmful. For every good-board story, there are more tales of crappy boards. They micromanage the staff. They get buried in operations, wasting their time scrutinizing font selections and toilet paper purchases. Worst of all are the boards that prevent progress, like the ones that refused to allow their organizations to publicly support Black Lives Matter, or to let the staff put their pronouns in their email signatures, thinking it's too "political." In a time when everything is on fire and our sector and its work are under serious threats, we don't need our boards to become obstacles.

But how could boards *not* be dysfunctional? We're talking about a structure where groups of volunteers who barely know one another, see one percent of the work, often don't reflect the communities we serve, and may have little to no experience running nonprofits are given vast power to supervise leadership and determine values, policies, and practices. Combine that with nonsensical philosophies such as "the board is the boss of the ED or CEO," and archaic and often inequitable practices such as Robert's Rules, and our default board structure looks like a lumbering, unwieldy, dysfunctional relic of the past.

Over the years, we have developed a learned helplessness around governance, thinking that the current widely used board model is the only one we have. So we put up with it, grumbling to our colleagues and working to mitigate our challenges, for instance figuring out ways to bring good board members on to neutralize bad ones or having more trainings or meetings to increase "board engagement." The more strategic among us may deploy tactics like the one I call Plaque and Sack, where we celebrate deadwood board members publicly and with great fanfare and shiny symbols of appreciation, all in a bid to get them to step down.

> *I think there is something to our default structure that causes dysfunction and turns nice people into assholes.*

There is a legitimate argument to be made that it's not the structure that's the problem. There are plenty of functional, helpful boards that use traditional structures and Robert's Rules. And there are plenty of horrible situations where there are alternative governing structures, ones that are flatter, less hierarchical, for instance. It may just be that when people are grounded in their values and the organization has invested enough time building up a cohesive culture of equity, trust, staff–board collaboration, and so on, it doesn't matter what structure they use.

I generally agree. But having been a leader overseen by boards and having served on boards overseeing executive leaders, I think there is something to our default structure that causes dysfunction and turns nice people into assholes. I've seen it happen to multiple people, including at my previous org. On occasion, I catch myself veering toward asshole territory when I am on a board: "I don't understand. Why do staff need...what do they call it...benefits?"

Not to say everyone becomes a jerk when they join a board, of course; there are lots of nice people who stay nice, and there are also assholes who turn nice. But it happens with enough frequency that we should discuss it.

Let's talk about what alternative governance structures may look like and what other organizations are doing out there. But first, as usual, we need to shift a few entrenched mindsets and develop some new ones when it comes to governance and boards.

Governance Should Be a Shared Responsibility

This idea that governance is the sole responsibility of boards is so entrenched that we often use these two terms interchangeably. When funders ask, for example, "How strong is your org's governance?" what they often mean is "How effective is your board?"

Reimaging Governance, a project of Toronto-based Ontario Nonprofit Network and Ignite NPS, writes the role of governance in an organization is

> *to provide stewardship, sensemaking and foresight that advance its purpose. Governance leadership takes responsibility for building and sustaining stakeholders' confidence in the organization's integrity, legitimacy and viability.*[1]

That definition may explain why boards are often so dysfunctional and overwhelmed. The people with the least amount of knowledge about the organization—the board members—have the sole responsibility for these critical tasks. Reimagine Governance has created tools and a learning community to explore models where "the board still plays a critical role, but governance leadership is more broadly distributed, and decisions are made in a collaborative way. It feels more like interlocking nodes that form a system of governance."[2]

Sharing governance addresses its complicated nature, clarifies who is responsible for what, builds more intention, creates more buy-in from internal stakeholders, and strengthens collaboration between board and staff. It also increases equity by distributing power and authority from the board, which tends to be very white and male dominated, to the rest of the organization, which tends to be more diverse.

In general, nonprofits are moving away from traditional hierarchical structures and toward more collectivistic models, like co-directorships and distributed power (see Chapter 5). Boards are no exception; in fact, given how much power boards hold, it's pivotal we prioritize boards and governance in this evolution.

The Board's Role Is to Advance Equity and Justice, Not Simply Protect Its Mission

A while ago, a colleague and I, both haggard executive directors with involuntary eye twitches, were having lunch. Our conversation led us to our boards, and he told me of how his board chair scolded him for the egregious crime of forwarding a funding opportunity to another nonprofit. "He was mad that I helped our 'competition' by letting them know of a request for proposals from a foundation. I figured why wouldn't we share RFPs with one another? Aren't we all trying to make our community better?"

Boards are often trained to only focus on their organization's survival. We need to move toward a community-centric board mindset, where board members understand and believe that what is ultimately best for the entire community must take priority over their nonprofit (or foundation)'s mission, as vital as it is. This means that:

- **Boards are grounded in racial, economic, and social justice.** Boards are often way behind staff in getting trained and engaging in conversations and reflection on these issues. This frequently sets back organizations, as board members are often imbued with formal power that they use to prevent progress from being made. Too often the work of examining systemic racism, white supremacy, privileges, and so on is seen as an afterthought by many board members, or something they reluctantly sign up for.
- **Boards reflect the communities being served.** Our sector is rife with white saviors, and this is especially present on boards. For a board to be effective and to minimize the potential harm it may cause, its members must reflect the community it's serving in terms of race, gender, income level, disability, and so on. As communities continue to diversify, the board must be constantly alert to ensure it's still reflective of the people it's serving.
- **Boards encourage mutual support and collaboration among nonprofits.** My colleague who shared a funding opportunity with another org should have been praised by his board. Board members should encourage their org to be supportive of other organizations, including sharing funding opportunities and even declining funding if another nonprofit, especially if it's led by marginalized communities, could benefit more.
- **Boards play a critical role in collective efforts to bring about racial, economic, and social justice.** Many boards not only stay out of taking critical stances against white supremacy, police violence, homophobia, transphobia, and so on, but actively

prevent their staff from doing so. Again, it is not good enough simply for an organization to grow and run its programs and services. Boards must constantly assess and reflect on whether their organizations are ultimately helping to restore equity and justice in the world.

The Board Is Not the Boss

Our default structures and philosophies and have conditioned board members to think they're basically the supervisors of the ED/CEO. It is ingrained in all of us, and many EDs/CEOs think along this line, too. Even I have introduced a board member at an event and joked, "This is one of my bosses!"

This line of thinking has caused tremendous problems, such as inflating board members' ego and sense of importance, decreasing of staff's authority and autonomy to do work, and furthering the board's meddling and micromanaging in programs and operations. It is problematic when board members rarely have even close to the same level of knowledge about what is happening on the ground.

Instead of thinking of itself as the boss of the ED/CEO or staff and thus imbued with power to make all the important decisions, a nonprofit board should consider itself a critical but co-equal element of the organization's work, serving as a partner and a check-and-balance mechanism. In Ananda Valenzuela's article series on governance, they mention the core role of the board to be "Loving Accountability,"[3] which includes monitoring team morale, financial stability, and impact on the community, having trusting and transparent relationships with staff, and stepping in to provide support when there are crises.

None of that though means that the board is the boss of the staff. Ananda emphasizes the board having "power-with" instead of "power-over" the staff. This is not a perfect analogy by any means, considering what has happened in politics over the past few years, but think of the branches of the U.S. government. The legislative branch can make laws. It can also impeach and remove the president. And the judicial branch could uphold these decisions.

Similarly, under the idea of "loving accountability," boards can pass policies, ensure the organization is complying with its values, checking regularly to make certain the executive leader is doing their job and is not abusive or corrupt, and possibly removing them when needed. But just as no one would consider the House of Representatives, Senate, or Supreme Court the collective "boss" of the president and the executive branch, no one should consider boards the "bosses" or "supervisors" of executive leaders and their team.

Fundraising May Not Necessarily Be a Main Board Function

This is probably one of the more blasphemous things I say. The expectation that most boards fundraise has negatively affected their ability to do their main duty well, which is to govern, and it may be time to separate these two roles by removing fundraising from most boards' roster of duties entirely. Who will be in charge of fundraising and how can nonprofits be sustainable if board members don't pitch in? The answer is simple.

The ED/CEO and staff will be responsible, as they've always been. Unless we're talking about large historic organizations like the symphony, where being on the board is a prestigious status symbol that requires hefty annual donations, connections to wealth, or ideally both, boards' fundraising activities and personal contributions only make up a small portion of the budget, but lead to all sorts of problems. Removing fundraising as an essential board role could:

Expecting governing bodies to do fundraising and governance means they often do a good job at neither.

- **Increase focus on governance.** Expecting governing bodies to do both fundraising and governance when they are both complex tasks and board members have extremely limited time means they often do a good job at neither. Removing one, fundraising, will allow the other, governance, to more likely succeed.
- **Improve morale among staff and board.** Nonprofit staff are often frustrated because their boards aren't pulling their weight with fundraising. Some board members are frustrated because

they just want to do governance, but they're expected to fundraise. Meanwhile, some board members just want to donate money and don't give a tub of moldy hummus about governance. Separating out fundraising from governance will clarify roles, decrease expectations, and allow people to choose how they want to be involved.

- **Allow boards to be diverse and reflect the communities they serve.** Believing boards are responsible for fundraising means nonprofits tend to prioritize recruiting those who have money, are connected to it, or who can fundraise. Since these folks tend to be white, this helps explain why the diversity of boards in the United States is so abysmal. Eliminating fundraising as a critical board function will balance this out, as nonprofits will focus less on who has money and more on who has the lived experience and skills to be effective on the board.

- **Create more egalitarian boards where all voices matter.** No matter how nice people are, it doesn't counter the fact that board members who give more money are allocated more power and influence at the organization than those who give less. Deemphasizing the board's role in financially sustaining the organization increases the likelihood that all voices, especially those from marginalized community members, are treated equally.

- **Let nonprofits align better with their values.** We all hear horror stories of board members who don't experience repercussions for being racist, sexist, transphobic, ableist, and so on, because they are also major donors or had connections to major donors, and the org is afraid of losing their donations or relationships. Eliminating fundraising as a function of the board will help lessen this type of values misalignment.

None of this is to say board members can't give to their organizations or help with fundraising. They certainly can contribute if they want. They can pass along connections to potential donors and funders as appropriate. They can even join the development committee and help that way, if they understand they're serving in a volunteer capacity and not as a board member.

Reconsider Board Giving and Compensation

A few years ago, when I led the Vietnamese Friendship Association (VFA), I remember trying to get board members to donate. Funders had been asking what the board giving rate was, and, if it wasn't 100 percent, to explain why. I've always found this practice grating, for a lot of reasons. First, it's completely meaningless. If each of the VFA board members had reluctantly yielded to my pleas and gave $5, for a total of $65, I would have been able to tell funders I had 100 percent board giving, but how is that meaningful? Wouldn't expectations like "100 percent of board members contribute time by volunteering at programs" or "100 percent of our board has personally experienced what it's like to be in poverty" be more relevant?

Instead of expecting board members to donate money, an increasing number of nonprofits are doing the reverse: Paying board members or providing stipends, which is way more equitable. Saskatchewan Arts Alliance is one such organization. Each board member receives a $155 stipend for each meeting, a cost to the nonprofit of about $10,000 per year. I talked to ED Em Ironstar, who reported this small change resulted in stronger board diversity and increased engagement.

"If we wanted to invite artists, especially those from marginalized communities, to serve on our board, we needed to recognize they don't always come from the same backgrounds as, for example, an ED from a multi-million-dollar organization. I don't know why [providing stipends] is so surprising in our sector when corporations and foundations pay their board members significantly more."[4]

Indeed, the median payment for board members of private companies was $32,000 in 2024, sometimes reaching up to half a million dollars for larger companies.[5] Meanwhile, a report on 238 private foundations found that 87 paid each board member $25,000 or more, and 19 paid more than $100,000 each.[6] Considering all that, nonprofits spending $10,000 for a more diverse, engaged, and equitable board seems like small fries.

Who the Heck Is Robert? Why Are We Still Using His Rules?

Henry Martyn Robert was born on May 2, 1837. He was an American soldier, engineer, and writer. In 1876, he published the *Pocket Manual of Rules of Order for Deliberative Assemblies*, which he modeled after the United States House of Representatives.[7] This manual, known as Robert's Rules for short, then became widespread.

But 1876 was nearly 150 years ago. Things have changed. Robert's Rules is a very white way of running meetings. Many communities are relational and use dialog, storytelling, and collective frameworks for making decisions. Using Robert's Rules means people from these communities are often left behind. I remember numerous occasions serving on boards and feeling overwhelmed and unable to participate because everyone around me—who were mostly white—had a grasp of these rules, but I didn't, even when they were discussing things in which I had more firsthand experience, such educational services for immigrant kids.

Instead of Robert's Rules, organizations can try alternatives that are simpler, more accessible, and more equity minded. For example, sociocracy and consent-based decision-making, which I elaborate on later.

Hiring the ED/CEO(s) Should Be a Collaborative Process

The idea that the board and the board alone makes the final decision on hiring the executive leader has been strongly held in our sector. But it makes little sense for a group of volunteers, who, again, see only a fraction of the work and interact with this executive director a scant few hours a month, to have more say in the matter than the people who will have to work with and report to this person all the time!

The board may have the legal authority to make final hiring decisions on the ED/CEO, but that does not mean it needs to jealously guard this power from staff like a group of Gollums from *Lord of the Rings* sitting in the conference room whispering "It's ours, Precious, our decision! We gets to decides who is the new leader!" Authentic collaboration and "power-with" regarding this vital decision will make for much happier staff and stronger likelihood the new leader will be successful.

ED hirings should be collaborative, with the search committee comprising half board members and half staff members. This committee would make the final recommendation to the full board as to who to hire, or even what new leadership structures should be considered.

When I left my previous organization, the board and staff collaborated closely. The resulting process led to an entirely new leadership structure with four internal senior leaders becoming co-EDs, which I discuss in Chapter 5.

Alternative Board Structures and Decision-Making Models

Erin Kang, Director of Network Engagement at Ontario Nonprofit Network, which stewards the Reimagining Governance project, elaborates on the idea that much of our sector has been stuck with this ingrained image of what governance/boards should look like:

> We have this standard, template idea of what boards should be: 8–12 people around the table who bring different skills or backgrounds to support the organization's purpose. And that may work for some organizations, but the important thing is it won't for them all.[8]

She uses an analogy I find helpful:

> Think about the nuclear family template, and how many families don't fit into that model. There are so many different types of families. We can't apply a singular template to all boards; organizations need to figure out what they need and how to make their governance and accountability work for them. That takes mindfulness.

Legal requirements for governance vary by country and state, but in general, there aren't many of them. Boards tend to have three formal duties: Duty of care, duty of loyalty, and duty of obedience. These are so broad that they can be interpreted in any number of ways. When it comes down to it, boards are legally required to exist, have at least three members, meet once a year or so, and file their tax reports. Some boards have legal requirements stating they must have certain types of compositions; for example, so many members must be from the community, so many must be appointed by the governor, and so on.

Outside of these very few formal requirements, a lot is open to interpretation. Which means we have endless potential to innovate beyond the stuffy traditional governance model. And there are organizations doing just that. Here are a few different structures colleagues have pointed out. I am familiar with some and not at all with others, so please think of this as a starting point to explore what may work best for your org.

The Minimally Viable Board (MVB)

This model comes from New Zealand-based group Enspiral. They have a video that explains the history of thinking behind the minimally viable board (MVB) model, which involves distilling the board's roles and responsibilities down to its essentials for the organization to remain in legal compliance. Depending on the country and state the organization is operating in, it may look like a board that has only three members who only meet once a year to approve the tax filing. This board could meet as needed when problems arise, but otherwise stays away from being involved in the other work of the organization.[9]

While it is not widespread yet, a few organizations have been exploring the MVB model. Canadian organization Never Too Late (NTL), for example, which focuses on serving youth who have or will age out of the child welfare system, has been using the MVB model, which it complements with a Trusted Advisory Council, a group of volunteers who have no legal obligations or authority, but whose time and expertise are called on as needed, a type of community board, which I describe in the next section. And it's working for them. I talked to Aviva Zukerman Schure, NTL's "Board Lead," who talked about the benefits of having this minimally viable mindset not just as it concerns the board, but in general. "It's astounding how better a decision is made when we ask ourselves 'What is the bare minimum the government requires from this?' and then it opens us up to new possibilities."

However, like with any model, there are challenges and considerations. Roles must be clearly defined. Aviva also finds that funders often look askance at their governance structure:

> When you go for funds, some funders look at you and go, "So you don't have a real board?" They think a traditional board makes you a better, more trustworthy organization. Even explaining our structure in grant proposals, with the Trusted Advisory Council, people are still confused.

The Community Board

If you use an MVB, it may be a good idea to pair it with a community board, or whatever cool name you may call it. If you are fiscally sponsored and aren't required to have a formal board, then you may also have something like this model.

The community board is kind of like a traditional advisory board, something many organizations have. They have no formal power but can be helpful in advising the organization on various matters. However, the Community Board takes it to the next level and strongly prioritizes engaging community members in the organization's work. The benefits include increased community buy-in; better input and feedback from community members on programs and strategies; increased volunteerism; strengthened connections among community members; and a wider donor base.

This is what my former organization had before I turned it into the traditional board, a decision that haunts me to this day. The model we used was never formally named; we just referred to the meetings as "quarterly gatherings." For RVC, the elements that made it successful were:

- **An open and welcoming environment** where everyone invested in the organization and the community it serves may participate. We tried to make it accessible by having meetings in the evenings, providing childcare and dinner, and being thoughtful about language and disability needs.
- **A combination of meaningful work and connections.** Attendees were engaged because the work they did was taken seriously. But also, it was done in a way where attendees got to know one another. For instance, small groups would discuss community needs, which would then lead to a full-group conversation. The next gathering may include choosing potential strategic directions.
- **Committees anyone could join based on their interests.** Smaller committees met between quarterly gatherings. These groups tackled a variety of work, based on what was needed at the organization, and disbanded and re-formed as appropriate.

Evolutionary Governance

Vanessa LeBourdais, former ED of DreamRider Productions, writes about her organization's experimentation with a model the org called Evolutionary Governance, which she acknowledges results from collective wisdom passed down from other leaders and communities, including Indigenous communities. This model has three core principles,[10] which I'm paraphrasing here, and which she warned me would be very "woo woo," meaning touchy-feely and in-tuned with the energies of the universe, I guess:

1. Everyone (board, executive leader, staff) trusts in emergence, which includes the willingness to "do nothing if nothing is necessary," minimal structure, shared power and responsibility, and egos being left at the door.
2. The board is genuinely and authentically supportive of the executive leader(s), serving as a place where they can share their fears, anxieties, hopes, dreams, and so on, anytime, without worrying about being judged. The board may provide observations and advice as needed and helpful.
3. The board tends to the holistic well-being of the organization and "the field," which includes staff, partners, funders, board, ED, community members, and even nature.

A follow-up article[11] describes several practices aligned with these principles, including board members and executive leaders each prioritizing doing personal inner work, such as building self-awareness, surfacing patterns that may arise out of trauma, increasing empathy, and so on. There is also the element of doing inner work on the organization, which involves everyone reflecting on white supremacy, conflict avoidance, power dynamics, and attachment to being the "good guy" no matter the cost, also known as white moderation, one of the Horsemen of Ineffectiveness.

Liberatory Governance

Change Elemental, a nonprofit that partners with individuals, organizations, and networks to build a just world by addressing inequity through some cool and transformative approaches to leadership, strategy, and collaboration, has been exploring what they call liberatory governance. Instead of a board of directors, it has a "governance team."

As explained on its website,[12] in this model, staff and governance team members work closely together to make crucial decisions grounded in shared values. There is a staff liaison who recruits people to work with the governance team on various projects and decisions, based on where their experience, knowledge, and connections would make the most sense. Governance team meetings may have staff join when it makes sense. There are also caucuses where staff and governance team members meet separately, then come back to share with the full group.

Change Elemental emphasizes the importance of shared values and the commitment to working together through conflicts in values that may arise. In searching for new governance team models, they prioritize people who align with their values, are open to experiment with governance based on those values, and "who already embrace and practice inner work, multiple ways of knowing, experimentation, and emergent strategy—and who are looking to upend traditional governance team models and create and remember anew." This is very different than traditional board recruitment practices, which often emphasize skills such as fundraising, law, and human resources, as well as wealth and connections to it.

Circle Process

The circle has been used by different Indigenous communities for thousands of years and contrasts greatly with the formal, rigid, and hierarchical structures we have as default. There are variations. Colleagues recommended the process described by Living Justice Press (LJP), a nonprofit that publishes books and provides resources on topics related to social justice, restorative justice, and peacemaking. This process, as described in LJP's website,[13] involves:

- A "talking piece" to help determine who is speaking and when
- Intentional conversations about values and guidelines for how the group operates

- Some type of ceremony to open and close the gathering
- Relationship building that is just as important as content and decisions and is prioritized first

While that seems simplistic on the surface, practitioners of circles say the process does more than just run meetings differently. It changes one's outlook on the world entirely, including our views on systemic injustice.

Sociocracy

Also using circles is sociocracy. In this system of governance, work is decentralized among semi-autonomous circles. Decisions are made based on consent, which means no one strongly disagrees with a certain decision. This is different from consensus, which requires everyone to agree. Linking allows circles to be informed of one another's work by having one person representing their circle in another circle, while double linking involves two individuals from one circle being members of a circle that's higher in the hierarchy.

SociocracyForAll.org[14] goes into significant details on this system, so check it out. I talked to Yodit Mesfin Johnson, the CEO of Nonprofit Enterprise at Work (NEW), who has had positive experience with sociocracy:

> *The benefits include the disruption of power hoarding and lack of transparency. It allows room for every person at the organization to be involved in governance, not just the board. The consent-based decision-making model encourages dissent, but also accountability for dissenters to come up with counter proposals.*[15]

Of course, this doesn't mean it works for every organization. Yodit adds, "You need buy-in from everyone. This is not a tool; it's a reworking and reimagining of how we steward and govern ourselves. It won't work if you try to overlay it on an org that isn't already interrogating power and systems."

Mindful Meetings

The Swell Collective, a nonprofit with the mission "to inspire, equip, and amplify change-agents representing historically marginalized communities using a positive-sum approach," has a free guide[16] on "Mindful Meetings," which is a thought-provoking foil to the stuffiness of how most meetings are run, especially when they use Robert's Rules.

Mindful meetings have an impactful agenda, use an equity lens to make decisions, foster authentic connections, and end with everyone being inspired and have clarity. There are five key phases, which I'm summarizing. Please see the full guide for much more detailed information:

1. **Check in.** This involves not just each attendee updating the group on what's going on with them personally but also provides space to discuss "rumors and elephants" that may affect the organization, celebrate victories, address lingering questions from previous meetings, add items to the agenda, and serve as an opportunity to learn and use one another's names.
2. **Calibration.** Grounds attendees in the purpose of the meeting and agenda items and sets up expectations for what will be accomplished. Takes information received from the check-in process and determines if the agenda should be changed to address emergent issues.
3. **Doing the work.** Agenda items usually fall into either of two categories: dialog or decisions. A process for keeping "group memory" is used, such as writing notes on paper taped to walls or through digital platforms. The group engages in dialog, creatively ideates, and makes and commits to decisions.
4. **Check point.** Reviewing notes, making sure decisions are recorded accurately, and checking time and agenda progress.
5. **Check out.** Discussing what worked and what didn't and plan for future meetings.

Heart and Brain

Nonprofit boards have been a huge source of vexation in the sector, but they don't have to be. Since there are very few strictly defined legal requirements on governance, most of the things we think we must do are mere traditions. They're like Taco Tuesdays. It's nice to have tacos on Tuesdays, and I'm a fan of any tradition that alliterates. But it's okay to have Teriyaki Tofu Tuesdays and have tacos on Wednesdays! Examining these practices through a lens of equity, as well as a lens of "does this make sense for what we're trying to do and the org we're trying to be?" reveals many of these practices need some updates. There is plenty of room to try out some new philosophies and practices. Experiment with what works for you and your organization. Be expansive. The governing body does not have to be the useless appendix or the painful wisdom teeth of the organization. At its best, it serves as the heart and brain.

Discussion Questions

1. If your governing structure were a body part, what would it be and why?
2. What is going great with your structure? What could be improved?
3. Should staff be involved in governance? How about volunteers? Clients?
4. What are the benefits and downsides of having a more diffused governing structure?
5. How can boards focus more on the entire community and not just their organization?
6. How can we make boards more equitable?
7. What are the advantages and disadvantages of removing fundraising as a board responsibility?
8. Should nonprofit board members be compensated or provided stipends for their time?
9. Besides Robert's Rules, what other traditional practices should be examined?
10. Which of the alternative board structures and decision-making models resonate with you?

5

Reimagining Leadership and Leadership Structures

I will take the Ring, though I do not know the way.

—Frodo Baggins

When I was Executive Director of the Rainier Valley Corps (RVC), the fellows in our leadership program wanted to take turns shadowing me for an entire day. The fellowship placed them to work full-time for two years at various organizations in Seattle led by and serving communities of color, with one of the goals being to create a bench of nonprofit leaders of color for the field. It would make sense for them to see what an average day is like for an executive director. To make sure it was an authentic experience, the fellows signed up for random days, not knowing what would be on the agenda.

Noir was one of the fellows. He was warm, caring, outgoing, and had a brilliant analytical mind. He had been placed as the Communications and Development Manager at the East African Community Services (EACS). I recalled reading the article[1] he had written earlier on RVC's blog, where he examined the idea of "perfection" and how his concept had been weaponized against poor and marginalized people:

Perfection is conditional, based on environment, community support or lack thereof, family situation, and so many other factors. Perfection is not binary at all. Any of us can phase in and out of perfection and imperfection, depending on the conditions of our lives. So we need to change how we qualify perfection.

At EACS, our vision is to build up East African individuals, families, and our community. Our EACS programs have assisted hundreds of refugees, including students. I often look at the people all around me—and you know what I think? I think they are perfect.

This sort of thoughtful, culturally grounded, equity-based perspective and approach is precisely what we need in leaders. After our 12-hour-long day of shadowing, I asked Noir if he would consider being an ED.

"Oh, hell no!" he replied.

Challenges with the Current Leadership Structure

Noir's answer echoed the response given by many of the other fellows who had shadowed me, and in line with the sector overall. Building Movement Project's report "The Push and Pull: Declining Interest in Nonprofit Leadership"[2] shows the percentage of nonprofit professionals who expressed no interest in top leadership roles has been growing. In 2016, 33 percent of white survey respondents and 25 percent of respondents of color reported they were not interested in taking on an ED/CEO role. In 2022, this grew to 44 and 32 percent, respectively.

Of those who do want to be an ED or CEO, many are not pulled into these positions by attractive forces such as encouragement, mentorship, the chance to make a difference, and so on, but rather by the push of escaping their challenging current work situation and other factors.

Who could blame them. Leadership in general can be hard, but nonprofit leadership comes with its own additional challenges, including the relentless fundraising cycle; never having enough resources; toxic, micromanaging boards; donors' and funders' ego and unpredictability; community members blaming you for all sorts of stuff outside your control; and complicated staff dynamics. And as with everything else, these things disproportionately affect leaders of color, who also face additional challenges unique to them.

Having been an ED for 13 years across two nonprofits, I can say that while the job is always meaningful and often rewarding, there is something fundamentally wrong with this model. Too much is put on the shoulders of one person, a soul-crushing level of responsibility. EDs are pulled in all directions, with pressure pushing back from all sides. In my two terms as an ED, there were a handful of days where I felt any sense of doing a good job; everything was always on fire, and the few victories my team and I achieved were overshadowed by constant looming stressors. As succinctly stated[3] by Ananda Valenzuela, who worked as Managing Director to lead RVC with me, "the executive director job is impossible."

Power Imbalance in Leadership

Besides the excessive responsibility borne by EDs/CEOs, there is also the concentration of power and authority among these leaders, which seems out of alignment with our sector's values of equity and community. Stories abound about abusive, egotistical EDs/CEOs using their power to make their team's lives hell, and often bringing their organizations to ruin. How does a sector that strives to create a just world default to a leadership model where one person at the top of the pyramid has vast authority over everyone else, only kept in check by a group of volunteers, the board of directors, which itself is another problematic structure?

With thoughtful, progressive EDs and CEOs, the traditional leadership structure becomes a benevolent dictatorship, but it's still a dictatorship in many ways. And it is ironic that we still hew so close to something we inherited from the corporate sector, a field dominated by white men, even though so many of our organizations are wrestling with dismantling injustice, which is rooted in white patriarchal capitalistic systems.

> *The leaders we need are the people who will not be leaders in any official capacity or conventional definition of leadership.*

This is not to say that the traditional model does not have its use. For certain organizations and purposes, hierarchy can be effective. The problem is when we believe that this is the only way to do things, a "best practice" that everyone must follow. This leaves little room to consider that other ways may be more effective for certain organizations and communities. And it also leads to orgs and communities being punished by funders and donors for not conforming to this established norm, reinforcing the same injustices we're trying to address.

The Kind of Leaders We Need Right Now

Before I talk about alternative leadership models, it's helpful to understand leadership archetypes and the evolution around them. While there are dozens of archetypes, a lot of the traditional ideas of leadership in the nonprofit field I see are based on three main ones:

1. **The heroic leader** is the solitary, brooding warrior with vision, courage, and a strong moral compass, who takes decisive action and inspires others to follow them into battle. Ideally, this is someone with steely, brooding eyes and a strong jawline.
2. **The charismatic leader** is defined by someone with a magnetic personality, who exudes confidence, has strong emotional intelligence, can present bold visions, and is great at convincing others through their ability to be dynamic and engaging in their communications.
3. **The servant leader**, a concept coined by Robert Greenleaf,[4] describes the type of leader who puts others' needs first, as opposed to someone who clamors for power and material gains.

Over the years, the servant leader archetype has been widely adopted, as it aligns more with our sector's purpose of helping people and strengthening community. Servant leadership offers a nice contrast against the individualistic, Western concept of leadership that is seen in the other archetypes and thus is more relatable for people of color and other marginalized identities. With everything our world is facing, however, we need to evolve our thinking around leadership even further.

In 2018, I was asked to reflect and write an article[5] in the *Stanford Social Innovation Review* about what is required for successful leadership in the 21st-century civil society. This was shortly after Trump assumed power the first time and unleashed cruelty and chaos daily. The essay that resulted, titled "The Best Leaders May Be Those Who 'Give Up'," started with a little story about my experience taking Seattle's Link light rail with my two kids, who were five and two at the time, the three of us having to stand during the tumultuous ride because there had been no open seats. Two kind women got up and offered to trade places with us, which I gratefully accepted, as my toddler was at risk of being flung out of my arms, which probably would have significantly dampened his love of trains.

The experience made me realize that the leaders we need now must put equity and justice at the center of their roles. This includes being aware of who has a seat and who doesn't, and who always gets to drive the train while others are forced to ride along. As importantly, it includes being willing to give up—for the sake of actualizing a just world—the things that make their lives comfortable and existence meaningful, including power and adoration and even formal leadership roles, like the white colleague who told me she would no longer apply for any ED or CEO position of any nonprofit located in and serving predominantly communities of color.

As we think about alternative leadership structures, it is helpful to acknowledge that the leaders we may need are the people who will not be leaders in any official capacity or conventional definition of leadership.

Creating a Leaderful Sector

Whatever archetypes and frameworks we use, a significant challenge for our sector is that leadership has traditionally been very individualistic. This is in line with every other aspect of our work. For example, fundraising, as I examine in Chapter 3, has always been about getting as much money for one's organization as possible, without concern about how it may affect other nonprofits and movements. Boards are often focused on protecting and sustaining individual missions, with little thought on how other organizations fare. In the same way, we traditionally think of leadership as comprising individual leaders who will serve one organization or movement each.

Over the past several years though, we have started shifting toward a more ecosystem-like approach, where effective leadership serves the entire sector and society, not just individual organizations, because all our missions are interrelated.

In their essay, "Cultivating Leaderful Ecosystems,"[6] published in the *Nonprofit Quarterly*, Aja Couchois Duncan, Susan Misra, and Vincent Pan expand on the concept and contextualize it for our field:

> A critical shift is happening across the social sector. More of our partners are expanding their focus of attention from single organizations, to coalitions, to movement networks oriented around a shared vision and values. . . This shift from competition to collaboration, from single issues to intersectionality, from equality and fairness to equity and justice, and from scarcity to collective abundance requires different ways of imagining and living into leadership.

They propose five key "nutrients" to enable this type of shift to happen. These include leaders who are engaged in the broader system and not just focused on individual missions, who intentionally build relationships with equity in mind, who are flexible, who value multiple forms of knowledge and perspectives, and who prioritize self-care and other types of inner work.

Effective leadership is in service to the entire sector and society, not just individual organizations, as all our missions are interrelated.

With all this in mind, let's do a quick glance at some alternative leadership models that are different from the traditional sole leader model we've become used to.

Co-directorships

There has been increasing curiosity about and experimentation around co-directorships, in which two or more leaders share the highest position of authority. Between 2019 and 2022, the number of orgs using a co-leader structure increased from 7 to 11 percent. Co-leader structures where one or more leaders are of color doubled from 6 to 12 percent, while all-white co-directorships increased from 4 to 7 percent.[7]

In 2021, the Asian Pacific Environmental Network published a report called "Nonprofit Leadership Models,"[8] where they examined the strengths and challenges of the co-directorship model in comparison to the solo-leader model, interviewing eight nonprofits with two-co-director models and three with sole leaders. They discovered the strengths of co-leadership include better alignment with visions and values around more democratic decision making; having access to more skills and experience instead of relying on whatever a sole leader possess; longevity of leaders staying in one place versus burning out and leaving; increased productivity; and better representation of communities being served in terms of race and other identities.

However, the organizations interviewed also revealed challenges with co-leadership. Co-leaders may not always be in alignment in vision, values, strategies, and communication and leadership styles, which may create tension and lead to slower decision-making. Plus, sometimes roles are not fairly or equitably distributed, resulting in conflicts. Power differentials and dynamics may exist if one leader feels more comfortable making decisions and the other does not. Sometimes staff members become deferential to the co-directors and rely on them to make decisions, even when it's within the staff's purview and authority to make decisions themselves. And finally, there is the potential for staff to form alliances with one "favorite" director, creating division and conflicts.

However, when done well, grounded in a strong foundation of trust, there is potential for the benefits of shared leadership to be infused across the whole organization and for the organization itself to be more aligned with our sector's value of equity.

Caminar Latino: A Case Study

While two-leader co-directorships are the most common, there are structures where three or more leaders exist. I had chance to interview the leaders at Caminar Latino, an Atlanta-based organization working at the intersection of domestic violence prevention and Latino identity. The nonprofit has a model with three co-CEOs.

Five years ago, Caminar Latino started growing. At the time, they had one CEO. Like with other organizations, with growth came significant additional stresses, too much for the organization's sole CEO to bear. The board agreed to a two-CEO model. While it did lessen the responsibilities each co-CEO carried, the organization was not prepared for a co-director model. Most of the board members came from the corporate sector and were used to hierarchical leadership structures, so they struggled with this shared leadership model. When one of the co-CEOs departed, the board considered going back to the sole-CEO model, but staff intervened, requesting to continue experimenting with shared leadership, but prioritizing more time to be very intentional. It was a structure they believed better aligned with Latino cultural strengths and values of relationships, community, and mutuality.

After much discussion among the board and senior leaders, Caminar Latino decided to try again, this time a triad model, with one CEO focused on Atlanta, one doing national work, and one concentrating on infrastructure and operations. All three co-CEOs would meet with the board chair every other week. All had clearly defined work plans with indicators of success. The trio uses a consent decision process where decisions can move forward unless there is strong objection.

While the organization is still in its early stage of experimenting with this model, the two co-CEOs and one team member I talked to reported positive results. Among them was the decreased stress and isolation many sole leaders often feel. As co-CEO Heidi Notaro put it:

"Being in that [sole-leader] position can be lonely at times. You can have your team and your board, but it's not the same. Now we have each other's backs. It's much less isolating."

Co-CEO Patricia Moen agreed. She had experience working with sole leaders in the past, as well as part of two-leader structures. "After having been a co-CEO, I don't think I would want to be a solo leader."

I asked Jaqueline Herrera, Director of Communications, Marketing, and Engagement, how having three co-CEOs affected the rest of the team. "It's still too early to tell," she answered, "But so far, it's been helpful. Previously, there was more bottlenecking, more waiting around because the CEO was too busy. Now I feel like I can ask any one of the co-CEOs. It's giving me more options to get answers."

Also too soon to tell is how this structure has affected staff's desire to assume future leadership, but that is something on the co-CEOs' minds. Said Heidi, "We want to support a pipeline of Latina leaders. But the solo-leader model is unsustainable; it's been taking a huge toll on leaders' health. What I want the younger leaders to see is not CEOs and EDs who are exhausted. I want them to think 'I want to be a part of that.'"

The organization's funders have been supportive of and excited about the new structure, one encouraging the nonprofit to share lessons with the wider field, which was how I heard about Caminar Latino's model.

Still there are plenty of challenges to work through. Some community members remain skeptical that this model will last. Both co-leaders I talked to mentioned needing to spend significant time analyzing alignment regarding a host of things, especially the level of risk tolerance concerning potential changes in revenues, such as an anticipated departure from federal funding that looms on the horizon.

I asked what advice they would give to other organizations considering going down this path. Heidi replied, "Try it, but don't romanticize it. Go in with the understanding that it's hard work. We think it's a better way to go, but prepare for things to be messy."

Distributed Leadership

Early career experiences where I saw supervisors crush my colleagues' suggestions and ideas out of spite or ignorance made me question the idea so prevalent in our society that leaders at the top of org charts call all the shots. As I mentioned earlier, the idea of a solitary person having that much power in the first place seems greatly in dissonance with our sector's values. But power dynamics aside, how is it even effective? Why hire competent people—people who have more skills and experience than you do in whatever area you hired them in—and prevent them from doing their job?

It is heartening to see the concept of distributed leadership taking root. As my former co-leader Ananda Valenzuela defines it, "Distributed leadership is a model where decision-making is consistently and methodically distributed out across the organization. For example, frontline staff making decisions."

For distributed leadership to work, certain elements must be in place. Our friends at the Building Movement Project researched and interviewed several organizations that used the shared leadership model and found several factors required for this type of structure to work.[9] Foremost, a high level of trust in other people to make good decisions, as well as high level of transparency, including around budgets and finances.

Other factors needed for successful distributed leadership include prioritization of learning, such as trainings on how to make informed decisions; strong alignment around values; and tons of patience and time for everyone to experiment with the model, reflect on what works and doesn't, and adjust as needed.

When done well and with everyone's buy-in, distributed leadership can lead to all sorts of benefits, including a stronger sense of autonomy, ownership, and meaningful work among team members; less decision fatigue among top leaders; and more innovation and collaboration.

Worker Self-Directed Nonprofits

Taking distributed leadership even further is the concept of worker self-directed nonprofits (WSDNs). This model is used and advanced by the Sustainable Economy Law Center (SELC). The organization defines it as "a nonprofit organization in which *all workers* have the power to influence the programs in which they work, the conditions of their workplace, their own career paths, and the direction of the organization as a whole."[10]

This model attempts to correct for many of the weaknesses of the traditional hierarchical leadership and governance structure, where a board passes down mandates to often-overpaid management staff who then pass down the orders to often-underpaid frontline workers, which recreates a lot of the power and inequities the sector is trying to fight, while also being very inefficient, as the frontline workers often have the most knowledge and skills, but must wait for instructions and permission from the people with the least.

On its highly informative website (theselc.org), the SELC provides toolkits, webinars, case studies, hilarious short videos in their "WSND TV" series, and other resources for organizations interested in exploring becoming WSDNs.[11]

I spent some time perusing the collection of videos and articles, and learned many things about SELC's implementation of WSDN that are worth considering, including teams are organized using a circles structure, roles and responsibilities are fluid, there is no boss, everyone may be paid the same, a board may exist but plays a different role than traditional boards, meetings have circular structures where people take turns to talk, and everyone is encouraged to work no more than 30 hours a week.

> *Distributed leadership can lead to all sorts of benefits, including stronger sense of autonomy, ownership, and meaningful work among team members.*

From my reading, there are some variations in how WSDN and other flat structures work, but overall, they are an interesting alternative to the hierarchical model we're so used to. However, like with other structures, the potential challenges should be considered. This includes what Jo Freeman in her 1972 essay calls "the tyranny of structurelessness," where power dynamics still exist, they're just masked better and thus are possibly harder to mitigate:

"As long as the structure of the group is informal, the rules of how decisions are made are known only to a few and awareness of power is limited to those who know the rules. Those who do not know the rules and are not chosen for initiation must remain in confusion, or suffer from paranoid delusions that something is happening of which they are not quite aware."[12]

There are also race, class, gender, and other variables to account for. Simon Mont, in his article in the Nonprofit Quarterly, titled "Autopsy of a Failed Holacracy: Lessons in Justice, Equity, and Self-Management,"[13] brings attention to these challenges that often occur in flatter structures, including the fact that white, male, able-bodied people may have a much easier time navigating them than those who are of marginalized backgrounds. He uses a useful analogy of a set of twins, one of whom gets tons of freedom and is encouraged to be herself, the other told that she doesn't deserve autonomy and is punished when she steps out of line. Now both twins are put into a room and told they are equal. As Simon writes, "the mere fact that the words were uttered would not somehow make them true. Each twin would be facing completely different internal psychological dynamics impacting her thoughts, feelings, behaviors, and the way she identifies and uses her own power."

All that said, flatter structures such as SELC's WSDN are worth exploring. To be successful, they require critical factors in place, such as a strong culture of feedback, trust among team members, a supportive and risk-accepting board, and strong analyses of race, ethnicity, gender, and other dynamics. When done thoughtfully and with these elements in place, it can lead to some awesome results.

RVC: A Case Study

In 2013, I founded RVC (Rooted in Vibrant Communities, originally Rainier Valley Corps), a nonprofit focused on increasing the capacity of organizations led by communities of color as well as strengthening the bench of leaders of color. At first, the org had a very traditional leadership structure. Everything was great, until the nonprofit grew significantly, and I was overrun and torn in different directions, leading to unhappy staff. I needed to focus on fundraising, but also I did not like nor have the aptitude for supervision, operations, and other internal stuff.

It was clear we needed another leader. So we hired Raul Alicdan as Associate Director. Raul was great, and things got better. But still, we still had a hierarchy where my input was needed for everything. We started moving toward shared leadership with the hire of Ananda Valenzuela.

As Managing Director, Ananda had autonomy to make decisions in his purview, so my time and energy were freed up to focus on external stuff.

Through the next several years, as RVC grew its budget and expanded its scope, with Ananda's guidance, the team started further exploring distributed leadership. Together over several months, we read and discussed Frederic Laloux's *Reinventing Organizations: A Guide to Creating Organizations Inspired by the Next Stage of Human Consciousness*, an eye-opening book. (I highly recommend the illustrated version, since the original can be very dense and academic.)

The book mentioned a radical decision-making structure called the Advice Process,[14] coined by Dennis W. Bakke in his book *Joy at Work: A Revolutionary Approach to Fun on the Job*. While there is significant nuance with this decision-making model, it boils down to every decision being made by the one person who is closest to the issue (due to their expertise, formal duties, or possibly energy and interest), provided they do two things: (1) Get advice from those who would be meaningfully affected by their decision and (2) Get advice from those who have expertise in the issue.

This was a very different way of doing things for all of us. For it to work effectively, there had to be a strong culture of feedback

(continued)

(*continued*)

and communication. Feedback, however, can be challenging in a sector that is often conflict avoidant. We spent significant time learning how to give and receive feedback and practicing doing so consistently, including expecting everyone to actively solicit feedback monthly from everyone else.

While everyone was generally on board with and excited about the new decision-making model, the implementation did run into some hiccups we had not learned about in our readings. Namely, the intersection of race, gender, and other factors affected people's comfort with power and authority. Women of color were especially hesitant, as many on the team had seen or experienced the negative consequences of making the "wrong" decisions at prior places they worked. These consequences not only affected them personally, but unfairly reflected on their whole race, gender, and communities. We agreed to be cognizant of these dynamics and commit to viewing decisions that led to unexpected outcomes as opportunities for the entire organization to grow instead of "failures" to be punished.

In 2019, having been with RVC for seven years, I decided it was time for me to step down. Ananda became interim ED. A long process ensued that ended in RVC deciding to go with a four co-ED model. Each co-ED has some executive leadership responsibilities while also engaging in various other programmatic, operations, and other duties. The co-EDs "supervise" one another in a circulatory structure, and one is assigned as liaison to the board. The rest of the organization also uses distributed leadership, the org chart resembling more of a flower with petals than the traditional pyramid. As it states on a blog post, "RVC is a liberatory, leaderful, self-managing organization where power is distributed in natural hierarchies."

> It has been several years since this model was implemented. RVC has faced some significant funding challenges, like many nonprofits during these tumultuous times under this administration. I caught up with Roshni Sampath, one of the co-EDs, to see how everything is going, and what lessons and advice the team has gotten from this experiment so far. While there have been challenges, including the time and energy it takes to ensure good communication and clarity of roles, Roshni indicated many benefits to RVC's leadership structure and culture.
>
> "When I'm with my team, I feel we can face anything together. Collective wisdom skills can be used very effectively. One person doesn't have to know anything. We can take breaks. Sabbaticals. Flex and manage. It's still hard to do it, but there is an ability to step back and know someone else can take forward. For the staff, the decisions don't have to come to you or through you. If there are clear processes about how to do this, everyone can innovate, create proposals, and free up the work a little more. People develop leadership skills."

Leadership, the way we think about it and the way it's being implemented at nonprofit organizations, has been changing. While the default hierarchical model—based significantly on white, patriarchal, capitalistic standards—is still prominent, flatter models with shared power and decision-making are on the rise, though they too have their challenges and pitfalls Ananda is quick to remind us not buy into the limiting binary of "hierarchy versus collective." Exploring alternative structures, while understanding the strengths of traditional ones, and perhaps combining the most effective elements from all of them, will help us get closer to leadership that's more aligned with our sector's values and vision. And it'll help the sector recruit and retain the brilliant, dedicated people we need to achieve our goals.

Discussion Questions

1. Why do you think fewer young professionals want to be in leadership roles?
2. What type of leaders (heroic, charismatic, servant) do you see most in our sector?
3. Given the sociopolitical landscape we're facing, what kind of leaders do we need now?
4. How have your own leadership philosophies and practices changed over the year?
5. How "leaderful" do you think our sector is currently?
6. What are the strengths and challenges of co-directorship?
7. Do you know of organizations in your area that are using the distributed leadership model?
8. What do you think of the advice process decision-making model?
9. What elements of the WSDN or other flatter models resonate with you? Which do you have concerns or questions about?
10. What similarities did you notice among the different organizations mentioned in this chapter that tried alternative leadership models?

6

Building Nonprofit Capacity to Fight Fascism

Can Equity's arrows seek truest rapture
Without the quiver of Infrastructure?
Can e'er Justice take flight and sing
Save with steadfast Capacity 'neath her wings?
—Unknown But Obviously Brilliant Poet

AFTER GETTING MY master's in social work, I wanted to break into international development. Applying for various positions and having no luck, I decided to spend a year in Vietnam, hoping to volunteer at one an international nongovernmental organization (INGOs) and build up my street creds. Thus, I found myself at a place founded by a white man, an American veteran who had spent time in Vietnam, married a local, and settled in Saigon. His organization was called Waifs of War (WOW), waifs referring to sad, abandoned children, the nonprofit's target demographic.

WOW's mission was to provide legal, educational, and other forms of support to children and young adults who were victims of the Vietnam War, often those whose fathers or grandfathers were U.S. soldiers. These Amerasian kids, called *bui doi*, "the dust of life," faced poverty and discrimination, ostracized because they looked foreign and reminded people of the war. The mission resonated with me, as my adopted older sister is Amerasian, and I wanted to help.

Helping anyone, however, proved to be challenging. We lacked funding, paid staff, accounting software, filing system, and basic equipment like desks and computers. The office was a tiny room on the sixth floor of a building, above a clothing store. Each day, sometimes soaked by afternoon monsoon rain, I would walk into the store, smile at the salesclerk, and trudge up to the office. There, the two other volunteers and I tried to do the best we could, but it was always chaos. Clients couldn't find us because the website was terrible, and when they managed to get to the office, we had no idea who to refer them to because the database was nonexistent.

Over the next several months, we tried to build out infrastructure, including changing the organization's atrocious name, but without funding and staff who had experience and who understood local dynamics, it was molasses. I'm not sure we ended up helping a single "waif."

That year of struggle and frustration taught me that when it comes to this work, passion and a good mission—the exciting stuff—are not enough. To do it well, organizations need to build up their capacity, which is the basic, often-overlooked stuff—office space, financial management software, computers, human resource policies, insurance, duct tape, decent chairs, and most importantly, staff.

Capacity Builders as Mycelium

I like to think of capacity building and the organizations that provide them—intermediaries, nonprofit state associations, even some funders—as mycelium. This is the underground, often invisible rooting structure of mushrooms. The mushrooms you see would not exist without this mycelial network.

Just as mycelium delivers nutrients, detoxifies the soil, fosters communications between different plants, breaks down dead material, and does other things that allow mushrooms to thrive, capacity builders play similar roles. They bring funding and skills to nonprofits, fight against bad practices, help nonprofits talk to one another, encourage organizations to collaborate, provide legal advice and support when organizations or the sector is attacked—which is now more relevant than ever—help maintain balance among large organizations and those led by marginalized communities, and facilitate the graceful sunsetting of nonprofits at the end of their life cycle.

While mushrooms are visible and appreciated, we don't think much about mycelium at all. Similarly, people may see the value in nonprofits, but they take for granted all the invisible things that are needed for nonprofits to be successful, including capacity building and intermediary organizations, who are often overlooked and underfunded.

Our sector now navigates an increasingly hostile environment, facing attacks by Trump and the Republicans, whose words and actions pollute and toxify the soil and environment for our community. Capacity building and capacity builders are critical. Yet, like everything else, there are some weaknesses we must address. This chapter talks about some harmful mindsets and practices around capacity building, new ones we need to adopt, and some of the organizations doing effective capacity building work.

Archaic Philosophies About Capacity Building

The way our sector, in particular the progressive wing of our sector, thinks about capacity is mired in a lot of old-school mindsets that make capacity-building strategies ineffective or even harmful to communities. Here are a few philosophies we need to adopt:

- **Give people the fish.** There has been this "teach a person to fish" mentality among many funders in our sector that for nonprofits to be effective, they need to develop their capacity among a dozen or so skills: fundraising, human resources, financial management, evaluation, and so on. This forces nonprofits to become generalists who are mediocre at most tasks. We need to stop and wonder if it makes sense for everyone to learn to fish. Maybe some people are better at baking, growing produce, making art, or whatever. In the same way, maybe not every organization needs to develop their capacity in bookkeeping or HR.

They could just hire an external company to do these specialized skills more quickly and accurately while they focus on what they're good at.

- **Consider cultural differences in capacity-building work.** A lot of capacity building is taking what works for large, white-led organizations and forcing them onto everyone else. Fundraising may be the worst in this respect. I was on the board of an organization a long time ago whose executive director brought in a consultant to increase fundraising capacity. He told us each to brainstorm a list of names of people in our networks who could each donate $10,000, whom we would then reach out to set up one-on-one meetings. This was a small Vietnamese organization. Philanthropy looks different in Vietnam, where it is often done through churches and temples. None of us knew anyone who could or would donate $10,000.

- **Training, workshops, and tools must be complemented with staffing.** Funders love paying for toolkits, training, and consultants to help nonprofits develop their capacity. The problem is that an organization could send someone to attend a thousand workshops or work with a consultant to develop a hundred strategic plans or whatever, but if it does not have dedicated staff who will implement these skills and plans, these efforts are pointless.

- **Organizations should stay the size that makes sense for them.** The report "Reexamining Capacity Building: Learnings from the Kenneth Rainin Foundation's Impact Grant Program"[1] discusses their efforts building capacity of their arts organizations grantees with less than $2 million in annual budgets. One of the challenges they found that affected organizations' capacity building was the "the tremendous pressure on nonprofits from the ecosystem to use growth as the most significant success metric." This is an assumption we've adopted from the corporate sector, where bigger equals better. But nonprofits are not corporations, and sometimes, staying small or medium-sized allows nonprofits to be most effective.

- **Fiscal sponsorship is equally valid as standalone status.** In *Pinocchio*, the wooden puppet strives to be a "real boy." In our sector, there's a similar widespread belief that organizations aren't "real nonprofits" if they don't have their own tax designation. Fiscally sponsored organizations are constantly asked if they will "spin off" from their fiscal sponsor, as if being under the umbrella of another organization makes them somehow less legitimate or effective. This incubation mentality prevents some creative ways our sector can reimagine and experiment with capacity building and how the nonprofit ecosystem can structure itself to be more effective overall.

- **Good work can be done through alternative organizational structures.** There are advantages to being a formal nonprofit, such as it's much easier to raise money. But some organizations can be a lot more effective in their work if they use an alternative structure such as LLCs, mutual assistance associations, and informal movements. It's important for all of us, but especially funders, to get out of this thinking that only formal organizations should be funded. With attacks from the right wing ramping up on traditional nonprofits, we should leave all options open, including using alternative structures that may be less vulnerable, which means thinking of ways tailored to building their capacity.

How the Right Does Capacity Building

There is a lot, as usual, we can learn from conservative organizations and foundations on how they think about and build capacity, which they have done quite brilliantly over the past several decades. Their secret is shockingly simple: MONEY. Lots of unrestricted money over many, many years, multi-year general operating dollars (MYGOD).

Sally Covington's seminal report "Moving a Public Policy Agenda: The Strategic Philanthropy of Conservative Foundations," which[2] I discuss in greater length in Chapter 8 on philanthropy, studies how conservative foundations and movements have run circles around liberal-leaning ones. In summary, they

People may see the value in nonprofits, but they take for granted all the invisible things that are needed for nonprofits to be successful.

provide significant general operating funds over long periods of time. We're talking 20–30 years or more. With unrestricted grants guaranteed over decades, it would be surprising if an organization does not develop its capacity.

Liberal-leaning foundations, in contrast, in trying to build nonprofits' capacity, often provide small, short-term, one-year grants, often restricted to capacity-building–related stuff, which often has the opposite effect and builds no capacity. I call this the *capacity-building irony*: Liberal-leaning funders' focusing on helping nonprofits develop their capacity prevents them from developing their capacity.

The conservative strategy of giving grantees a ton of cold, hard cash for as long as they demonstrate progress in advancing conservative goals has proven to be super effective. It is something liberal foundations that want to build strategies in progressive organizations should emulate. What prevents liberal-leaning funders from doing so includes toxic intellectualizing, white moderation, and the other Horsemen I mention in Chapter 2.

But there is another factor: Many liberal-leaning funders view nonprofits the way society sees poor people, and capacity building serves a purpose like society helping the poor develop financial management skills, find employment, and otherwise "pull themselves up by their bootstraps."

This patriarchal, paternalistic treatment of low-income individuals often backfires and keeps them in poverty. It does the same to nonprofits. Direct cash transfers to low-income individuals and trusting them to manage their own funds have been shown by research to be extremely effective in pulling people out of poverty.[3] In the same vein, giving organizations significant funds and getting out of their way has been shown by conservatives to greatly increase organizations' capacity and impact, and it's something progressive-leaning funders must take seriously.

Shared Spaces

Office and programming spaces are vital to building capacity. However, our individualistic Western culture has encouraged every nonprofit to have its own space, which is often expensive, leading many organizations to take what they can get. We need to explore new ways for nonprofits to be structured that would allow our sector to be more effective and efficient. One solution is shared space.

EquaSpace, located in Minnesota, for example, is a beautiful, functional building where organizations have their own office space but share the kitchen, bathrooms, and meeting rooms. Twenty-one organizations reside there. Among its many offerings, EquaSpace provides workshops, monthly meetups for EDs, similar gatherings for young professionals, quarterly breakfasts featuring various leaders in the field, and "office hours" with experts on various topics from human resources to mental health to mergers to supporting communities during the barrage of attacks by Republicans.

Spending so much time together has led to an organic increase in collaboration, which EquaSpace's executive director Sarah Clyne reports is a common outcome when organizations share the same spaces.

"We have one organization that had to lay off the entire team and now the ED is running it solo. She has a three-day conference coming up and when other leaders got wind of this, two orgs stepped up and offered their entire teams to help—no questions asked."

This sense of community and mutual support is particularly important during these times. EquaSpace has been playing a vital role as Trump and the Republicans continue to attack nonprofits, especially those serving the most vulnerable:

> We rally to support orgs that need protection. There is some cover by being inside EquaSpace. For example, we have an organization that does East African advocacy. They are immigrants, Muslims, and they fight for worker rights in Amazon warehouses. Folks are trying to shut them down. We are here to support them in whatever way we can.

The waitlist to get into EquaSpace has been growing. Despite its obvious success, there have been some challenges, including the common one of funders not being interested in funding capacity building. Shared spaces and other deeper forms of capacity building are things that funders need to support if we want to equip nonprofits to do their work effectively in this sociopolitical environment.

The *Star Trek* Model (aka the Community-Alliance Model)

In *Star Trek*, there are various starships. Each has a different captain and a different mission. However, they are bound together by Starfleet, a central organization that supports and coordinates the work of all the ships and does back-office stuff, allowing Captains Picard or Janeway to lead the exploration of space and build diplomacy across the galaxy instead of entering numbers into the finance database and writing HR policies.

The nonprofit sector as it exists can be compared to *Star Trek*, but without many Starfleet-like organizations to coordinate everyone or do back-office support. Every organization is expected to do its own HR, finance, evaluation, communications, IT, fundraising, governance, and so on, which is not efficient. Meanwhile, we compete with one another for resources, and we often have no idea what other nonprofits are doing.

The *Star Trek* analogy is not perfect. Starfleet is extremely rigid, militaristic, and hierarchical. Many of those philosophies and practices will not work or would even be harmful when translated into the nonprofit sector. Still, we can use these lessons to implement a better model—let's call it the community-alliance model. Here's what it may look like:

- **There will be more central supporting entities that provide shared back-office support.** These entities will have teams handling critical services like bookkeeping, taxes, insurance, and so on; not teaching them how to do it but just doing it for them, "giving them the fish" as mentioned earlier (though nothing prevents them from learning if they want). Alliance members pay a sliding-scale fee based on their budget for these services. This will create an economy of scale that will benefit all members.
- **Fiscal sponsorship will be something not frowned upon but encouraged.** There are a lot of stigmas around fiscal sponsorship, which results in many organizations becoming or remaining 501(c) organizations despite their complete lack of interest in or capacity to handle administrative functions. Being fiscally sponsored will allow more efficiency in back-office tasks and provide some legal protection.

- **Executive directors will be more focused on the mission.** According to a report by CompassPoint and the Meyer Foundation,[4] the lack of administrative support is a key contributor to executive director burnout in small and medium-sized organizations. In the community-alliance model, EDS/CEOs will be able to devote more time and energy to fulfill their missions, including collaborating with other leaders.
- **Boards will be more focused on vision, strategy, and advocacy.** Many boards, especially in smaller organizations, spend a lot of their time in operations, which leaves little time for the board's most important roles: representing the interests of the community at large and ensuring the organization is achieving its mission, vision, and values. In this community-alliance model, they can now focus more on these critical areas.
- **Fundraising will be a combination of individual and joint efforts.** Each organization in an alliance continues to raise funds (fiscally managed by the supporting organization) for its own individual mission. However, there may also be joint efforts to raise funds for the entire alliance. Some alliances may explore a co-op-like model where funds are raised and then shared equitably among alliance members. The combined power of organizations working together will significantly help to bring about effective funding practices and increase funding overall.
- **There will be a system of mutual support among members.** Effective alliances are grounded by a set of strong and deeply held values, one of which is the mutual care and respect that members have for one another and between members and the support organization. The support organization will step in to coordinate assistance during crises, for example, providing an interim executive director during leadership transitions, or creating a pool fund that members can tap into when undergoing cash-flow issues.
- **Organizations focus on programs but also work together on systemic issues.** As operations are taken care of by the support organization, each organization and its staff have significantly more time to work on planning and running programs. This is

what many organizations and leaders were meant to do, what they are good at, and what they should be doing. In addition to their individual work, they also have more time and resources to deeply collaborate to address the systemic challenges facing our communities.

- **Organizations may spin off or remain permanent members as appropriate.** Some organizations are big and may need their own internal operations and have no interest in shared services (although, this may be an issue of perception, as there are organizations that are currently fiscally sponsored that have annual budgets in the millions). They may need to spin off from their fiscal sponsor. However, there is no pressure to force nonprofits to become independent organizations.

I know the alliance model sounds idealistic or fantastical, but this is not a new idea. Organizations such as TSNE, Tides, Community Partners, The National Network of Fiscal Sponsors, and others have been pioneering many of these concepts for years. Rooted in Vibrant Communities (RVC), the organization I founded and led for several years, piloted something like the alliance model.

RVC's Comprehensive Capacity-Building Model

Years of leading the Vietnamese Friendship Association (VFA) and talking to other leaders taught me that much of the capacity-building philosophies and strategies forced onto smaller, marginalized-community-led organizations were not only not working, but oftentimes harmful to these orgs, and a new model was needed. For instance, funder's definition of readiness—which is the measure of when an organization has enough capacity to be given grants of significant sizes—often leave these groups behind.

This is something I call *the capacity paradox*, where organizations need significant funding to build their capacity, but funders refuse to provide significant funding to nonprofits unless they already have capacity. Kind of like how young professionals can't find work because they have no experience, but they can't get experience if no one hires them.

RVC was founded as an intermediary organization to help grassroots nonprofits break out of this paradox. Since the organizations we talked to all indicated the need for staff, we started with a fellowship program that recruited dedicated leaders of color who wanted to do this work, provided them with ongoing training and mentorship, and had them work full-time for two years at host organizations. These leaders had a variety of critical responsibilities, including running programs, fundraising, managing operations, and whatever else was needed.

After a year, we checked in with host organizations, who reported how helpful the fellows were. But having fellows who were sometimes the only full-time staff at these organizations was not enough. The nonprofits were still overwhelmed by the sheer number of tasks required: fundraising, financial management, HR, and so on. RVC was reminded that we were still using a "teach a person to fish" paradigm of capacity building, but this time by sending fellows over to learn how to fish for their host sites. We realized these organizations had no time or interest in learning a variety of skills, nor should they, as their role should be to run programs, mobilize community members, and whatever else their missions called them to do.

With this realization, we expanded our services to include fiscal sponsorship and back-office support. Organizations under our fiscal umbrella receive financial, HR, and other types of operations support, which frees up their time to focus on their missions. In addition, capacity-building coaches provide guidance around a host of issues. An organization could have one or more full-time fellows, most of its back-office needs taken care of, and a coach to help plan the board retreat or do a strategic plan.

The model is expensive (estimated to cost between $100,000 and $200,000 per organization per year, most of it going to fellows' compensation), and there were various other challenges, including fellows and host sites not always being good matches. Despite this, the model has been effective in building capacity. In a nod to capacity-building irony, by removing the obligation for organizations to develop their capacity in different business departments, they could focus on delivering programs and services. Thanks to that, several were able to receive significant funding, which allowed them to grow their capacity.

Transformational Capacity Building

The lessons we learned at RVC led to the creation of a model we call Transformational Capacity Building. RVC leaders April Nishimura, Roshni Sampath, Anbar Mahar Sheikh, Ananda Valenzuela, and I wrote about it in detail in an article published in the fall 2020 edition of the *Stanford Social Innovation Review*.[5] I'm summarizing the seven key approaches to this model:

1. **Build trustworthy and culturally resonant relationships.** Building relationships with nonprofit leaders allows for deeper understanding of what the best approaches are, what cultural contexts should be taken into consideration, and what factors may pose as barriers. While it does take time to do well, these rapports significantly increase the chances of capacity-building strategies to succeed.
2. **Address underlying patterns of behavior rooted in history and culture.** An organization based in a community where women aren't usually expected or allowed to handle to money, for example, or younger people generally defer to their elders, or war trauma has affected whether people are even comfortable with their name being listed in any sort of roster, will have to consider these factors in their efforts to build capacity in finances, board development, and evaluation.
3. **Encourage nonprofits to be specialists, not generalists.** As I mentioned, forcing organizations to engage in 20 different things means they often are overwhelmed and don't do an effective job at any of them. Let organizations focus on the things they are good at, which are often the things only they can do because of their relevant language, cultural skills, and connections—and allow them to outsource other vital tasks.
4. **Cultivate networks to generate power and change systems.** Traditional capacity building often focuses on individual organizations' growth and survival, further perpetuating the Hunger Games nonprofits have been forced to play. Transformational Capacity Building recognizes nonprofits exist in an ecosystem and encourages the building of cohorts, networks, and movements, and interdependence among nonprofits.

5. **Invest in the inner well-being and growth of leaders.** The success of organizations and movements is tied to the people leading them. Taking care of people's physical, emotional, mental, and even spiritual well-being—through sabbaticals, executive coaching, therapy, and space for connecting to others—leads to stronger capacity among the organizations and movements they're involved in.
6. **Provide simultaneous, multilayered capacity building activities.** In direct service work, we often talk about "wraparound services," where clients receive multiple complementary forms of support: housing, employment assistance, case management, and so on. This wraparound approach is effective for capacity building, as we found out at RVC, where organizations are provided fellows, back-office support, grant-writing support, and capacity-building coaches.
7. **Offer significant, direct, flexible, multi-year funding.** MYGODs allow organizations to do what they need and respond to changing community needs and the sociopolitical landscape. Give organizations tons of unrestricted cash over several years, instead of tiny grants restricted to capacity-building work, and they thrive.

Multi-entities

Creating multi-entity structures, where nonprofits establish several organizations under their names, is something we have been underusing. As we face off against threats to the sector, this is a model more organizations need to consider, and more funders need to support. Having some combinations of C3, C4, C5, C6, for-profits such as LLCs and S-Corps, political action committees, and other legal structures allow nonprofits access to more tools to effect change. Being both a C3 and C4, the most common type of multi-entity, for example, holds a couple of key advantages, namely the increased ability to do advocacy, lobbying, and political work; and stronger legal protection and reduced risk.

Several organizations are multi-entities, including Planned Parenthood, the Sierra Club, and the ACLU. I am on the board of Progress

Alliance of Washington, which has a C3 to organize donors and provide resources to organizations advancing progressive values, and a C4 to engage in political actions, a significant and impactful one being the First Mile Circle, which gathers financial and other forms of support for progressive candidates of color in Washington State.

> *More nonprofits should consider becoming multi-entities, and more funders must fund them.*

If we want to be effective in fighting back against the right-wing movement, we need to be more politically active as a sector, and that means having more 501(c)(4)s and more C3s converting into multi-entities. This also means that capacity building will need to change to accommodate multi-entities, as there are more legal complexities to deal with within that structure.

Luckily for our sector, we already have some awesome organizations leading the work in this area. New Left Accelerator (NLA), for example, works to build the capacity of multi-entities on the front line fighting for justice. I had an energizing meeting with Deborah Barron, NLA's executive director, who reinforces the importance of nonprofits becoming engaged fully and strategically in power-building and politics. She reminded me that our current structures, which rely heavily on 501(c)(3)s, actively prevent risk-taking and power-building, as 501(c)(3)s originated partly from the government's strategy to curb the influence of Black churches. "A C3 is necessary but insufficient, which is why the right-wing often uses corporate entities." As 501(c)(3)'s ability to do systems change work is getting more and more restricted by an increasingly fascist government, we will need to invest more time and resources into different structures. More nonprofits should consider becoming multi-entities, and more funders must fund them.

Movements

In 2020, the other leaders of CCF and I met to discuss its future. We had an important decision to make: Formalize CCF into a traditional 501(c)(3) nonprofit, or to turn it into a global movement.

The former path would allow us to raise more money for sure, but then we would have to spend significant time and energy building organizational capacity. The latter path would mean less capacity, structure, and funding but may allow CCF ideas to better proliferate, which may result in tangible changes across the sector.

We discussed Creating the Future's founder Hildy Gottlieb's article "Building Movements, Not Organizations,"[6] where she states many of the significant social changes we've seen over the past few decades were not led by individual organizations, but by movements, and names some key differences between these two structures, including "Movements define success globally. If a movement is successful, things change for everyone. Organizations, on the other hand, often define success internally, by what the organization accomplishes for itself."

The CCF team voted to become a movement, a decision I believe has led to the growth of CCF ideas across the United States, as well as into other countries, at a scale and speed that probably would have been difficult to achieve had we incorporated as a 501(c)(3) nonprofit.

Informal networks can do incredible work and are less likely to be targeted by the right, although they will try.

This isn't to say that all formal nonprofits should disband and become movements. There are certainly advantages and disadvantages to both structures. But if our sector wants to be at our most effective, we must let go of the assumption that change can only be accomplished through formal organizations. Often, it is movements that will have the greatest impact, and capacity-building strategies must take that into consideration.

Alternative Structures

Besides movements, there are other structures we can use to do important work while lessening their probability of being attacked by the right. Thaddeus Squire, Founder and Chief Commons Steward at Social Impact Commons, which is a field builder and supporting organization for fiscal sponsorship and nonprofit resource sharing, recommends our sector explores a few alternative structures as a survival strategy[7]:

- **Operate under a fiscal sponsor.** Being under the umbrella of another organization provides some legal protection, increased confidentiality to donors, and the flexibility and ease for sponsored groups to change their names and migrate to another sponsor or spin out on their own as needed. As Thaddeus puts it, "The fiscal sponsorship community could become a kind of present-day Underground Railroad for the nonprofit community."
- **Become a small, private entity.** We've been so used to donations to nonprofits being tax-deductible that we forget people often donate money without considering how it helps them pay less taxes. A limited liability corporation (LLC), for instance, can still do amazing charitable work, and people can still donate to it. And it'll less likely be attacked because of how excessively entrenched and worshipped capitalism is in society.
- **Create informal networks.** In many communities, it is not formal nonprofits that provide services, but neighbors helping one another out, paying for funeral and other major expenses, creating loan circles, and so on. We're seeing more of that. Informal networks can do incredible work and are less likely to be targeted by the right, although they will try.
- **Form a religious organization.** There are very few legal requirements for starting a religion, and once you do, there is almost zero oversight from the government. I can start Vuism today, open the Temple of Vu, and begin accepting tax-deductible donations immediately! While we should change laws to make religious institutions more transparent and accountable, we might as well take advantage in the meanwhile to do advocacy, community organizing, and other critical work being challenged by the right.

Time to Start a Religion?

Having strong infrastructure is vital to nonprofits' work. Capacity building goes beyond financial management, HR, and other important skills. It's also about peer learning, creating collective wealth, collaborative and strategic advocacy, and building community power. However, it's often unappreciated, along with the organizations that provide capacity building.

As threats to our sector intensify, all of us must think differently and more creatively about how we are structured and what tools would be most potent in fighting back and protecting our communities. Getting rid of some outdated philosophies would be a good first step, followed by experimenting with collaborative models like sharing spaces, forming alliances, nurturing movements instead of organizations, becoming multi-entity structures, and doing good work through for-profits or even religious institutions.

Funders, meanwhile, must increase support capacity building as well as intermediaries and other organizations that are doing the needed but often invisible work of providing nonprofits and leaders with the skills, resources, and connections necessary to survive and fight, especially in this fraught sociopolitical context.

Discussion Questions

1. What are examples of the "boring," often invisible things we take for granted that allow nonprofits to be effective at their work?
2. In what other ways is capacity building and capacity builders like mycelium?
3. Which of the archaic philosophies that need to die have had the most effect on our sector? Can you think of other ones to add to the list?
4. How have these philosophies been affecting organizations led by and serving marginalized communities?
5. Do you agree that funders often see nonprofits the way society sees poor people? If yes, why do you think this attitude exists?

6. What are the advantages and disadvantages of collaborative models such as the ones advanced by EquaSpace or RVC?
7. Which, if any, of the Transformational Capacity-Building model key approaches resonate with you?
8. What's currently preventing nonprofits from growing the capacity to do advocacy and political work?
9. Should more organizations become multi-entities?
10. What are your thoughts on alternative structures, such as forming a religious organization?

7

Advocacy, Community Organizing, and the Levers of Power for Systems Change

Every moment is an organizing opportunity, every person a potential activist, every minute a chance to change the world.

—Dolores Huerta

A FEW YEARS AGO, I was out of town giving a keynote speech at a conference. One of the topics I addressed was the need for our sector to push back against the hyperfixation with overhead. During the Q&A, a colleague raised her hand and described how in her city each year, the local newspaper published a list of the top 10 organizations with the highest overhead rates in a bid to publicly shame them, resulting in nonprofits being terrified to end up on the list.

"You said we need to stop apologizing for our overhead and invest in our staff and other things we need to do the work effectively, but how do we do that here when we're all scared that our organizations will end up on that list in the newspaper, which would affect our funding?" Everyone in the room was empathetic to the colleague and her dilemma. Solutions were proposed for how to fly under the radar of this overhead witch hunt, perhaps by using different formulas for allocating expenses in the books. I was about to answer when another colleague raised her hand:

> Why do you let this newspaper have so much power? Why don't you get a bunch of nonprofits together and write a letter to the editor or an op-ed to educate people why overhead matters and how this list is harmful to our work?

I watched from the stage as people's eyes lit up. It seemed that organizing and fighting back was not something they had even considered.

As brilliant and courageous as people in this sector are, we do have a problem with collective learned helplessness, a psychological phenomenon where people feel powerless to change things. They give up even trying and gradually internalize the idea that these things are normal and everyone should conform. It happens with overhead, and it happens with all the societal problems the nonprofit sector is trying to solve.

In that room, it was exciting to see wheels turning. But they need to turn faster, with more urgency, and on every issue. Advocacy, organizing, and work to change systemic inequity are things every nonprofit must engage in.

State of Nonprofit Engagement in Advocacy

"The Retreat of Influence: Exploring the Decline of Nonprofit Advocacy and Public Engagement," a study published by Independent Sector in July 2023,[1] finds nonprofits engaging less in advocacy than they had 20 years ago:

- Only 31 percent of survey respondents reported doing advocacy or lobby work over the past five years and 25 percent reported ever lobbying, in contrast to 74 percent who reported engaging in lobbying in 2000.
- Only 32 percent reported being aware that 501(c)(3) organizations could do advocacy around federal legislation, in contrast to 54 percent in 2000.

- A whopping 56 percent said policy engagement was not applicable to their missions; 18 percent indicated they believed their missions would discourage advocacy.

This is disappointing, but not surprising. There has been rampant misinformation about advocacy work. A colleague who started working with a large, well-known organization texted me: "Just went through new employee orientation. One slide of the PowerPoint read 'As a 501(c)(3), we are not legally allowed to conduct any advocacy or lobbying.'" This is not true. C3s can spend up to 10 percent of their budget on advocacy and lobbying; they just can't endorse political candidates; 501(c)(4) nonprofits can endorse political candidates.

Various factors may explain the low engagement in advocacy. Quorum's 2024 State of Government Affairs Survey[2] asked people what their biggest hurdles were in doing advocacy. Forty-seven percent reported understaffing, 34 percent named lack of funding, and 74 percent indicated political partisanship.

With funders' disdain for advocacy and thus lack of funding for it; widespread misinformation about what nonprofits are allowed to do; and our tendency to be conflict avoidant, over time, we've internalized the message that advocacy is bad because it is too "political," or if it is legal to do, it is form of mission drift for organizations whose central focus is not on systems change.

However, with the Trump administration posing an existential threat to our sector and the people we serve, our relationship with advocacy, lobbying, and political engagement must change. Systems change work is no longer something most of the sector can ignore while a few poorly funded organizations continue heroically doing. It is something all of us must prioritize, no matter what our mission is, and something funders must all fund, or at the very least not prohibit nonprofits from doing. As Kevin Dean, President and CEO of the Tennessee Nonprofit Network writes:[3]

> [T]he very systems that perpetuate inequities in income, housing, education, and jobs require systemic shifts achieved through advocacy. Restricting funding for these crucial efforts hinders our ability to address the root causes of the challenges facing our communities and perpetuates the very problems we are trying to solve.

Whatever the challenges may be, the results of years of underinvolvement in advocacy and lobbying, and underfunding by funders, are abysmal to our sector and the efficacy of its work in addressing some of the most entrenched problems in our world.

The Loudest Voices Win

A while ago I read Jan Masaoka's thought-provoking article "Aspirin and Democracy,"[4] where she discusses the effects of the professionalization of the nonprofit sector. One such effect, according to Jan, is that:

> [N]ew executive directors can write personnel policies and grant proposals while practicing self-care, but they don't know how to get 5,000 people to a protest demonstration or 50 parents to a city council meeting.

Jan's statement struck me for how true it is. I remember in grad school, where I was getting my master's in social work, learning about the nonprofit sector's role in grassroots movements. Through persistent advocacy, our sector helped advance civil rights, labor rights, disability justice, environmental policies, and so on. I learned about the different principles and strategies of community organizing from texts such as *Rules for Radicals* by Saul Alinksy and *Organizing for Power and Empowerment* by Jacqueline B. Mondros and Scott M. Wilson, such as "power is not just what you have but what your opponent thinks you have."

Working in education equity, I was told by an elder, "If you can get 20 angry parents to dress in the same T-shirts and pack the school board meeting holding signs, you can get whatever you want." This is sad, but unfortunately this is also how most of the world works: the loudest and most organized voices tend to win, and they are often from those of privilege, who benefit most from systems staying the same. Our sector, founded to help lift the voices of those who don't always get heard, has in many ways lost sight of that. Many of us are starting to lose our community organizing skills. We barely learn or teach them anymore.

Because of our decreasing engagement in advocacy work and the losing of skills, we've allowed the loudest, most privileged voices to win over the past several decades, leading our communities to face the increase in injustice we see now with this administration. We need to let go of some long-held mindsets, adopt some new ones, reclaim one of the most important and impactful skills we possess, and learn lessons from the few organizations doing incredible work in this area.

The Wake-Up Call for Our Sector to Be Political

Imagine for a moment that there are people who continually run around setting fires. The fires are burning down houses, killing people directly by burning them or indirectly by destroying their crops and leading them to starve. Neighbors start rallying to support one another. Some develop fire-resistant building materials. Others create treatments for burns. A few engineers create crops that grow fast and are fire resistant. Other people coordinate workshops on how to put out fires. The people who set fires keep doing it, but people get better at mitigating the damages.

After a while, this is just accepted as normal: Some people set fires, others help victims of the fires. White papers are written about how fires disproportionately harm people of color, disabled people, and trans people. Conferences are held on burn treatments.

The people setting fires, though, get smarter and more coordinated. Instead of setting random fires, they set targeted fires aimed at weak points at times in the year when the fires would likely spread the fastest. They set thousands of fires simultaneously to overwhelm people and destroy their morale. They release propaganda to convince people whose houses they would burn down that it was their neighbors who set the fire, and that they—the arsonists—were the only ones who could stop the fires.

The townsfolks, stretched to their limits, are tired. A few tune out. Some move out of town. Those who stay work together to create masks that prevent smoke inhalation. They have even more workshops on fire safety and how to survive fires. There are countless deaths, but there are also countless lives saved. A spirit of camaraderie develops. Still, the fires keep increasing in number and intensity.

Throughout all this, a few tiny voices keep piping up to say, "We need to stop the people who are setting fires!" But everyone ignores them, countering with "Uh, no, our job is helping victims of fires and shine bright lights on the inequity around who gets burned and who does not get enough food after their houses burn down. Stopping the people who set fires is the job for someone else."

So the fires rage on and worsen, as the fire starters get bolder, knowing that no matter what they do, the townsfolks will only respond to the effects of the fires, not try to stop them from setting fires. Soon the whole town is consumed, and the fire starters move to different towns to burn them down, too.

That's basically our sector right now. If we, as a sector, are allergic to advocacy, then we have severe disgust, if not full-blown phobia, of actual politics. We believe politics is beneath us. We don't want to get our hands dirty. Politics and anything associated with it is an ugly, terrible thing; we should focus on more noble, feel-good pursuits while rabble-rousing about how we need to change systems, yet simultaneously avoiding doing the thing that would significantly change systems.

And by *we*, I mean the progressive wing of our sector. Right-wing groups have brilliantly and effectively run circles around progressives at every single turn, as you learn in Chapter 8. While progressives help folks affected by their cruel policies, they create more cruel policies. While we debate theories of change and read white papers, they elect racist presidents and senators. Conservatives' embrace of politics and consistent implementation of effective strategies have enabled power to be concentrated in their hands.

The right-wing is full-in on using politics as a powerful and effective weapon to advance their often-abhorrent values. They embrace politics, knowing that if they can get people who align with conservative values to be in power—if they can get a single right-wing judge on the Supreme Court—they will influence thousands of wide-reaching issues for a long, long time, so they invest and strategize. They cut out all the barriers to achieve these goals.

This is where the left needs to be. We must get out of this "neutrality" mindset and not only engage with politics, but to fully embrace it, using the same strategies the right has used, but with progressive values. Considering all the suffering and deaths of countless people, the dismantling of democracy, the rise of fascism, the destruction of vulnerable communities and our planet, and the pain that will intensify in the coming years under this current administration, it is our moral obligation to get over our disgust of politics and use it as an instrument of justice. We can no longer continue to only respond to the fires, we must stop the people who keep setting them, who keep fanning the flames. We need to wake up to reality, acknowledge that everything we do is political, and fully and unapologetically engage with politics through such vehicles as 501(c)(4)s and political action committees (PACs) to advance the community we care about.

The Progressive Theory of Change

For all the money, energy, and time progressives spend on intellectualizing in various ways—individual theories of change, logic models, outcomes, metrics, and so on—we have little agreement on a grand vision and strategy that would solve every problem we're working on. This is another lesson we can learn from conservatives, who, for all their differences, are guided by a few philosophies and strategies, including packing all levels of government with right-wing politicians and judges, allowing capitalism to run unchecked so wealthy people and corporations can hoard as much money as they want, sowing discontent through media like Fox News, building strong institutions like the Heritage Foundation to implement these and other strategies, and so on.

Do all those things effectively, and every issue conservatives care about—deregulation of corporations, stronger borders and fewer immigrants, no restrictions on guns, no abortions, weak social safety nets, no curbing of environmental destruction, and so on—will be taken care of. We see how effective this has been for the right.

What would this look like for progressives? What are the few key issues that if progressive nonprofits and funders could all focus on would address homelessness, poverty, hunger, climate change, gender-based violence, mass shootings, infant mortality, cruelty to animals, the foster care system, elder abuse, disability justice, and so on?

I'm going to get us started. Every societal problem facing our communities stem from a couple of things: unchecked capitalism and greed from oligarchs and corporations, and conservatives being in charge and imposing their will and values on everyone. Here then are the levers of power progressives need to focus on, based on the perspectives I've gathered talking to the people in the field doing the work:

- **Elect more progressive women of color into office at all levels.** There are too many white dudes in power making decisions for everything. While some of them mean well and come up with good policies, it should be a fundamental progressive belief that the people who experience the most injustice would be the ones to best understand it and thus be the most effective at addressing it. The number of progressive women of color in elected office should be used as one of the main indicators of how well we are doing at effecting systems change.
- **Change the tax code so wealthy corporations and individuals pay their fair share of taxes.** Currently, nonprofit and philanthropy have been serving as a conscience-laundering and charity-washing arm of capitalism, where wealthy individuals and corporations get to hoard money and then donate to charity a fraction of what they should be paying in taxes. It's time we had fair, progressive tax laws.
- **Control the narrative regarding important issues and how we talk about them.** It is hard to do anything about gun violence and other issues in the United States because decades of propaganda, misinformation, and brainwashing from Fox News and other conservative outlets have seeped into people's unconscious. Conservatives are masterful at messaging and communications. We need strong, active, unapologetically progressive platforms and pundits to help counter misinformation and advance values of equity and inclusion. This means buying up some conservative platforms and converting them, the way Elon Musk took over Twitter.
- **Protect and enhance voting rights so that the most oppressed people can and do vote.** Yes, people sometimes vote against their best interests, but often the people who are most marginalized in society, when given a chance, tend to vote for progressive policies. Conservatives know this and that's why when they're in power, they work to eliminate voting rights. Since the

right-wing-controlled Supreme Court gutted the Voting Rights Act, hundreds of voter suppression laws have been passed across the United States,[5] including making it illegal to give food and water to people who are standing in line to vote. Progressives must ensure the people most screwed over by an unjust system have the right and the support to fully participate in civics. We must fight to strike down voter suppression laws, rally behind things like Election Day,[6] and provide support—transportation, childcare, whatever it takes—for people to vote.

- **Remove the influence of money on politics.** Money plays a significant role in our political structure, allowing corporations and wealthy individuals to exert inequitable influence on our society. We must reduce the influence and power of corporations and the wealthy on who gets elected and which laws get passed. Reversing Citizens United, the Supreme Court decision that allowed corporations to be legally treated like individuals, which means they can donate as much money as they want to influence elections, would solve many of the problems we have.

Mission Creep

In Jim Collins' book *Good to Great: Why Some Companies Make the Leap . . . and Others Don't*,[7] he references the ancient Greek parable "The fox knows many things, but the hedgehog knows one big thing." This hedgehog concept has embedded itself in our thinking. We think about effective organizations each having a core competency that they stick to. Any organization that strays too far away from its central focus and competency is in danger of mission creep.

We've been trained to think mission creep or mission drift is no good, very bad. When orgs don't stick to their missions, it often leads to confused constituents, annoyed partner orgs, irritated funders, and a less effective field.

But like with everything else, there comes a point where philosophies and concepts are misused or are taken to the extreme, to the detriment of the sector and the people we serve. Our acceptance of the idea that all orgs should specialize in a few things and not do too many things has been having some negative consequences.

For instance, many organizations led by communities of color and other marginalized communities don't have the luxury to focus on one thing. What may seem like mission creep is just us responding to interconnected needs our constituents have indicated we should focus on. Funders and donors' not understanding these dynamics may be a reason why it continues to be so difficult for grassroots, culturally focused organizations to get funding for their vital work that no one else could do as effectively.

Meanwhile, progressive-leaning funders fear creeping away from their mission. This leads them to become entrenched in single issues and solutions. Homelessness. Environment. Early learning. These single issues are often based on whatever the board members at the foundation care most about, but are devoid of any analysis of systemic injustice and what strategies would be most effective to tackle it. Once they are locked in, it's impossible to convince foundations to shift their priorities. I learned this firsthand after approaching a local foundation to ask for funding to increase voter engagement among eligible voters in communities of color.

Worst of all, the hyper-avoidance of anything perceived as mission creep has weakened our sector's ability and readiness to work collectively on vital issues that affect all of us, especially around the levers of power talked about in the previous section. All organizations should advocate for their communities, no matter what their mission focus is. Advocacy around the levers of power that would affect every issue we care about is never mission drift.

Consider voting rights, for example. With exception of a few organizations challenging the hundreds of voting suppression laws that have been passed, the sector's collective response has been lacking, a "meh. . .not our purview" attitude among many organizations. Other leaders, meanwhile, wrung their hands anxiously but refused to engage, afraid they'd step outside their mission.

It is not mission drift to protect and advance voting rights and participation. Every single nonprofit and foundation out there, no matter what its mission is, should be participating in voter engagement.

According to the Nonprofit Power report[8] from Nonprofit VOTE:

> [V]oters who were engaged by nonprofits about voting were much more likely to cast a ballot than comparable voters—10 percentage points more likely (56 vs 46 percent). The turnout boost was even higher among historically underrepresented groups. Younger voters (18–24) engaged by nonprofits were 14 percentage points more likely to vote than comparable young voters. People of color engaged by nonprofits were 12 percentage points more likely to vote. Low-income voters also saw double-digit boosts in turnout. These findings provide a compelling case for more nonprofits to engage the communities they serve in voting and elections.

If we have a hope of effectively and permanently solving the issues we care about, then all nonprofits must be engaged in advocacy and community organizing, and all funders must fund advocacy and community organizing work. We should follow the lead of the organizations whose hedgehog concept is advocacy and systems change work, but all nonprofits and all funders need to get involved. The following sections take brief glances at a few cool and creative advocacy projects that brilliant leaders and organizations have been doing.

Vietnamese Rainbow of Orange County

In 2012, five Vietnamese people in Orange County formed Vietnamese Rainbow of Orange County (VROC) and applied to participate in the Little Saigon's Tet Parade in celebration of the Lunar New Year. The group that organized the parade rejected their application, stating that lesbians, gays, bisexual, and transgender people didn't exist in Vietnamese culture.[9] (This is disappointing to me, a bisexual Vietnamese man, but not shocking, considering how conservative Vietnamese culture can often be.)

Fueled by the anger at the discrimination and the ignorance on display, VROC started mobilizing the LGBTQ community and allies in Orange County, working to not just be included in the parade, but to educate the public about LGBTQ issues and increase the visibility of LGBTQ Vietnamese people. Using the radio, television, and newspapers, VROC gained support from political leaders and national organizations such as the ACLU and GLADD.

The group tried several strategies that ultimately proved unsuccessful. VROC filed an injunction with the Orange County Superior Court, though the court was bound by existing laws governing private events. VROC worked with Westminster City Council members, the city attorney, and others to get the city to include a non-discriminatory clause in special events permits, which was rejected, though the city did require the Tet Parade organizers to pay over $18,000 in legal fees.

The following year, however, the organizers of the Parade put it to a vote of its general members, and the vote was to exclude Vietnamese American LGBTQ individuals from marching. Having been equipped with the political connections, visibility, and better organized than from the previous year, VROC mobilized and pushed harder. Once the parade organizers lost $60,000 in sponsorships with VROC's advocacy, it forced them to hold a second vote with its members. This time they overwhelmingly voted to allow Vietnamese American LGBTQ individuals to march in the parade.

Since 2013, VROC has been incorporated as a 501(c)(3) organization. It continues doing advocacy related to LGBTQ issues such as protesting anti-trans policies at school boards, while also conducting research such as on the mental health of LGBTQIA+ youth of color, educating the community on issues like workshops for parents on how to accept their queer kids, and building collective power by working in partnership with other grassroots organizations focused on equity.

UnKoch My Campus

Conservative donors have been extremely strategic in how they spend their money to shape politics and culture. And few are more effective than the Koch brothers and their network. Among their strategies is to infiltrate and influence higher education, using significant donations to shape their political agendas at universities, hiring professors who are aligned with conservative ideas, shaping curricula, bolstering conservative student groups, and suppressing the work of progressive students and faculty. UnKoch My Campus was founded in 2014 to expose and counter the influence of the Kochs and other right-wing billionaires on higher education.

UnKoch My Campus organizes a network of student activists, arming them with information regarding how much the Kochs spend at their universities and on what, and training them in tactics like using online petitions and organizing rallies and protests to pressure their schools to break ties with the Kochs.

The organization's work has led to significant victories. George Mason University, for example, received over $129 million from the Koch Foundation and was hit with a lawsuit in 2017 by student activists supported by UnKoch My Campus. It became the first university to change its gift acceptance policy based on UnKoch My Campus's recommendations. In Tucson, the group and its local partner successfully pressured Tucson Unified School District to remove the Koch-funded high-school curriculum. They also stopped Arizona State University from requiring all students to take the Koch-backed "Philosophy, Politics, Economy and Law" class, which was rife with right-wing ideas. Meanwhile, UnKoch My Campus worked with New Hampshire–based progressive advocacy organization Granite State Progress to prevent a Koch-backed attorney general from gaining power as chair of the New Hampshire Supreme Court.

The group's focus has expanded beyond the Koch brothers, into structural inequalities in general, such as ensuring education and other common goods and institutions are free from the influence of the wealthy and corrupt. One of its campaigns is #CopsOffCampus, a movement to get campuses across the United States to stop working with local police forces.

UnKoch My Campus, however, has predictably faced significant backlash, and not just from the right. Its assertiveness goes against the white moderate tendencies we're so used to, which means lower chances to get funding. But the group is undeterred. According to Jasmine Banks, founder and executive director, "While our strategies and tactics were not always popular with 'mainstream' liberal nonprofits claiming to be about social justice, we have known that naming bad actors with massive positional and economic power is a critical part of disrupting injustice."[10]

Fighting against billionaires and the racist system of policing and incarceration, and getting flak from all directions, must seem like an extremely daunting uphill battle. But the courage UnKoch My Campus shows should inspire and guide our sector if it hopes to successfully stand up against injustice.

Democracy Vouchers

As mentioned earlier, money has been a major factor in our political system. Those with money have played a significant role in who gets elected, tending to favor white and male candidates. Estevan Muñoz-Howard, Senior Director at Ktisis Capital, which serves as a strategic advisor to progressive donors and institutions, wanted to do something about it. He had been inspired by his time living and working in Ecuador, where civilians mobilized to counter the harm that wealthy individuals had inflicted through bribery and corruption.

After he moved to Seattle, Estevan started volunteering with an organization called Fix Democracy First, formerly Washington Public Campaigns. He and a group of like-minded activists started meeting weekly to discuss what public financing of elections would look like in the city and how to advocate for it. They had a chance in 2013, when the Seattle City Council asked the Seattle Ethics and Elections Commission (SEEC) for recommendations on this issue. The group mobilized to influence SEEC. The measure the City Council would put on the ballot for a vote was a matching fund for small donors, where if they donated $10 or more, they would get a sixfold match from public funds.

It was voted down, but by a surprisingly narrow margin. The effort had built momentum. The next day, the group got calls from local and national donors. Armed with money and interest, they tried again, this time proposing the ambitious Democracy Vouchers Program, which would provide each eligible Seattle resident with four $25 vouchers they could use as donations to their favorite qualified local candidates. The program would be funded by taxing Seattle homeowners an average of $8 a year. With the $1.5 million they raised, the group mobilized, collecting the required signatures to get the proposal directly in front of voters as a ballot initiative. It passed with over 60 percent of the votes.

I caught up with Estevan and asked for any advice he had for the sector regarding advocacy work. He warned against the tendency of thinking of any one proposal or project as a silver bullet that would address all the problems we currently have in society. He reiterated the importance of seeing setbacks and failures as part of the necessary process toward success. Above all, Estevan stressed the importance of having a long-term view, not just during the advocacy phase, but also during implementation once you achieve victory:

> We have this need for immediate gratification. People, especially funders, have short attention spans. We need to be more committed both to our fights as well as our wins. It takes years. During those first two years when we met weekly to work on this issue, some of us wondered "Is this pointless?" I'm glad we stuck with it.

A lot of us are glad they did too. Since its implementation in 2017, the Democracy Vouchers Program has played a significant role in increasing the voting participation of Seattle's low-income residents and people of color. According to a study done by researchers at the University of Washington's Center for Studies in Demography & Ecology, participants in the program were more likely to live in poorer neighborhoods than those who donate cash. Among those who used their vouchers, there was a larger share of people earning $30,000 or less a year, which suggests the program has increased the diversity of the donor pool.[11]

The program has also increased the number of candidates of color, women, and younger candidates running for office, as well as significantly boosted voter participation.[12]

Let's Put Out Those Fires and Stop the Arsonists

Out in the real world, I see the incredible work our sector does every day. And I also see we have developed a learned helplessness and an avoidance of advocacy, lobbying, and work that would change the inequitable systems oppressing the most marginalized people in our community. Given the dire situation of our sector and the world, we must fully embrace advocacy as central to every organization's work, not something outside its missions. Advocacy must be something we must all engage in, and something all funders must fund. Everything is political, and we must engage in politics too, by forming multi-entities such as C3s/C4s/PACs and working to get progressive candidates elected.

Luckily, we have brilliant organizations out there leading the way. We just need to follow their lead, and funders need to provide support by funding advocacy efforts. If we can be louder than the voices calling for hate, cruelty, and injustice, we can stop those who are setting fires and achieve the kind of world we know is possible.

Discussion Questions

1. What are some examples of learned helplessness you've seen in our sector?
2. What are some other factors that may explain why advocacy engagement has been dropping so significantly since 2000?
3. Who have been the loudest voices in our society? What allows them to be so loud?
4. Why do you think nonprofit organizations and professionals avoid politics?
5. Which of the levers of power listed most resonates with you?
6. Do you think it is mission creep for non-advocacy-focused nonprofits to work on systems change?
7. Which of the tactics used by the featured organizations should more organizations use?

8

Reimagining Philanthropy, Foundations, and Funder–Nonprofit Dynamics

While we do our good works let us not forget that the real solution lies in a world in which charity will have become unnecessary.

—Chinua Achebe

I WAS IN MY parked car one day, eating a bánh mì between meetings, covered in crumbs, when a phone call came from Philip Li, the CEO of the Robert Sterling Clark Foundation (RSCF). I had reached out earlier to see if my organization Rooted in Vibrant Communities (RVC) might be a good match for the foundation's priority around leadership.

"We're interested in RVC and its work but need some more information," he said. I was about to ask him for more details about RSCF's grant application process and the deadline, when Phil continued. "I know you're busy, so do you mind finding me a grant proposal you already wrote for another funder and emailing it to me? And don't worry about editing it or even changing the name of that other funder, just forward the whole package over."

I hung up and chewed slowly on my spicy tofu sandwich, a single teardrop rolling poetically down my face. Surely I was in the middle of one of my daydreams, as the process was never that easy, and funders never that accommodating. Many funders think the word *philanthropy* comes from the Greek root words *philos*, meaning "love of," and *anthropos*, meaning "burdensome and pointless grant applications and other status-quo-upholding shenanigans based on the whims of the wealthy."

I looked through the email archive on my phone and found a grant proposal I had submitted to another foundation. It was a large proposal that had taken me 40 hours to complete, comprising a 10-page narrative and a dozen attachments, including a bespoke budget tailored for the foundation using their tedious format and chart of accounts, a theory of change, a logic model, a work plan, the tax exemption letter, the latest financial statements, and, though I may be misremembering, the blood type of every staff member. I forwarded the email and all the attachments to Phil. It took me about three minutes to do. We found out a couple of weeks later that we received a significant multi-year grant.

RSCF's process was simple and yet truly groundbreaking. The foundation got all the information it needed, and it only took me a few minutes, instead of the hours that would normally be required preparing a new proposal package, pointlessly trying to fit within arbitrary character limits many funders like to impose. I could now spend these hours I saved on more meaningful work.

How Current Funding Practices Perpetuate Inequity, and How to Address It

Foundations and grants are a vital part of our sector, providing support to many leaders, organizations, and movements. Some of the people I admire most in the field—yes, some of my best friends—are foundation professionals and board trustees, many of whom work hard to make things easier for nonprofits. This brings to mind the program officer who called me up clandestinely to recommend I change one thing that would have tanked my organization's application ("You and I did not have this conversation," she whispered before hanging up), and the program officer who let me sneak out of his foundation's office with several dry-erase markers and a bag of pistachios. These are expensive items that would certainly have increased my organization's overhead rates if we had bought them ourselves.

However, while foundations do some good and are filled with many good people, the funding system they rely on is one of the biggest sources of stress for nonprofits, and more seriously, one of the most significant barriers to our effectiveness in driving social change.

The funding-dynamics struggles nonprofits deal with are too numerous to detail in one short chapter. They include the *shiny object syndrome*, where funders gravitate toward the latest trends, often abandoning programs with proven track records; the *game of funding chicken*, where funders wait to see who else will invest in a new project first before they themselves jump in. And, of course, the *snowflake application*, where funders require grants to be written in their format and with their character limits, forcing nonprofits to waste hundreds of thousands of hours collectively each year translating the same answer from one proposal to another, because one funder wants an answer in 1,000 characters while another wants the same answer in 750 characters.

These things stifle imagination and force nonprofits into a survival mindset, where most organizations no longer have the luxury of dreaming boldly and planning ambitiously, but instead struggle to simply keep programs and services going for our community members who need them, alleviating symptoms of inequity but seldom successful at eradicating it for good.

And as with everything else, communities of color and other marginalized communities are disproportionately affected. The current funding system is designed by white people to ensure funding goes mostly to white-led organizations. As Vanessa Daniel, author of the book *Unrig the Game: What Women of Color Can Teach Everyone About Winning*, observes in her op-ed to *The New York Times*[1]:

> I've seen repeatedly that it's far easier for a young affluent white man who has studied poverty at Harvard to land a $1 million grant with a concept pitch than it is for a 40-something Black woman with a decades-long record of wins in the impoverished

community where she works to get a grant for $20,000. This, despite the epic volumes of paperwork and proof of impact that she will invariably have to produce. She reads as risky, small, marginal. He reads as a sound investment, scalable, mainstream.

Because larger, white-led organizations can play the game better, on occasion they receive significant funding that trickles down in smaller amounts to organizations led by marginalized communities. Of the few grants directly accessible to smaller organizations, many are onerous and downright paternalistic, like the time a foundation staffer told me their grant committee made the process for their $5,000 grants difficult on purpose to give these smaller orgs a "real grant-writing experience" to help them develop their skills.

All of this may explain why so few philanthropic dollars in the United States go to organizations led by communities-of-color. I spoke to Edgar Villanueva, author of Decolonizing Wealth,[2] who told me "Less than 10% of philanthropic funding reaches communities of color—the very communities whose labor and land built this nation's wealth. This is not generosity; it is a moral debt long overdue."

Edgar's number aligns with research from Philanthropic Initiative for Racial Equity (PRE),[3] which found that organizations and programs focusing on communities of color only receive 6 percent of foundation and corporate grantmaking. Furthermore, according to Lori Villarosa, PRE's founder and executive director, "Even within that small percentage, more than a third of the top 20 recipients of funding focused on communities of color were founded by white billionaires or large corporations advancing their own top-down theories of change, such as charter schools, as the solution to racial disparities."

The lack of funding going to communities of color is why the work of foundations focused on bringing resources to marginalized communities is so vital. The Black Future Co-op Fund, for example, invests specifically in Black nonprofit leaders and Black-led organizations that focus on serving Black communities. This is critical when it's estimated that only. 1.8 percent of philanthropic dollars go to Black-led organizations.[4] I talked with Andrea Caupain Sanderson, BFCF's interim managing director, who reinforced the importance of philanthropy having a restorative and justice-grounded lens:

"We are seeking to change the paradigm of philanthropy, funding only Black-led organizations to respond to the economic segregation and philanthropic redlining that has devastated our communities. We are putting ourselves in the driver's seat, taking every right action to ensure our future descendants have a vibrant and thriving life."

Another example is Headwaters Foundation, which supports nonprofits focused on helping residents of the Flathead Reservation and Montana's 15 westernmost counties. According to a report by Native Americans in Philanthropy and Candid, Native Americans are 2.9% of the US population but receive less than one-half of a percent of philanthropic dollars,[5] In addition to their regular open grants, the Headwaters partners with the Confederated Salish and Kootenai Tribes to ensure funding is going to Indigenous communities in Western Montana, and in a way that respects Indigenous tribes' agency. As CEO Carly Hare said when I caught up with her, "By working directly with Tribal leaders, we ensure our support aligns with the Tribe's priorities and vision for health. This partnership reflects our respect for Tribal sovereignty."

Trust-Based Philanthropy

I'm appreciative of the efforts, including many led by funders, to challenge the existing toxic funding practices and dynamics. In particular, the trust-based philanthropy movement that influences the Robert Sterling Clark Foundation and other funders' grantmaking philosophy and process. As written on the Trust-Based Philanthropy Project's website,[6] the approach is grounded in several key values: *work for systemic equity; redistribute power; center relationships; partner in a spirit of service; be accountable;* and *embrace learning.* Among the practices it recommends are:

- **Move in solidarity with nonprofits** by checking in with grantee partners, offering support beyond money, being transparent and responsive, advocating for the sector, and collaborating with other funders to reduce burdens on grantees and be helpful to them in other ways.

- **Mobilize money in a trust-based way** by committing to multi-year unrestricted funding, increasing grantmaking budget especially over the next four years, offering rapid response funding, streamlining and simplifying grant processes, giving "gifts" instead of grants when possible, and being flexible on grant disbursement timing.
- **Nurture possibility and innovation by** funding big bets (large, catalytic grants), supporting connection and convenings, and exploring funding beyond just 501(c)(3)s to include LLCs, 5101(c)(4)s, mutual aid networks, donor circles, and so on.

These practices are vital in shifting power to communities most affected by systemic injustice and enabling our sector's fight for an equitable world. As Pia Infante, one of the main leaders in the founding and growth of the trust-based philanthropy movement, states in this article in SSIR[7]:

The ultimate work of trust-based philanthropy is to build a democracy that acknowledges the role of structural racism in the creation of wealth in the United States.

This broader view is critical, and something that's been missing in how many funders approach their work. This is particularly true of *progressive-leaning* funders, who express alignment with values of equity, justice, and democracy, but whose actions, or lack thereof, often constrain our sector so it cannot achieve those goals.

The Differences Between Progressive and Conservative Funders

In 1997, Sally Covington published a report commissioned by the National Committee for Responsive Committee. "Moving a Public Policy Agenda: The Strategic Philanthropy of Conservative Foundations"[8] presented the analysis of the differences between conservative-leaning and progressive-leaning foundations in how they act and fund, and why the former have been so much more effective in advancing their agenda. As stated in the report's foreword by James. A. Smith, executive director of the Howard Gilman Foundation and author of *The Idea Brokers: Thank Tanks and the Rise of the New Policy Elite*:

> Proclaiming their movement to be a war of ideas, conservatives began to mobilize resources for battle in the 1960s. They built new institutional bastions; recruited, trained, and equipped their intellectual warriors; forged new weapons as cable television, the Internet, and other communications technologies evolved; and threw their full resources into policy and political battles.

In contrast:

> [T]he majority of [liberal-leaning] foundations, if they are engaged in the public policy realm at all, tend to operate not with a long-term policy perspective but with a problem-oriented and field-specific approach. The ideological proclivities of most foundations, if they can be characterized in ideological terms at all, are grounded in the traditions of American pragmatism. Their commitments are short-term and project-driven, often looking for measurable outcomes rather than such vaguely definable goals as pushing public opinion in one direction or another.

According to Covington's research, conservative foundations operate on a whole different, much more effective level. They focus on the big picture and get out of the weeds, act quickly, provide significant general operating funds, build institutions, fund them for literally decades, support leaders, and engage in policy and politics.

Progressive funders—with a few exceptions—intellectualize, are severely risk-averse, focus narrowly to fund isolated strategies and programs, treat grantees like parasites and freeloaders who need to be micromanaged through onerous grant applications and reporting processes, and avoid politics.

Nearly three decades later, the report is still relevant. In fact, liberal-leaning foundations may have become even more entrenched in their ways. These destructive habits have been so ingrained in the way these funders operate that even the most "innovative" foundations and program officers still follow many of these destructive behaviors.

These differences explain why conservative movements and organizations have made so much progress in pushing their agenda over the past few decades to the detriment of democracy and the well-being of everyone in society who is not a rich, straight, white man. The rise in fascism we see today is a direct result of the effective work right-wing funders have done over the past several decades.

In talking to progressive-leaning funders about how they could be more effective, I often hear this phrase: "There's no roadmap for making philanthropy more effective." That's entirely wrong. There's already a very well-tested set of strategies that's been created and used by conservative funders. The rest of this chapter summarizes these strategies. The funders who believe in a just world need to follow it, but with progressive values grounding their work.

Rethinking Strategic Philanthropy

One of the most toxic and destructive philosophies held by progressive-leaning funders is the concept of strategic philanthropy. It's the idea that funders should have specific issues they tackle and how they go about tackling them. Over the past several decades, this means that foundations adopt narrow issues, ignore other issues, and change their focus year after year. This year, it's early learning. Next year, it's the arts. The following year, it's the environment.

And all of it glazed with a thick, delusional layer of toxic intellectualizing (one of the Horsemen of Ineffectiveness I discuss in Chapter 2) in the form of theories of change, logic models, and endless, redundant, and expensive research forced on the entire sector.

This concept has done significant damage. So much so that its originators have published articles apologizing for unleashing it on everyone, including a letter[9] by Hal Harvey, one of its founders, called "Why I Regret Pushing Strategic Philanthropy," where he laments how the concept has created a field of funders who think they are way more knowledgeable and qualified than the communities and leaders who are closest to the problems being addressed.

Strategic philanthropy ironically has caused progressive-leaning funders to be extremely *un*strategic, delving into the weeds and into single issues, obsessed with short-term metrics and outcomes, instead of addressing the systems of inequity that are the root causes of all issues.

What Strategic Actually Looks Like

If we want to see what effective strategy looks like, and what we must emulate, let's study right-wing funders, who have been running circles around progressive-leaning funders. First, they have a vision. Not just for their work, but for all of society. It's a vision most of us would consider horrifying, for sure, but it's there, and it unites conservative funders and movements and guides their work.

Their vision is a society where government is limited, capitalism runs unchecked, white Christian men are in charge, taxes are low for the wealthy, guns are accessible, immigrants are few, schools teach the bible, women stay at home, gay people have no rights, the poor remain poor, and a strong and lethal police presence exists to keep everyone in their respective places.

They have relentlessly pursued this vision for the past several decades, and their strategies have followed that. These strategies, as we see from the Covington report, are simple, easy to understand, and devastatingly effective.

Build and maintain institutional bastions: Conservative funders set up powerful institutions responsible for shaping public opinions, influencing legislation, and elevating conservative voices into positions of power. Among the most influential are:

- **The Heritage Foundation,** which has been shaping domestic and foreign policies, playing a major role in Reagan's policies, and has been a main driver of Project 2025.
- **The Federalist Society,** which has successfully shaped the judiciary in the United States to be right-wing, including pushing the appointment of right-wing Supreme Court Justices Scalia, Thomas, Gorsuch, Kavanaugh, and Barrett.
- **The Cato Institute,** which has been a major force pushing for free-market principles, including school choice and deregulation.
- **The American Enterprise Institute,** which has been instrumental in pushing for the gutting of the federal welfare program, while pushing for tax cuts for the wealthy and for corporations.

Recruit, train, and equip intellectual warriors: Conservative funders know that individual leaders are vital to their movements, so they focus on creating pipelines of leaders from a young age and supporting them throughout their careers and across fields. Some of their activities include:

- **Training and supporting future leaders** through various opportunities such as fellowships like the Claremont Institute's Publius, Lincoln, and John Marshall Fellowships and Heritage Foundation's Young Leaders Program.
- **Engaging young people** through conservative activism on college campuses by funding conservative speakers, conferences, and projects such as Turning Point USA's Professor Watchlist, which targets professors accused of being leftist. Turning Point has also started targeting high school students.
- **Providing support and platforms** for conservative voices to gain prominence, creating a cadre of influential speakers, podcasters, media pundits, authors, and so on.

Shape cultural narratives through controlling the media. The hatred and anger we see toward "woke-"ness, trans people, DEI, taxes, gun reforms, and the government did not come from nowhere. Conservative funders have known that shaping society requires shaping the narrative, which requires a robust media strategy, so they have invested heavily in this area. Among their strategies are:

- Maintaining a powerful network of news media that dominates the airwaves. Fox News, The Daily Caller, Breitbart News, and the Washington Examiner are a few of the most influential, flooding the United States with a barrage of conservative messages.
- Investing in digital media and online influence such as PragerU, The Daily Wire, The Blaze, assorted YouTube and podcast channels. These are especially important in reaching young people.
- Supporting talk radio, such as Rush Limbaugh, who was one of the most influential conservative voices until he died.
- Funding the creation of alternative platforms such as Truth Social, Parler, and GETTR, and buying up platforms such as Twitter.

Get conservative leaders elected at all levels: Conservative funders understand that to actualize their vision, they needed conservatives to be in power politically at all branches and levels of government.

> *If we want to see what effective strategy looks like, and what we must emulate, we need to study right-wing funders, who have been running circles around progressive-leaning funders.*

- Providing substantial financial support to Republican candidates, using Super PACS and dark money.
- Investing significantly to shape the judiciary by supporting conservative judges and ensuring they get elected and appointed, including to the Supreme Court.
- Funding organizations and movements that work to elect conservative candidates. Susan B. Anthony Pro-Life America, for example, funds political candidates who oppose abortion rights.
- Backing efforts to suppress voting and increase gerrymandering to ensure conservative voices are present, even when they are outnumbered.

Levers of Change

The strategies of conservative funders have not been a secret. They spell it all out, both their vision and how they will go about doing it. If progressives want to address more than the symptoms of injustice, we need a clear agreement on some policy levers that would positively affect every single issue we're working on, the way conservatives have centered their work on free-market, limited government, unregulated corporations, and so on. Here are some of these levers:

- Changing the tax codes so that wealthy individuals and corporations pay their fair share of taxes.
- Electing progressive candidates into every branch and level of government, focusing especially on women of color to balance the overrepresentation of white men.
- Protecting and expanding voting rights, including automatic voter registration and making Election Day a national holiday.

- Limiting the influence of corporations on politics, specifically reversing Citizens United, the Supreme Court decision that allowed corporations to spend unlimited money to elect candidates who are less likely to regulate and increase taxes on businesses.
- Shifting the cultural narrative by fighting misinformation and spreading progressive philosophies of equity and inclusion.

If we can accomplish these goals, most of the issues we're working on would instantly be better. Let's dive into the strategies to accomplish these, learning from conservative funders. With everything being so urgent, I'm going to start with what may be hardest to convince left-leaning funders and donors to do.

Fully Fund and Engage in Politics Right-wing funders have been effective because they see clearly that politics is the most potent weapon, and they invest heavily and unapologetically in it. Conservative funders have no qualms supporting right-wing political candidates, while liberal-leaning funders have been horrified at the idea. I talked to a colleague who had been a part of right-wing circles before she realized they didn't align with her values. She said, "Conservative donors and funders are not afraid to buy political candidates."

The Federalist Society, for example, is a vastly influential organization that has worked for several decades to shape the judiciary system. It's funded by conservative foundations like the Charles Koch Foundation, Bradley Foundation, Scaife Foundation, and Mercer Family Foundation, along with dark money groups like DonorsTrust. Its key leader is Leonard Leo, one of the most powerful figures in the conservative sphere. Leo and the Federalist Society helped Trump confirm more than 200 right-wing judges, including Supreme Court Justices Gorsuch, Kavanaugh, and Barrett.[10]

The Federalist Society was founded in 1982 and has been so effective that conservative funders and donors have doubled down on them. Three years ago, billionaire Barre Seid donated $1.6 billion dollars—the largest donation to a political group in U.S. history[11]—to a new organization run by Leonard Leo, to continue shaping the judiciary until it's entirely right-wing. This $1.6 billion, focused on seating conservative judges, will have ripple effects that will cost our sector multiple times more to address.

In contrast to this, left-leaning funders mostly tend to avoid funding politics, viewing it as beneath them. What we need from left-leaning funders in this moment is acknowledgment that their disdain of and refusal to engage in politics has been a fatal mistake, followed by a full-throated commitment to fund and engage in countering the right's political engagement over the past several decades.

It means at the very least, left-leaning funders need to invest a minimum of $1.6 billion dollars immediately to place progressive judges across all levels, with the Supreme Court as a long-term target, to counter Leonard Leo and the Federalist Society's actions. Ideally, they'd invest $20 billion (to start with) to make up for decades of investing little to nothing in this area.

Progressive-leaning judges have served as a firewall against the injustices we're seeing; we need more of them at all levels and jurisdictions. When it comes to literally saving democracy, $1.6 billion is not a lot of money. A lot of foundations have that just sitting in their endowments.

And that is just the judiciary. We need funders to back progressive political candidates across other branches of government, and at all levels—city, state, and federal. Since 501(c)(3)s cannot endorse political candidates, funders need to significantly ramp up funding 501(c)(4)s, PACs, Super PACs, and other organizations that can fully work to elect progressive candidates into office.

Over in Seattle, I have been on the board of the Progress Alliance (PA) of Washington, another network of progressive donors working to advance equity and justice. It is both a 501(c)(3) organization and a 501(c)(4) organization. One of PA's signature programs is the First Mile Circle, which supports progressive candidates of color being elected into office in Washington State. In 2023, the Circle provided financial support to 43 candidates. Nearly half, 19, got elected, including my friend and colleague James Lovell, VFA's former senior staff, who oversaw the organization's academic programs.

First Mile has a budget of less than a million dollars each year. Imagine what could be achieved if left-leaning funders funded politics with the same level and commitment as right-wing funders.

Build Progressive Institutions Doing these things well requires the existence of progressive institutions that are financially secure for decades so they can do their work. We have seen clearly how effective conservative institutions have been. Some combination of the Heritage Foundation, Federalist Society, Cato Institute, American Enterprise Institute, Turning Point USA, the Hoover Institution, the Claremont Institute, the Leadership Institute, Judicial Watch, and a host of other right-wing organizations is involved in almost every domestic and foreign policy as well as every aspect of the United States and even global culture.

We do have many progressive organizations that do important work. The Center for American Progress (CAP), for example, which was founded in 2003, works to counter the Heritage Foundation. CAP influences Democratic policies around healthcare, climate, and the economy. The Institute for Policy Studies (IPS), founded in 1963, has long been advocating for tax reform, opposing war, pushing for racial justice, and advancing other progressive issues.

The problem is that they are often not funded by progressive-leaning funders to the same degree or in the same way that conservative funders fund their institutions. CAP, for example, reported on its 2022 990 that its expenses totaled $48.2 million, with $26.6 million going to salaries, and net assets totaling $47.7 million.[12] IPS that year reported spending $5.4 million, including $2.9 million for salaries, and net assets of $10 million.[13] Meanwhile, in the same year the Heritage Foundation reported spending $93.7 million, with $44 million of that in salaries, and net assets totaling $332 million.[14]

While there are incredible organizations doing pivotal work, progressives need our own versions of the Federalist Society, Heritage Foundation, Turning Point USA, and so on, and we need to fund them to the same degrees as the right does, if we hope to be successful in countering their work.

Fund Advocacy, Policy, Lobbying, and Organizing Work At RVC one time, I was skimming through the contract for a grant of $25,000 from a local foundation when I saw a confusingly worded item that said something about my organization agreeing not to engage in advocacy or lobbying work. I called up the program officer. "It's not that we don't allow that type of work," he said, "it's just that we don't want any of the grant money we're giving you to be used to do that work." This is typical of many left-leaning funders: indifferent to, if not deathly terrified of anything remotely considered political, including things that are adjacent to but are clearly not political, like advocacy or voting rights.

Fortunately, there have been some progressive funders who have been doing incredible work in this area. The Solidaire Network, for example, is a network of progressive donors aligned on fighting for a just world. It connects and engages donors around various progressive issues, mobilizes resources for progressive movements, and shifts the paradigms in how donors and funders perceive and engage with leaders who are on the front line. An example of its work is the support of protestors charged with domestic terrorism, as well as bail fund coordinators and other activists facing prison time, for opposing the Copy City in Atlanta. As Solidaire's executive director Rajasvini Bhansali says,[15] "[W]e believe strongly that *funders are not just bystanders*—we must act as agents to safeguard our constitutional right to free speech and peaceful assembly."

Meanwhile, the Florida Rights Restoration Coalition received funding from Michael Bloomberg and other celebrities to pay the fines imposed on formerly incarcerated people so that they could vote. It is unjust that people must pay to vote after they've served their time, especially when the criminal justice system has been proven to be so racist, but until that problem is solved, funders supporting nonprofits that work to restore voting rights is the right thing to do.

Create an Army of Progressive Leaders At the end of 2019, I left my job after being an ED for 13 consecutive years across two organizations. One day, I got an email from Angie Kim, President and CEO of the Center for Cultural Innovation (CCI), whom I had never met or interacted with prior. "I'm wondering if you have a soft landing? Can our work potentially fund you, give you a business card, and act as a platform so that you continue to be in the field in ways that might work for you?"

Through our conversations over the following months, I got to understand what she meant by "soft landing." Angie and CCI were doing what conservative funders have always done, which is to support their leaders as individuals, not simply as batteries to power specific programs. They do this through fellowships, mentorship, career connections, and internships; they help them build platforms and large followings through book deals, spots on large media platforms, podcasts, and so on; and they provide them with funding for legal defense and litigation.

Plus, conservative funders' support of their leaders starts early. They spend three times more than progressive funders on investing in young leaders such as college students. As Generation Progress's report "Building Tomorrow: The Need For Sustained Investment in America's Progressive Youth"[16] shows:

> [T]he top 10 conservative youth organizations had a combined total revenue of approximately $142 million, while the combined total revenue of the top 10 progressive youth organizations was $55 million [...] And in 2014, the single largest conservative youth organization (in total revenue) had more money than the four largest progressive youth organizations combined."

All this explains why so many of us can name dozens of influential right-wing figures off the top of our heads, while we struggle to agree on a few progressive leaders. It's not that we don't have brilliant leaders. We do, like Ta-Nehisi Paul Coates and Nikole Hannah-Jones. But they are not supported at anywhere near the same level as leaders supported by the right.

Funders need to give these and other progressive leaders millions of dollars to build up platforms that would rival the right's pundits. Meanwhile, help create pipelines to increase the number of progressive voices by a hundredfold through fellowships, internships, career connections, mentorship, and so on, starting from high school, as the right-wing's Turning Point USA has been doing. Help them develop successful books, podcasts, radio shows, YouTube channels—whatever it takes to spread progressive messages.

Fund Media, Messaging, and Cultural Narrative Work The right has Fox News, Breitbart, Infowars, podcasts, radio, and social media. They've even managed to turn historically progressive-leaning or centrist media such as CNN and the *Washington Post* into propaganda machines for the right.

The left, meanwhile, has outlets that are supposed to lean progressive, such as *The New York Times*, but these outlets are neoliberal and platform or support heinous views, like *The New York Times*'s fueling of transphobia.[17]

Funders need to vastly fund truly progressive journalism and media strategies at all levels and across all platforms. Support integrity-based journalism. Support local newspapers. Create the equivalent of Fox News and other powerful media platforms.

Or even better, just pool your money and buy up these platforms outright, as *The Onion*, a progressive-leaning parody site, tried to do with Infowars, the platform right-wing conspiracy theorist Alex Jones used to effectively spread all sorts of horrific misinformation, including that the mass shooting massacre at Sandy Hook was fake. A federal judge halted the sale, but imagine if more progressive funders thought like *The Onion*.

Imagine the difference it would make in society if a progressive billionaire or funder successfully bought Fox News and it started spouting ideologies around equity, diversity, and inclusion instead of transphobia, racism, and general fear and hatred.

This Is the Rainy Day. Give Out Money Now. If you're reading all this and thinking "That's great, but where is all of this money to fund these things going to come from?" you're not alone. Years of funders telling the sector, "There's only so much money to go around" has led many of us to believe this lie. U.S. foundations' cumulative assets have grown 15 times over the past 35 years, including an astounding 46 percent during the pandemic. There's now over $1.5 trillion hoarded by private foundations, and it's still growing (unless the market crashes or something).[18]

Foundations, meanwhile, tend to spend out only the minimum of their assets as required by law each year, which is about 5 percent, even though their endowments have been growing significantly more than 5 percent each year. In 2024, it's estimated that U.S. foundations' collective assets grew by nearly $170 billion, or about 11.5 percent. This means if foundations increase their payout on average from 5 percent to just 6 percent, it will free up an additional $15–20 billion each year.[19] We need funders to go way beyond 5 percent, to 10 percent, to 25 percent, to whatever it takes. Your endowments mean nothing if society falls to fascism.

So what's the holdup? Why are so many funders saving for a rainy day when the world is facing multiple simultaneous existential crises? Many funders have locked into this concept of their foundation existing in perpetuity, which means not spending out each year more than their assets can grow. But why? Dimple Abichandani, in her book *A New Era for Philanthropy*[20] wrote:

> The most pervasive story in the philanthropic sector is the story of scarcity. This is the story we tell about how our resources are not enough. This "not enough" story shapes our philanthropic practices, relationships, strategies, and, most importantly, in this moment, our understanding of what is possible.

This scarcity mindset, one of the Horsemen of Ineffectiveness, has shrunken many progressive-leaning foundations' imaginations, and stunted imagination is another Horseman. It creates a self-reinforcing cycle, as future problems are often caused by current problems we fail to adequately address.

Fortunately, there are funders who see the urgency of taking care of current problems before they grow exponentially. Many are spending down their endowments and possibly sunsetting their foundation. The Freedom Together Foundation announced a payout increase to 10 percent. Woods Fund Chicago (WFC) increased its payout rate to 14 percent in 2025, aiming for 15 percent in 2026; in their newsletter published August 2024,[21] WFC's President Michelle Morales explains the Foundation's philosophy:

> [W]e determined that we wanted to turn the concept of being *fiduciarily responsible* on its head [. . .] Traditionally, fiduciary

responsibility emphasizes adherence to a minimal payout, protecting the corpus so that it can continue perpetually. *At WFC, we believe we are fiduciarily responsible to the community and prioritize impact over returns.*

Funders should all follow WFC, Freedom Together, and other foundations in getting out of this scarcity mindset and in giving out more money now instead of saving for a future that will not exist for anyone except billionaires. Stop saving for a rainy day when there is currently a monsoon flooding our communities.

Funding More Effectively

It's not just what conservative funders fund and how much, but also how they do it that also allows their grantees to be so effective. Covington's report spells out several of these major differences between conservative and progressive-leaning funders.

Give Only Multi-Year General Operating Dollars (MYGOD)

General operating funds over several years are a hallmark of conservative funding. It allows conservative organizations, movements, and leaders the flexibility and stability to do whatever they need to advance conservative values, including engaging in politics. There is now so much data and evidence on how effective general operating funds are, including for advancing equity.[22] Giving restricted short-terms funds is so archaic and embarrassing that any foundation still doing that should just have all its staff and board members wear codpieces and powdered wigs.

Fund Organizations for 20 or 30 Years at a Time

Conservative funders are in it for the long haul. According to the Covington report,[23] "[M]any of these foundations have engaged in similar funding efforts for as long as *two decades* [emphasis mine]."

This steady stream of support for decades, and again mostly in the form unrestricted funds, means right-wing nonprofits can plan and dream and have flexibility to change their strategies as needed to be effective.

In contrast, most grants from progressive-leaning funders are one year in duration, which keeps nonprofits constantly in survival mode. Three-year grants are better, but it often takes that long to build capacity and connections, so right as organizations are starting to hit their strides, the funding ends and they must start over.

Let's learn from conservative foundations and commit to providing progressive nonprofits and movements with two or three decades of funding at a time.

Reduce the Administrative Burden on Nonprofits

The grant application process has been one of the most archaic and destructive rituals in this line of work, wasting hundreds of thousands of hours of nonprofit leaders' time each year. With things being so dire, all funders need to reexamine their processes and simplify everything, including their timelines. Nonprofits are fighting to protect communities and democracy. They need funders to make grant decisions in four weeks or less, with as little energy spent as possible, not the months of anguish and uncertainty most grant application processes put them through.

There are efforts to make grant processes better, such as PEAK Grantmaking's Project Streamline,[24] the JustFund Common Application[25] that allows nonprofits to apply to over 170 foundations with one proposal, and funders like Robert Sterling Clark, who just accept whatever informative grant proposals potential grantees have already written. These are great starts.

Treat Grantees as Actual Partners

Conservative funders treat their grantees as actual partners, while progressive-leaning funders often treat their grantees with suspicion and disdain. Why, for example, do so many funders require nonprofits to fill out the same grant application for funding renewals, despite having worked together for several years? Knock it off. Give general operating funds. Check in on grantees. Encourage honest feedback, including about challenges grantees are going through. Help problem solve.

Bring the occasional basket of gluten-free mini muffins. It'll take a while to reverse the fear and anxiety you've conditioned in nonprofit leaders, but we need real partnerships if we want to create lasting change in the world.

Change the Charters

A lot of funders have been using their founding charters as excuses to avoid engaging in more effective strategies. These documents are not written in stone. Work with your legal counsel to change your founding charters so you can increase your payout rate and fund differently and more effectively, including funding progressive individuals, movements, mutual aid, LLCs, religious orgs, 501(c)(4)s, PACs, and so on. Stop letting policies written during different times and by people who are often dead or otherwise less likely to suffer under this fascist regime dictate your actions in the present moment.

Funders, Own Your Power

I know foundation funding is just one element in the fight for social justice, but it is a critical element, as we see when studying how conservatives have been so successful. Progressive-leaning foundations must own the power they have and the responsibility that it entails. If we as a sector are to be effective in addressing injustice and creating a diverse and inclusive society, funders who believe in progressive values must be willing to do some difficult soul-searching on their philosophies and practices and make some significant changes in how they operate.

We can combine what we have learned from right-wing funders with the values and practices recommended for trust-based philanthropy. Add to this observations by individuals and organizations from marginalized communities who have been at the forefront tackling societal issues. Together, these elements provide us a path toward evolving funding practices that enable our sector to be at its most effective and to help create a world where charity and philanthropy, in their current forms, are no longer necessary.

Discussion Questions

1. What do you think philanthropy is currently doing well?
2. How have current philanthropic practices been affecting marginalized communities and the organizations led by them?
3. Which of the trust-based philanthropy practices resonate most with you?
4. Do you agree that there are major differences between conservative and liberal funders?
5. Do you think the "levers of change" listed (changing tax code, protecting voting, electing more progressive women into office, limiting the influence of corporations on politics, and fighting misinformation) are the right ones?
6. Why don't more progressive-leaning funders support advocacy, organizing, and political work?
7. Do you believe foundations should exist in perpetuity?
8. What are some ways that funders and nonprofit leaders can shift their dynamics to be one of true partnership?

9

Reimagining Hiring Practices

When you've worked hard, and done well, and walked through that doorway of opportunity. . .you do not slam it shut behind you. You reach back.
—Michelle Obama

THE PERIOD AFTER I graduated with my master's in social work was surreal. I had moved back to Seattle and into my parents' house. I was hoping to find a job but didn't have much luck, even after several months. Caught in the experience paradox, where I didn't have enough experience to be hired, but I couldn't get experience because no one would hire me, I stayed cooped up in my room, futilely sending out resumes and cover letters during the day. At night, I wandered out of the house to stare at the sky, wailing, "I may be unemployed, but I'm still a human being! A human being!"

Hope came one day in the form of an invitation to a first-round interview for a case manager position. I was excited, grateful that this place would give me a chance. I didn't have a car, so my older sister dropped me off. I was there early, dressed in my best button-down shirt and slacks, hair combed, breath minty. I felt excited and confident. As an immigrant with a social-work background I was perfect for the job helping low-income immigrant families.

The interview did not go well. The panel of four people sat on one side of a long table, and I sat on the other. I was nervous and started sweating, which created an anxiety loop I could not get out of. At one point, I was asked what my strengths were, and I said something like, "Well...uh...I...um, I'm a...I think...I think I'm pretty good...at communicating..."

I did not get that job. Devastated and kicking myself for bombing so badly, I started studying for the Law School Admissions Test. If the nonprofit sector wasn't a good fit for me, then maybe the legal field would be. Several weeks of practice followed by truly abysmal practice test scores and an even worse actual test performance sent me back to trying again in this sector, this time applying and getting into an AmeriCorps program. It paid a third of what the case manager job would have paid. I ate pasta with jarred tomato sauce for the next two years, but at least I finally broke into the sector and was on my way to making a difference in the world.

Our Hiring Practices Are Archaic and Inequitable

Hiring people is something most organizations must do from time to time, and considering how vital staff are to the work, it must be done well. And yet, there are endless stories of how badly it goes. Many of our current hiring practices are crappy, thoughtless, and inequitable. We leave so many behind, having bought into harmful beliefs like:

- "If someone is even slightly late for an interview, they're obviously disorganized and disrespectful."
- "If someone has a typo on their resume, they're sloppy and not detail-oriented."
- "A formal college degree means this person is educated and disciplined."
- "If an interviewee can answer our complicated questions quickly and thoroughly, it means they're quick thinkers."
- "People who make eye contact and have firm handshakes are confident."
- "Candidates who send thank-you notes after the interview are appreciative and competent."

These beliefs and practices disproportionately affect people of color, women, disabled people, LGBTQIA people, neurodivergent people, and other marginalized people. Like with most things, we inherited them from white corporate culture. It is a culture that rewards people for being able to navigate white cultural norms (such as thank-you notes), encourages competition, and is rife with asymmetry in power and expectation of gratitude. And then we wonder why our teams often aren't diverse.

We need to have our equity lens on and practice seeing through them. A candidate could be a few minutes late because they could only take so many hours off from their current job, they rely on public transportation, and their bus could be late. For another candidate, English may not be their first language. They speak with an accent and make mistakes from time to time. But the fact that they're fluent in multiple languages should outweigh a typo on their resume or cover letter. We need to hire differently, starting with changing a few mindsets we've internalized.

Recruit and Invest in Talent for the Entire Sector, Not Just Individual Organizations

In Chapter 3, I mention the "Nonprofit Hunger Games," where nonprofits are forced to participate in an endless competition for funding, constantly trying to write the best grants, tell the most compelling stories, build the most stable relationships with donors, and so on, all to ensure our own organizations have the best advantage for survival.

A manifestation of this is through our hiring philosophies and practices, a "Talent Hunger Games," so to speak. There are thousands of articles on staff recruitment, hiring, retention, and so on, but they all have something in common: It is always about the well-being of the organization. We get the best talent to ensure our own organization's success. We strive to compensate workers fairly and provide them career advancement opportunities. . .namely so they can stay at our organization and help our siloed mission.

Currently, we recruit professionals to fulfill our individual missions, paying little attention to how our treatment of them might affect their work at their next organization or the way they perceive the entire sector. Let's switch to a more expansive and abundant view, that we not just hiring to get stuff done at our organization, but that our organization is one entryway into a sector that needs and values its most important asset, the people who decide to do this work each day. The problems we are trying to address are profoundly interrelated. Our missions are interconnected, unified by a vision of a just and equitable world.

We need to recruit, hire, train, mentor, compensate, and even fire staff with the mindset that our actions affect the success or failure of the whole nonprofit community. On one of my blog posts on this topic, colleague Lisa M. Stone wrote these inspiring words in the comment section:

> I tell all new staff persons at the beginning of their time with us [. . .] that if they identify another job they want, whether because of their passions, or for advancement, or because it pays more (only please talk to me about pay before taking another job, so we can reassess our standards), to tell me about it as early as they can, so I can help them get it. I have great colleagues, and I don't want them to leave, but I also view their success as everyone's, so if I can help them move on/up/elsewhere, then that's my job.

This generosity of spirit and long-term vision for our sector's work is how we should begin our hiring process. This process is usually the first meaningful experience with an organization, and sometimes with the sector, so special care and respect should be given. Let's think of every job candidate as a vital leader in our sector's collective mission to make the world better, whether they end up working with our specific organization for a short while, a long while, or not at all.

Have Gratitude and Respect for Job Candidates

In our society, those who have less money and power are expected to be grateful and demonstrate that gratitude to those who have more. Service and retail workers are expected to be grateful to customers, but rarely are customers expected to be grateful to cashiers or restaurant servers.

I'm going to call this ingrained notion of who is expected to be grateful to whom the *asymmetric requirement of gratitude* (ARG). In our line of work, ARG manifests itself in several ways. Primarily, nonprofits are expected to be grateful to donors and funders, trained to be constantly appreciative of people who give us money to do the work.

Similarly, job candidates are expected to be grateful to people doing the hiring. This helps explain why employers feel perfectly entitled to make job applicants go through inane hiring processes with interminable rounds of interviews and unpaid assignments. (After job candidates are hired, staff are expected to be grateful to their employers for giving them a job, which includes the expectation that they put up with unreasonable stuff all the time.)

The attitude is so ingrained that many of us in the sector don't even realize it. There is still the idea among many people, for example, at least in the United States, that job candidates should send thank-you notes (ideally handwritten, but email will do), to people who interviewed them.

Job applicants and employers are in a process to determine if they are a good match to work together. They need each other. But right now, only the former has the expectation to show gratitude through a series of rules—many unwritten—and get punished for how well they do it. Let's restore some balance.

Think about all the things job candidates have to go through and then take a moment to be grateful that they are willing to go through all that with you and your organization. Hold on to this sense of gratitude as you plan and implement your process and let it dictate how you treat all candidates in every step of your process.

Move Beyond Whiteness as Proxy for Professionalism and Qualifications

Since there are so many job candidates and there's only so much time to get to know them, we start using shortcuts, instant proxies for what is professional and what defines candidates as qualified. These shortcuts are rife with problems. Namely, they've been defined by white people, especially white neurotypical people.

"Professionalism" has been a concept that tends to favor white, male, cisgender, straight, and neurotypical colleagues. Aysa Gray enumerates in an article in *Stanford Social Innovation Review*[1] how this idea of "professionalism" manifests and has been weaponized against people of color and other marginalized identities:

> The story unfolds many ways: in white and Western standards of dress and hairstyle (straightened hair, suits but not saris, and burqa and beard bans in some countries); in speech, accent, word choice, and communication (never show emotion, must sound "American," and must speak white standard English); in scrutiny (black employees are monitored more closely and face more penalties as a result); and in attitudes toward timeliness and work style.

In Alice Wong's book, *Year of the Tiger: An Activist's Life,* she discusses how her voice, affected by her disability, may not seem as professional in comparison to the voices we generally hear on the radio, which tends to be of straight white dudes, and how this exacerbates inequity. "By accepting the default 'good voice' as one that is able-bodied, one that is pleasant, clear, articulate, and devoid of any markers of disability, you erase disabled people, rendering them the Other."[2]

This conceptualization of professionalism then translates to the conceptualization of qualification. Someone who has natural hair, for example, or who doesn't like to make eye contact, or who wears their culture's formal attire to an interview, could be seen by the interview panel as "unprofessional," which also means they're not qualified. Combine this with other white-people-determined markers of qualification, such as formal education degrees, and it creates a strong bias toward those who are white, male, neurotypical, able-bodied, and so on, during the hiring process and after they've been hired.

Mitigate for Unconscious Biases

A lot of biases, however, are unconscious, also known as implicit, meaning most people aren't even aware they have them. In one seminal study,[3] researchers from the University of Chicago and the

Massachusetts Institute of Technology sent out 5,000 fake resumes with either common white-sounding or Black-sounding names to real job openings in Chicago and Boston. They found that resumes with white-sounding names were 50 percent more likely to be asked to come to interviews.

That was in 2003. In 2021, researchers at the University of California, Berkeley, and the University of Chicago did a similar study, sending out 83,000 fabricated applications for 11,000 jobs across 108 Fortune 500 companies. They discovered that applications with white-sounding names were called for interviews on average 9 percent more than those with Black-sounding names. A couple of companies were 24 percent less likely to call back applicants perceived to be Black versus those perceived to be white.[4] While 9 percent is way better than the 50 percent from 20 years ago, it's still significant.

Besides race, there are also biases, both conscious and unconscious, across other identities. The Muse and Recruitment Marketing's 2024 Workplace Experience Report summarizes their findings from an online survey of over 1,000 women respondents. They found that 42 percent indicated they experienced gender-biased or inappropriate questions, and 41 percent said they were discriminated against due to gender during interviews.[5]

Meanwhile, the American Bar Association Commission on Disability Rights posted a guide on addressing implicit biases against the disabled people. They cited a study that found significant unconscious bias toward people without disabilities, with 76 percent of respondents showing an unintentional preference for non-disabled people.[6]

Implicit biases are ubiquitous, with all of us having some form, but there are things we can do to mitigate them. All hiring managers and everyone on a hiring team should be trained to understand and look out for unconscious biases. Hiring teams themselves need to be diverse. Recruitment should be thoughtful, such as using media controlled by communities of color, instead of just relying on word of mouth from existing staff. Job postings and interview questions should be audited to ensure the language is neutral and inclusive, as certain words and titles tend to be male-coded (such as competitive, driven, leader) while others are female-coded (such as supportive, collaborative, interpersonal), which may bias not just hiring teams, but even applicants.[7]

The End of Cultural Fit

One of the most insidious and toxic ideas we still cling to is the concept "cultural fit." Strong work cultures can be great when they are grounded in equity and with clearly spelled-out rules. What tends to happen, however, is that it becomes another way to perpetuate the status quo while absolving people of guilt and enabling them to rationalize terrible, thoughtless hiring and management practices that punish people from marginalized communities.

I know countless people, mostly of color, who have been rejected from jobs despite having all the qualifications, and those who have been hired but then demoted or fired, with supervisors claiming they don't fit the culture. It happens a lot, especially when it comes to staff of color who seek to make their organization more equitable.

People are increasingly questioning this concept of "cultural fit" entirely; *Forbes* published an article asking if cultural fit is "just a new way to discriminate."[8] The problem is that there's no good definition or agreement of what constitutes "cultural fit," so it's usually based on a series of unwritten rules, such as "those who go to happy hour and socialize with one another after work tend to be viewed positively by their supervisors."

Having unwritten rules is one of the best ways to perpetuate inequity, racism, sexism, ableism, ageism, and so on, because those invisible rules tend to favor the dominant culture. For these and other reasons, let's never use the term "cultural fit" again.

Equitable Hiring Practices

With all this in mind, let's talk about what we can do to ensure we have happier nonprofit employees, starting with hiring practices. While there are many, I'm highlighting a few we all need to adopt, if we haven't done so already.

Disclose Salary Ranges and Never Ask for Salary History

Not disclosing salary in your job posts furthers racial and gender wage gaps. According to this March 2024 fact sheet by National Women's Law Center:[9]

When employers negotiate without giving pay range information to job applicants, applicants are more likely to rely on their past pay as a negotiation reference point, which perpetuates existing pay gaps. Given that women and people of color are typically paid less than white, non-Hispanic men in the same occupations, they would have to request a particularly large percentage increase over their current pay for their request to be on par with their white, non-Hispanic male counterparts.

The research is so clear now on how salary cloaking perpetuates inequity that multiple states have passed laws requiring employers to disclose pay information on job posts[10] and/or making it illegal to base pay on salary history.[11] There is no valid excuse, **none**, for any organization to not list the salary on all job postings, or to ever ask anyone for their salary history.

And none of us should help spread the word on job postings that don't include salary information upfront. Job boards should mandate it and refuse to list any postings that won't disclose.

Pay Job Candidates for Their Time Spent Interviewing

On Twitter (I refuse to call it X, and I don't use it anymore), a user named Racquel Coral (@Withloveracquel) posted:

> A job that I interviewed for a month ago selected another candidate. This afternoon, I received an email from them asking for my information so they can send me a stipend of $150 for all the time that I put into my application, interview process, and final stage project.[12]

The post went viral for how much sense such a practice makes. Those of us who are secure in our jobs sometimes also forget how expensive it can be to look for a job. People must take time off from existing work. There are gasoline, bus fares, and other transportation costs. Parents and caregivers must find childcare or other forms of support to do interviews. There are costs associated with looking the part, including dressing in business clothing and having a "professional" hairstyle. It is inequitable to ask people who are often economically vulnerable to spend hours doing multiple rounds of interviews while people on the hiring team, who are often other staff and thus are compensated, get paid for doing the hiring.

Companies are increasingly adopting the practice of paying job candidates for their time spent in interviews and in doing special tests and assignments.[13] This needs to become a default practice. Build it into your budget to pay job candidates once they make it to the interview stage. Pay them by the hour based on how much the position would pay. This will help make it more equitable as well as help cut down on the excessive hoops that many organizations make candidates jump through.

Accept Assignments in People's Portfolios; Do Not Ask for Unpaid Work

There are still many organizations that ask job candidates to do unpaid labor as part of their hiring processes, including creating a sample fundraising plan, developing a PowerPoint presentation, writing a sample appeal letter, and so on. My friend and colleague Irene Nexica, an equity-minded recruiting and hiring expert, told me:

> I received an assignment as the second round for something that they described would take three to four hours (already too much to ask), and actually took me more like 16. The assignment was basically designing the first 30 days of the job for this new role.

Irene was also forced to endure six rounds of interviews.

Besides being inequitable, these assignments are not good gauges of candidates' skills, as they won't have all the information needed to be accurate. Sometimes, it is unethical, as organizations have been known to use the work produced by job candidates without their permission and without compensating them.

Don't ever ask candidates to complete a special assignment unless you are willing to pay them a consulting rate to complete it. Instead, just accept work the candidates have already produced. Ask them to elaborate on their thinking process, results, lessons learned, future work, and so on, based on the samples of their past work.

Prioritize Relevant Experience Instead of Requiring Formal Education Degrees

There are still a lot of positions that require a college/university degree, even for entry-level work. This is inequitable, favoring those who are privileged enough to be able to pursue higher education and have the neurotypicality that makes it easier to succeed in a traditional academic setting. It is a poor and ineffective proxy to determine if a candidate has the skills needed for a job. You are leaving behind many candidates who may have incredible experience and talent, but who may not have the degrees.

Yes, some specialized positions do need a degree or certificate (doctors, accountants, mental health counselors, etc.). But most do not. I've been an executive director across two organizations for over 13 years, and as difficult, complex, and volatile as this position is, there is nothing about it that a hardworking, dedicated person cannot learn to do—even if they don't have a BA. The main qualification someone needs to be a good executive director is not a degree, but a high threshold for pain and chaos!

Instead of this arbitrary requirement, focus on whether people have the skills and experience for the job, especially firsthand experience in whatever issues the position calls for. Cultural and language skills and alignment around values like equity are particularly vital and should be a lot more valued than formal education degrees and other arbitrary and inequitable markers of qualifications.

Hire Formerly Incarcerated People

We know the criminal justice system is inequitable, with people of color, especially Black people, more likely to be monitored, stopped at traffic lights, arrested, falsely convicted, and harshly sentenced.[14] This then greatly decreases their chances at getting employment and being financially stable. It affects not just the person incarcerated, but their families and communities. As this article by the Center for American Progress states, families of currently or formerly incarcerated people experience increased financial instability, have harder time paying bills, and even have less likelihood of obtaining loans, all of which contribute to the racial wealth gap:

For Black and Hispanic families, this vicious cycle is particularly pronounced. These families are more likely to face arrest, conviction, and incarceration, even for the same crimes as white people—a consequence of widespread systematic racial biases in the criminal justice system.[15]

Meanwhile, Black and Latino/Hispanic families, due to centuries of systemic discrimination and oppression, have built less wealth than white families, compounding the problem.

Hiring formerly incarcerated people is one way we can help fight this form of inequity, while also gaining staff who may be most qualified to do this work because they have lived experience with the unjust systems our sector is trying to change. There are many amazing nonprofits focused on helping formerly incarcerated individuals, but every organization should be thoughtful and equity-minded in this area.

No More Thank-You Notes

I like thank-you notes; I write them, and I keep every note that people send me. On crappy days, I sometimes pull them out and read them to remind myself that I do add value to the world and my work matters, no matter what my relatives in Vietnam say when I visit. And I can't stress enough how much I dislike the idea that job candidates are expected to send follow-up thank-you notes to interviewers. It is a very white-coded and U.S.-centric practice, as not many other cultures or countries have this practice. In Vietnamese culture, you thank people after a job interview by saying thank you as you leave the job interview. Rewarding or punishing candidates for whether they write a note or not will advantage candidates who are familiar with and experienced in white culture, who will most likely be white.

Also, it is an unwritten rule, and unwritten rules are great ways to discriminate not just people from different cultures, but also neurodivergent people who have trouble navigating these weird invisible expectations.

So, no more post-interview thank-you notes! Employers, stop expecting it, and stop favoring job candidates who do it and punishing those who don't. And all job candidates everywhere, you are hereby excused from ever having to write another thank-you email or card ever again! Go! Be free! Reclaim your time! Watch your favorite shows! Write a sea shanty!

Other Important Hiring Practices

Due to space, I can't elaborate on a bunch of other practices that we should be adopting, but I'll mention them briefly here.

- **Spell out your *entire* hiring process and timeline in your job posting.** If you plan to have finalists do five interviews, a presentation, and a Thunderdome battle with only office supplies as weapons, say so upfront. Job candidates deserve to know how much time they will need to spend with you, and whether it's reasonable.
- **Send interview questions in advance.** We need to stop equating being extroverted, charismatic, and good at talking, with a high degree of intelligence and qualification. Most jobs require thinking, research, and deliberation, so give job candidates interview questions to think about ahead of time.
- **Do not require vehicle or driver's ID unless it's an essential function.** Requiring a vehicle and driver's license leaves out candidates who may not drive because of disability, or who may not be able to afford a car. Assess whether this is necessary.
- **Reserve plenty of time for candidates to ask questions.** Don't interrogate candidates for 50 minutes and then give them two minutes to ask questions at the end. Candidates deserve an equal amount of time to gather information to make their decision about whether they should work for you.
- **Get back to all candidates in a timely manner.** One of the biggest complaints from job candidates is going through hours of a job process and then never hearing from the employer again. Have the courtesy to notify everyone who took the time to engage with you, at every stage of your process.
- **Be thoughtful about your "creative" interview questions.** If you were an ice cream flavor, which one would you be? How

many gummy bears would fit in this interview room? Creative questions can be fun and even helpful in breaking the ice, but just make sure you're not leaving behind people from different cultural and economic backgrounds.

- **Do not require people to be able to lift 25 or 50 pounds if it's not an essential function.** This is another requirement that discriminates against disabled candidates or others who may not be able to lift heavy things. Unless it's essential, don't include it.
- **Pay candidates what is fair, not what you can get away with. Don't tie people's pay to their ability to negotiate.** Women, people of color, and especially women of color are systemically underpaid, in part because negotiations are rife with inequity and unconscious biases. So pay people fair salaries, even if in the negotiation process you could get away with lower offers.
- **Have a thoughtful and robust onboarding process.** On occasion, organizations spend a lot of time conducting a great hiring process only to leave new hires to flop around in their new role. Make sure you put effort and consideration into this area.

Invest in Our Sector's Future

In middle school, when I was still back in Seattle, I remember some engineers from Boeing came to visit and talk about their profession. This was followed shortly after by a field trip, where we got a tour to see firsthand where they worked. It was inspiring. It makes me think now about how people enter our field. I don't recall an executive director or program manager or major gifts officer ever visiting a classroom to inspire kids to go into this line of work.

The people who do end up here, despite the lack of information and dearth of visible role models, are here for a reason, probably some combination of chance and the desire to make the world better, safer, more vibrant, more inclusive. When they send in their application, when they sit, nervous, in front of us, and throughout every step of the hiring process, let's view them as the assets they are for our sector and treat them with gratitude and respect.

Discussion Questions

1. Think about the best experience you had when you were looking for a job. What made it so great?
2. Think about your worst experience. What factors made it terrible?
3. What other ways can we end the Talent Hunger Games and invest in talent for the entire sector, and not just for specific organizations?
4. How else does asymmetric requirement of gratitude (ARG) manifest in society and in our sector? Are there situations where this asymmetry is valid?
5. What other examples can you think of whiteness being used to gauge professionalism and qualification? How do we counter it?
6. Besides names and the race associated with them, what other ways do implicit biases manifest? What can we do about it?
7. Do you agree that we should end the concept of cultural fit entirely, or can we modify it?
8. Among the equitable hiring practices listed, which ones resonate with you? Which one do you disagree with?
9. What other hiring practices not listed here should organizations consider?

10

Reimagining Work Culture

We will not go back to normal. Normal never was. ... We should not long to return, my friends. We are being given the opportunity to stitch a new garment. One that fits all of humanity and nature.

—Sonya Renee Taylor

In 1995, after several years of living in Seattle, my parents decided to move our family to Memphis, Tennessee, where they bought a convenience store/gas station. I had just started freshman year of high school, and a month later had to leave all my friends behind, uprooted from my home for a second time.

My older brother, Phong, stayed behind to go to college, leaving me the oldest child at 14, which meant I was expected to help at the store. Two or three times a week after school, and on some weekends, I was there, mainly working the register, sometimes stocking the shelves. In the back of my mind was the constant fear that we'd get robbed by someone with a gun.

My parents never paid me for the four years I worked at the store. It just didn't ever occur to them that they would have to compensate their own child. Wasn't the fact that they removed me from a war-ravaged country and provided food and shelter enough? I had no money of my own and had to ask them to buy me anything I needed, and they were also unreasonably frugal. One time I asked for some new pens for school, and my dad handed me a dozen random swag pens he had lying around.

All of this was made worse by the fact that I noticed how horrible our work structure and conditions were, but had little agency to change anything. My parents saw me as a teenager who knew nothing, while they were wiser, more knowledgeable adults. They were exhausted constantly, working 7 am to 11 pm each day without any days off, but my hints about cutting down store hours, closing a couple of days a month, hiring and paying other people (gasp!), or just selling the business and moving back to Seattle were never considered.

Bitter and resentful but unable to quit dramatically like I often daydreamed about, I resorted to stealing candy from them. Each time I was at the store, I would take several king-sized chocolate bars and bags of chewy treats. I brought dozens to school, snacking on them all day, indulging in a sweet and high-calorie form of revenge. I also gave them to classmates. If I had been more enterprising, I could have sold the treats to make money.

The pilfering lasted a while until my parents found out and chastised me for pinching candy we needed to sell to earn money to send home to our relatives in Vietnam. Did I not consider each Reese's peanut butter cup to be a day of sustenance for my impoverished cousins, each Skittle an hour of reprieve from the constant hunger of my ailing grandparents?

The four years of experience at a young age working in a place where I was underappreciated, told to be grateful, guilt-shamed via others' suffering, constantly dismissed for questioning why we did things the way we did them, and supplementing my lack of compensation with snacks, prepared me for a lifelong career in nonprofit.

Let's Talk About Burnout

A few years ago, my team and I at RVC took the burnout quiz from Beth Kanter and Aliza Sherman's book *The Happy Healthy Nonprofit: Strategies for Impact Without Burnout*.[1] More than half of us realized we were on the verge of burning out. This, of course, was nothing surprising. Burnout is a very common problem in our sector.

Recently, I attended Fund the People's Talent Justice Summit, where Dr. Christina Maslach, an expert on burnout, was a keynote speaker who recently came out with her book *The Burnout Challenge: Managing People's Relationships with Their Jobs*. During her presentation, Dr. Maslach talked about society's tendency to pathologize burnout as if it were a medical condition, something that needs to be cured in the individual—maybe with a green smoothie and a couple of days off! In reality, it is indicative of something not being right with the work environment:

> "Burnout is a canary in the coal mine. It's the warning sign of a toxic work environment. What we shouldn't do is question why the canary isn't tougher."

Besides burnout, there are other critical problems affecting the sector, namely recruiting and retaining staff and motivating people to assume the mantle of leadership. Clearly, it's in our sector's best interests to do some things differently. As younger workers continue to enter the sector, a lot of the crappy stuff we've been putting up just doesn't cut it anymore. Why are we doing the same stuff, like working five days each week? Why are we still in the grips of capitalism and its toxic idea of productivity?

A lot of stuff we got from the corporate sector, some we inherited from white-dominant culture. We can have happier, more effective people and thus a stronger sector, if we start changing these mindsets and the practices stemming from them. In the chapter on leadership, I talk about different leadership and decision-making structures, moving from more hierarchical models toward flatter, more democratic ones, including having co-EDs or not having any leaders at all. Here are some additional considerations we should explore as a sector.

End the Culture of Toxic Productivity

Overwork has become so ingrained in our sector that we just accept it as normal without even realizing it. Another friend of mine, Erica Barnhart, once said something that haunts me to this day: "Why do we talk about work-life balance? Why does work come first in that phrase? Why not life-work balance? Or just balance?"

We have a productivity complex, and it's causing serious damage in several different ways. The more meetings we attend, the more stuff we do off-hours, the more projects we take on, the more we reinforce this idea among one another that this pace is normal and expected. If you're talking about how you have 12 meetings today, for example, even if you say it with an air of apology and exasperation, it still sends the message that others are supposed to do that, too. It becomes a self-fulfilling prophecy.

Plus, being productive in the way we currently define it requires time and other resources that are not equitably distributed. For example, during the pandemic, it was clear that those who could afford childcare for their kids were able to get more work done than parents who couldn't. In general, people of color and other marginalized identities have fewer resources and more responsibilities, such as taking care of their extended family. We also need to factor in the fact that frontline staff tend to be BIPOC and women, while senior leaders tend to be white and men, which brings up a whole host of other variables regarding who can do work how and when.

If we denormalize these toxic U.S. philosophies and practices around productivity, it'll make it easier to adopt the things that may be working for our colleagues elsewhere.

Another subtle but insidious result of our hyperfocus on productivity is that we reinforce the valuing of individuals not by their intrinsic worth, but by how many hours they put in at a job. This further devalues and dehumanizes disabled people, elders, and others who may not be able to work in the ways that society expects. Everyone has intrinsic worth and should be treated with respect and dignity, whether they can work or not. Our value to society should not be dependent on what we contribute to it in the form of work hours.

We all daydream about the labor practices of European countries like France or Sweden. I've never worked in Europe, but I hear rumors of people being able to leave work at the end of the day, emails being forbidden from being answered off-hours, mandatory six-week vacations, months of paid family leave, and more.

Evolve Our Concept of Professionalism

After the first few weeks of the pandemic, I was home-schooling my two small children while trying to get my own work done and putting out various fires, frazzled like all of us were. The four-year-old constantly escaped his preschool Zoom meeting to stand in our front yard, yelling at passersby, "Put your mask on! Do you want to get coronavirus?!"

I was disheveled for my own virtual meetings, hair uncombed, wearing the same shirt for days. Occasionally the seven-year-old would burst into the room to bury his face in my chest, crying because he didn't want to do a dance or participate in other physical activities his teacher was leading because exercise was part of the curriculum, even in a virtual classroom.

After the pandemic, our idea of what is and isn't "professional" should have radically changed. Why was eating on camera during a virtual meeting unprofessional? Why were all my colleagues apologizing when their kids or pets or spouses popped into view, as if acknowledging the existence of their personal lives was considered unprofessional?

The old ideas of what is and isn't "professional" have been stifling. Let's evolve our thinking around what is a good org culture and what is professional beyond the white, male, cisgender, able-bodied, heteronormative, neurotypical, and Christian default, and allow people to be their authentic selves at work. Especially when this work is so relational and human-centered, it will enable us to be more effective. So, if you feel like eating an entire pint of ice cream straight from the container during your next video meeting, go for it. There are more important things to focus on, as we'll see in the sections to follow.

Diversity, Equity, and Inclusion in Work Environments

The topic of being equitable and inclusive in the workplace warrants entire books. It is something on which we need continual training, discussions, and practice. Although DEI and those who believe in it are being villainized, it is still core to our sector. Here are a few things we can think about and act on. I've divided them up into a few broad categories. By no means are these categories or the actions associated with them comprehensive, and it's best to check in with colleagues who have lived experience in these areas:

- **Race.** Ensure everyone is trained in recognizing and addressing racism, anti-Blackness, privilege, microaggressions, and unconscious biases. If a DEI committee is formed, make sure leadership is actively involved in it, and do not ask people of color to take on the work of this committee without additional compensation. Conduct regular audits and address disparities that come up, such as racial wage or leadership gaps.
- **Culture.** Acknowledge and celebrate cultural holidays and traditions; heritage months may be a good place to start. Allow people to wear their cultural attire to work and work-related events. Avoid jargon and use clear language, which will be helpful to people for whom English is not their first language. Rotate different types of meals for work events and not rely on one type of cuisine (such as pizza) all the time. Have welcome signs in different languages and culturally diverse decorations. Avoid assuming white cultural customs—such as eye contact, hugging, and people of different genders shaking hands—are universal.
- **Disability.** Ensure physical spaces are accessible to people using wheelchairs and other mobility devices. Make sure captions are available on videos and anytime someone speaks during webinars or events, and ensure people always use microphone for people who are deaf or hard of hearing. Provide alt-text and captions on all images, ensure online communications are screen-reader compatible, and describe charts and other visual elements when doing presentations for people who are blind or have low vision. Discuss as a team what other accommodations would be helpful, as many disabilities, such as sensory and cognitive differences and chronic pain, are not visible.
- **Gender.** Have an anti-discrimination statement and make sure it includes gender identity among all the other protections. Provide all-gender restrooms. Make sure healthcare covers

gender-affirming care. Encourage people to list their pronouns in their email signatures and in their bios on the website. Avoid using *guys* when addressing everyone. Discourage misogynistic jokes and comments. Men should be aware of when they're dominating conversations, undermining women and nonbinary people, and taking undue credit.
- **Sexual orientation.** Make sure healthcare includes LGBTQIA-specific needs such as fertility treatments and allows coverage of same-sex partners. Ensure parental leave policies cover adopted kids, same-sex parents, and other family structures. Lessen heteronormative defaults and include more LGBTQIA in communications such as on websites. Discourage homophobic jokes and stereotypes.
- **Religion.** Create quiet, private spaces for people to pray or meditate. Be thoughtful about dietary restrictions (at my last nonprofit, we made a rule to never order anything with pork ever). Map out major religious and cultural holidays and avoid planning important meetings and events on those days). Have dress codes that allow for religious attire. Allow flexibility in work schedules so people can observe their religious practices; for example, many organizations close several days around Christmas, but it may be helpful to give colleagues options to take those days off at another time if they don't observe Christmas.
- **Caregiving status.** These are people who take care of small children, aging relatives, or sometimes both. Have a robust paid family leave policy in place. Allow flexible hours, remote work, and job-sharing arrangements. Have private, quiet spaces for breastfeeding and pumping. Make sure all bathrooms have changing tables. Be thoughtful around not creating a culture that rewards people who can be present for after-hour work or socializing. Have events where children and relatives are welcome; hire childcare providers for those events. Subsidize childcare costs in general if possible.
- **Neurodiversity.** See the strengths that people with different brains bring. Avoid creating a culture where extroverts are rewarded, while leaving behind those who tend to be quiet, need

time for reflection, and are thoughtful in their approach. Be clear in communications and do not assume everyone can read minds or unwritten social cues. Examine how neurodiversity factors into things, especially conflict management, where we have been trained to use neurotypical skills to resolve tension. For instance, when someone doesn't make eye contact, it doesn't mean they're being dishonest or disrespectful.

- **Age.** Recognize that having people of different generations is a strength. Foster an environment where people of different ages can collaborate and peer-mentor. Discourage jokes and stereotypes about young or old people. Offer training, upskilling, and promotion opportunities for everyone, regardless of age. Provide desks, chairs, and lighting suitable for people of different ages and physical needs. Avoid using biased terminologies such as "digital native" and "fresh blood." Plan team activities that appeal to all age groups.
- **Income.** Cover costs of work-related activities. Do not make employees pay for event tickets if they must be there to work. Be thoughtful about social activities and how much they cost, as they may leave behind coworkers who can't afford to participate. When splitting bills during outings, pooling money to buy gifts for coworkers, having potlucks, and so on, be mindful that not everyone has the same budget. Allow for flexibility in scheduling for people juggling multiple jobs. Eliminate all employee giving campaigns; never ask people to donate to organizations they work for. Be aware of how those with more financial stability can inadvertently harm those with less; for instance, workers with spouses who make a lot of money may not fight as hard for pay increases because it's not as relevant to them.

Thriving Wages and Equity-Based Compensation

In 2021, Choose 180, a nonprofit focused on youth, decided all staff would receive a minimum salary of $70,000 a year. This was a transformative change for many team members, especially those who had been working multiple jobs to stay afloat. It added significantly to how much they needed to fundraise, but it was aligned with the nonprofit's values. I asked Sean Goode, Choose 180's former ED, how he felt about it.

His answer: "The difficult part wasn't raising wages or finding the money to sustain it; the difficult part was reconciling why it took so long for me to do it in the first place."

The scarcity around staff compensation is one of the biggest barriers for our sector. It's a problem we all acknowledge, but something we have mostly accepted as unavoidable, even when it is horribly ironic, like when nonprofit professionals qualify for the services their organizations offer.

It's not entirely nonprofits' fault, though. Funders have a great part to play in this. Fund the People's Talent Justice Report, which surveyed 1,480 nonprofit professionals, found that "84 percent of nonprofit and foundation respondents stated that competitive salaries and benefits are needed for entry-level nonprofit jobs. Yet only 41 percent of foundations provide funding to grantees for these purposes."[2]

Funders' reticence to provide consistent and sufficient funding has created a pervasive learned helplessness and scarcity mindset around compensation, which has been leading to some very bad habits, such as using random intuition to set salary.

Even our "best practices," such as basing pay on sector averages, is something we need to be thoughtful about. As my colleague, Pragya Madan of Pragya Madan Coaching & Consulting LLC, says:

> It's deeply frustrating that nonprofit compensation practices continue to rely on benchmarking against already underpaid sector salaries, perpetuating a harmful cycle. This approach ignores the systemic undervaluing of nonprofit work and reinforces the narrative that passion should come at the expense of fair pay.

Women, people of color, disabled people, and older workers continue to be underpaid, so it's vital to examine our existing compensation gaps and make plans and adjustments accordingly. Let's follow the lead of organizations like Choose 180. We need to compensate people not just "living wages" but ones that allow people to thrive, build wealth, and eat the occasional handful of organic blueberries. This means we must snap out of the scarcity mindset, stop being apologetic for overhead, build our budget accordingly, and educate funders and donors on the real cost of doing this work. We must instill in them—and ourselves—the worth of nonprofit professionals.

Pay Ratios and Alternative Pay Structures

To use the equity lens further, we should also look at the disparity between how top-level leaders versus frontline staff are paid. While it's not as egregious as in the corporate sector, where CEOs can make hundreds of times more than the lowest-paid worker, it's still present in our sector. Some nonprofits have instituted ratios where the highest-paid person cannot make more than x times the lowest paid, with x often being two to five. Whatever the ratio is, the disparity in pay between top leaders and frontline staff is something we need to think about more seriously, especially as EDs, CEOs, and other administrative staff tend to be whiter, while frontline staff are significantly more likely to be people of color.

Nonprofits are also increasingly exploring more radical pay structures, including everyone being paid the same, such as the case at the Sustainable Economy Law Center, whose Workers' Self-Directed Nonprofit model I explored in Chapter 5. Other organizations are basing pay on individuals' financial needs, for example, paying more for those who have children or are taking care of aging parents. These are not silver-bullet solutions. They have their own challenges, but it's good for us as a sector to explore and experiment.

The Benefits of Sabbaticals

There is now significant research and resources on the benefits of sabbaticals. The Durfee Foundation[3] has been a pioneer in supporting sabbaticals for over 20 years. Durfee's uses case studies to illustrate the countless benefits of sabbaticals, including:

- **Increasing retention of nonprofit leaders.** Having sabbatical policies in place will help with staff retention. Supporting staff enough to provide them paid breaks after several years of hard work will increase their motivation to stay.
- **Shifting perspectives and allowing for new thinking.** So many of us are mired in the grind that we have little time and energy to think broadly and creatively about our sector, our community, our leadership styles, and other critical things.

- **Changing organizational culture around work/life balance.** From the case studies in the Durfee report, and from colleagues I've talked to who have taken sabbaticals, people return after an intentional break feeling more energized and committed to doing things differently, including how they engage with life/work balance.
- **Providing leadership opportunities for other team members.** Our sector sucks at succession planning. Leadership transitions often lead to fear, anxiety, and chaos. It does not have to be this way. Giving internal staff leadership opportunities when a senior employee is absent allows them to practice vital skills (and see that maybe it's not so bad). And it allows the person on sabbatical to realize that things don't have to fall apart when they're gone, which counters this myth of the indispensable solitary leader.

With so much compelling data, nonprofits should all have sabbatical policies in place. And it should include all staff, not just the ED/CEO. And funders need to fund sabbaticals; if you don't know where to start, again, our good friend the Durfee Foundation has a how-to guide.[4]

The Rise of Four-Day Workweeks

In 1938, the U.S. government passed the Fair Labor Standards Act, which made the 40-hour, five-day workweek standard.[5] Before that, people often worked 60 or more hours each week, hardly sleeping, spending time with their children, or, I imagine, hanging out smoking at the local speakeasy.

Franklin D. Roosevelt signed the law into effect, but five years prior to that, he had supported efforts to make the workweek even shorter, at 30 hours.[6] John Maynard Keynes predicted that we'd all just be working 15 hours a week by the year 2030, due to improvements in standards of living and advancements in technology.

The point is that we do not need to be married to the idea of working 40 hours a week for five days, then relaxing one day on Saturday before freaking out all day Sunday due to all the anxiety of having to return to work on Monday. Three-day weekends are amazing and truly restful; can you imagine having that every single week?

Luckily, the four-day workweek (4DW) is on the rise. There is a movement trying to make this a standard practice for everyone in the United States. The nonprofit organization WorkFour is one of the leaders in this issue. The organization provides several compelling arguments for the 4DW, including cutting down on burnout, increasing worker productivity, increasing employee retention rates, improving recruitment of new employees, and enhancing workers' health. While there are challenges, such as frontline staff perhaps not being able to cut down on hours the way other staff can, several organizations have been piloting this new structure, with overall great results. The Montana Nonprofit Association, for example, tested it out and reported:

> So far, our experience has been good but not perfect. It has definitely increased employee well-being. And by every objective metric, we are maintaining or exceeding the productivity and impact that we want and need to achieve.[7]

Another organization, Common Future, adopted the 4DW in 2021. According to its Co-CEO Jennifer Njuguna:

> We've seen first-hand that a 32-hour workweek works well. We started exploring this idea as we were going through the pandemic—we wanted to reduce stress, improve flexibility, and empower our teams – and this move helped us do that.[8]

The benefits are not just for employers and employees. WorkFour also mentions general societal benefits such as reducing mass unemployment as artificial intelligence advances, and even mitigating gender inequity.

It's been over 85 years since FDR signed the law that made the 40-hour, five-day workweek the standard. Things have changed significantly since then. With advances in technology and with so much compelling evidence of the benefits of the four-day workweek, this is something we should seriously consider making a sector-wide practice.

The Increase in Nonprofit Workers' Unions

Workers' unions have been vital for bringing about many of the rights and privileges we enjoy today. The five-day workweek itself, for example, did not just appear out of nowhere and become law. It was the result of labor organizers working for over a hundred years.

There have been a growing number of employees of nonprofit organizations unionizing, including at Southern Poverty Law Center and Minnesota Council of Nonprofits. Even smaller organizations with a handful of team members have started unions. Among the unions that were formed, there have been some major wins. The workers at Southern Poverty Law Center, for example, successfully negotiated an increase of minimum pay from $15 to $20 an hour; some staff had salaries increase from $38,000 to $60,000.[9] Included in the contract was also the banning of nondisclosure agreements, which are legal documents often used by employers to silence employees who experience discrimination and abuse.

I'm all for nonprofit workers unionizing. If forming unions allows nonprofit workers to be fairly compensated, get sufficient paid family leave and other benefits, be treated well, and for our sector to advance radical ideas such as four-day workweeks, then we should be recognizing, supporting, and encouraging unions.

At the same time, having been an executive director, I saw firsthand how difficult raising money can be. Unlike for-profits that can generate their own revenues, nonprofits often rely on the whims of funders and donors, which makes it challenging to meet some of the collective demands of workers. As the number of nonprofit workers' unions rise, I hope we can break out of the adversarial relationship between management and staff, a relationship we inherited from the for-profit sector, and create one of effective collaboration, such working together to push funders to increase funding.

Normalizing Mental Health

Content warning: This next section talks about suicide.

In 2023, a close friend of mine died of suicide. She had been battling depression, anxiety, and suicidal ideation all her life. Despite various challenges she experienced in her life, including homelessness, she successfully dedicated years of her life to advancing social justice through her nonprofit and community work, affecting the lives of many people, especially the numerous kids she taught and mentored.

Sadly, she wasn't the only colleague I knew who has died of suicide. In Seattle, the loss of a brilliant and beloved activist of color at the beginning of the pandemic sent waves of shock and grief. Mental health challenges, lack of support and resources for, and related deaths of people in our field are things that affect us all, and yet we rarely talk about them.

This is due in part to the stigma in society about mental health, with people often equating mental health illnesses with character flaws. It is also perceived as "unprofessional" to talk openly at work about our struggles with mental health.

But stigma around mental health issues fades as more people talk about their own mental health, and workplaces become more supportive. A significant number of people experience mental health challenges (23 percent of the U.S. population in 2024[10]), but that mental illness doesn't have to be a weakness, and in fact has been a strength among many leaders throughout history.

As my friend and colleague Kevin Dean, CEO of the Tennessee Nonprofit Network, says in a post on the nonprofit's website[11] where he talks about his own struggles with depression: "You should know that acknowledging your mental health status is the first step to emerging triumphant and being an instrument of change."

Mental health challenges and suicide among nonprofit professionals and social justice activists need to be recognized as an issue we address openly. Many of us entered this line of work because we have dealt with trauma in our own lives. We have seen and felt firsthand the effects of injustice, and it drove many of us into the field. Our traumas make us more empathetic and often more effective. But it often comes at significant costs. Nonprofits can help mitigate these costs by creating workplaces where it's as normal to bring up mental health struggles as it is to bring up physical ones, ensuring mental health services are included in medical benefits, providing resources and support, and encouraging workers to prioritize their mental health.

Nonprofit professionals are the most valuable resource we have. While volunteers are vital, staff members drive a lot of the programs and services our sector delivers. But the many work culture philosophies and practices we've inherited and have taken as immutable have not only been burning people out but also preventing new ones from entering the profession. We need to evolve the way we think about things such as professionalism, productivity, cultural fit, and mental health. We should also consider offering thriving wages, sabbaticals, and four-day workweeks as not the rare exceptions in our sector, but the default. All these things will allow for happier employees who are more effective in their work of bettering our world.

Discussion Questions

1. Why is the rate of burnout so high in our sector? What do you think should be done about it?
2. What messages have we been taught regarding workplace productivity? How have these messages been manifesting in the ways we work and live?
3. What are some things we've been told are "unprofessional" in the workplace? Where did these beliefs come from? Do they still make sense in the context of a changing and diversifying workforce?
4. What are some DEI practices you have seen that have been beneficial, either at your current or previous places of work? What areas do you think could be improved?
5. What do you think of the idea of all workers making a minimum salary, such as $70,000, regardless of their position or years of experience? What is the ideal ratio between the highest-paid and lowest-paid worker?
6. If you work for an organization, does it have a sabbatical policy in place? Have you had a sabbatical yourself? What would you do if you were to have a sabbatical?
7. How do you feel about a four-day workweek? What do you think are challenges preventing a global adoption of this idea as a norm, and how do we overcome it?
8. Why has there been an increase in nonprofit workers' unions in recent years?
9. What are some beliefs you've been taught around mental health? Do you think they still ring true?
10. What other changes are needed as we reimagine nonprofit work culture?

11

Don't Bring Spreadsheets to a Knife Fight

Using Data to Effectively Advance Justice

Research is not an innocent or distant academic exercise but an activity that has something at stake and that occurs in a set of political and social conditions.
—Linda Tuhiwai Smith

EVERY LUNAR NEW YEAR, I invite my friends and family to go to the local Buddhist temple at midnight to get our fortunes for the year by kneeling on the floor and shaking a container of sticks until one falls out. There are 80 or so sticks, and each one has a number corresponding to a particular fortune.

One time, I got the worst fortune ever, something like, "This stick represents a bird in the storm. Danger unfolds from four directions. All your endeavors will lead to failure. For every path you take, there is only pain and despair, and your hopes will be dashed upon the rocky shoals of futility."

That's terrifying (though poetic), so I did what you are supposed to do when you receive a bad fortune for the New Year. It is a secret technique I learned from my father, and he learned from his father, and something I will pass down to my sons: When you get a bad fortune, put the stick back in the container and keep shaking until you find a fortune you like.

I put it back and got this fortune instead: "This stick represents taking a lantern to go find the light. In the darkness, you search for the flame. On the treacherous and winding path, you use a lantern to illuminate your way. Tormented will be your quest, until you realize the light is within your hand."

I wasn't sure that fortune was better, but the line to shake the container again was long, so I accepted this fortune, my mind starting to ruminate on what the lantern I'd be holding in my hand the rest of the year symbolized. Maybe it was family. Or love. Wi-Fi? I do use a lot of Wi-Fi to search for stuff.

Expending energy trying to find the right stick, ignoring the ones we don't like, and wasting time looking for something that's right under our noses—these things all remind me of our sector's obsession with research, data, and evaluation, and its destructive tendency for toxic intellectualization.

Toxic Intellectualizing: How Our Obsession with Data Has Affected Our Work

I always joke that if MLK Jr. were here and he said, "I have a dream. . .," the response from many funders and leaders in the sector would be, "Your dream is great, but where's your data? Do you have a track record? Are you scalable? What's your theory of change? Where's your logic model? Hm, your theory of change makes sense, but have you run a double-blind controlled experiment to prove that your strategies would achieve this dream? Anyway, it'll take us 12 months to do our own due diligence and research to determine if your dream aligns with our priorities and strategies for this year before we sign on to support it."

Progressive-leaning funders' obsession with data and research has infected the entire sector, conditioning us all with a propensity to overdo it with the outcomes and metrics and proof of concept. Instead of acting, we discuss. Instead of taking risks, we research. Instead of learning by trying and failing, we waffle and equivocate. Measure twice, cut once, as the saying goes, but we've reached a point where we measure a hundred times and barely cut anything. I cannot imagine conservative leaders and movements having this level of toxic intellectualizing, where they spend endless time—years, often—ruminating and pontificating, and consider it forward momentum.

In 2025, during the second week of Trump's return to power, his administration released a memo to freeze all federal funding. They did not wait years to collect data. They didn't need a new logic model or theory of change. They didn't read white papers and put on summits where they placed sticky dots on easel paper to vote on which community they wanted to prioritize hurting first. They immediately acted. Chaos and panic ensued as nonprofits, which heavily rely on government grants, faced cuts to vital programs and services. Millions of people around the world would have suffered or died. Children would be left hungry. Seniors would not get life-saving medication.

In response, to our sector's credit, within a day of the order's release National Council of Nonprofits, Democracy Forward, and other nonprofits filed a suit to stop it. Because of the suit, a federal judge immediately called for a hearing, which then led to the court's decision to temporarily stay the order, with the main reason being that it was not well thought out and was confusing. The administration then rescinded it, but they are likely to refine it, back it up with more data, and release it again.

There are many lessons from this whole episode. Data and research are meant to be used to advance an agenda, to act. While appreciating knowledge for its intrinsic value is wonderful, we have taken it too far, and the obsession with it has often become a barrier impeding action. Also, data can be collected through implementation; by launching a poorly planned memo, the Trump administration got vital data on what kind of resistance it would face, how the courts would act, how the public would respond, and so on, which would help it draft a much more effective order down the line.

Most importantly, data can be used as a tool or a weapon. One of the factors in the rise of Trump and MAGA has been misinformation, the spreading of false data on everything from immigrant crime rates to climate change to egg and gas prices. It does not matter that none of these data are accurate or backed by research. The fact that they are out there, amplified by effective messaging, means much of the public will believe it. And even if later data repudiates these erroneous claims, the damage is already done.

These are lessons progressives should be learning. Instead of using data to fuel our progressive agenda, our default is to spiral further and further into toxic intellectualization. This prevents us from taking meaningful action. To be effective, we must find ways to break out of this spiral. That will require us to change our understanding of and relationship to data and evaluation, and to ground it in equity and justice.

Weaponized Data and How It's Been Hurting Marginalized Communities

The use of data as a weapon to perpetuate injustice is not new; it's a common occurrence throughout history. Phrenology, for example, the study of various bumps on one's head and how they correlate to qualities like intelligence and temperament, was once considered a valid science and was used to "prove" the superiority of white people and the inferiority of other races, which then justified colonization, slavery, and other forms of injustice.[1]

Between 1948 and 1994 of South Africa's Apartheid period, a test was used in which a pencil was pushed through someone's hair. If it slides right through when they shook their head, it means they were white or mixed; if the pencil remains in place, they were considered Black. Even though this "pencil test" was so inaccurate that it often categorized people of the same family into different races, its results were considered valid data to legally determine people's race, allowing for discrimination.[2]

While right-wing movements continue to use false data to harm people and communities, among progressive-leaning nonprofit organizations and funders, it is more subtle. Dr. Jondou Chase Chen coined the term "weaponizing data." My organization Rooted in Vibrant Communities (RVC) was lucky enough to work with him to develop and implement our evaluation strategy. Jondou defines "weaponizing data" as "When people, and especially people with systemic power, use data in ways that cause harm, especially to those who are already systemically targeted." He elaborates on how it often plays out:

> So often, I've seen particular types of data—test scores, financial information, etc.—be used to lift some people up and put other people down. And when we look at collectively who this is, it's clearly systemic. And while some might question whether the original intention of using the data was to cause harm to our communities of color, when it continues to happen after the harm has been named, it is clearly being done to harm.[3]

Here are ways data is weaponized in our sector, and many of us don't even realize we're complicit in it:

- **Data is used to hoard resources.** Because of funders' hyperfixation on data and evaluation, many will only give funding to organizations that have "strong" data, which forces nonprofits into the data-resource paradox, where you need adequate funding to collect robust data, but funders won't give a nonprofit significant funding unless it has robust data. This then allows larger, mostly white and mainstream organizations that already have resources to get additional funding. Organizations led by communities of color, disabled communities, rural communities, LGBTQIA communities, and so on are left behind, finding it challenging to break out of this Catch-22.
- **Data is used as a gatekeeping strategy.** Similarly, I've seen data used to prevent strategies from being deployed. When community leaders advocate for solutions, the response is often, "Yeah, that sounds good, but where's the data proving that will work?" And when data is presented, it's often still dismissed for not being rigorous and quantitative enough, not using double-blind, chi-squared tests with the right Pearson correlation coefficient or whatever.
- **Data is used to rationalize terrible decisions.** A few years ago in Seattle, a local university decided they would discontinue a

staff position focused on recruiting Asian students because the data shows that there are enough Asian students. When the data is disaggregated, it shows Southeast Asian students were significantly underrepresented. The data, flawed as it was, was a convenient way for the school to justify its thoughtless decision. (The community banded together and pushed back, using disaggregated data, and the position has been reinstated to focus specifically on Southeast Asian students.)

- **Data is used to pathologize whole communities.** Probably the most dangerous way data is weaponized in our work is it's used to issue blanket statements about whole groups of people, usually that they are deficient in some areas.

Relevant to this last point, Rochelle Gutierrez of the University of Illinois at Urbana–Champaign talks about "gap-gazing"[4] as a type of intellectual fetish many researchers have, and a harmful one that offers "little more than a static picture of inequity, supporting deficit thinking and negative narratives about students of color and working-class students [. . .] and promoting a narrow definition of learning and equity."

Gap-gazing often pathologizes those most affected by injustice, focusing the blame on individuals or communities. This leads to ineffective programs, instead of addressing the systemic factors, such as racism and sexism, that are usually the causes of these problems. One example is financial literacy programs to teach the poor how to manage their limited dollars instead of working to change unfair systems, such as increasing minimum wage.

While the weaponizing of data can be done intentionally, oftentimes it's done without intention or malice. The way we think about data, evaluation, metric, outcomes, theories of change, logic models, and so on, affects how funders fund and how nonprofits do their work. We need to de-weaponize data.

The Role of Evaluators as Agents of Justice

Evaluators often think their job is to be neutral, to simply reveal the data as disinterested observers. Many think that the work to advance equity and justice should be left to frontline colleagues, while their role is to simply provide information. This is similar to how many fundraisers believe they should raise money, but that it's up to program staff to use the money to effect change. However, we're fighting inequity and injustice, and we need evaluators (and fundraisers) to see themselves as agents of justice. This means evaluators must:

- **Understand that evaluation is political.** Everything we do is political, and data and evaluation are no exceptions. They are powerful tools that can be wielded for good or evil. They have been used to reinforce existing structures of power and inequity. The right, in particular, weaponizes misinformation to proliferate inequity, while the left often uses research to justify complacency and avoidance of meaningful action.
- **Prioritize communities over funders and even organizations.** So many evaluators, despite believing data should be objective, cater to the needs of funders and sometimes strong-willed organizational leaders, over what is best for the community. Prioritizing communities means designing logic models, strategies, metrics, outcomes, and reports based on what communities need, and not withholding information that might be upsetting to funders or organizational leaders.
- **Advocate for organizations and communities.** Evaluators know better than anyone how complex the work is. They should use their voice to help leaders push back against funders and others in power when their demands are excessive, unreasonable, or not aligned with equity.
- **Help people reimagine what evaluation can be.** Right now, it is often a tool used to prove the worth of programs and communities to funders and policymakers. It often reinforces white-dominant standards of success while punishing communities that cannot conform to those standards. You can play a part in helping reimagine what data and evaluation can be: Tools for learning, for building community power, for advancing liberation.

Things We Need to Unlearn

Some things have been so ingrained in all of us that we don't stop to think how they are affecting how we see and do things. Here are few things we all need to unlearn:

- **The illusion of objectivity.** Data is supposed to be objective, but humans are subjective, with biases that influence how they collect and interpret data. Therefore, there's no such thing as objective data. Also, people will find the data that supports their established position, and ignore anything that doesn't.
- **The delusion of validity.** Since many nonprofits lack the resources to gather robust, scientifically accurate data, but we are all somehow forced to, a lot of the information we gather is not accurate. It's full of various biases and confounding variables. We just delude ourselves into thinking it's valid.
- **The assumption of generalizability.** People are varied, but we tend to assume that findings in studies can be generalized to everyone. Then, we make decisions based on those assumptions. So many studies do not focus on kids of color, for example, and yet assume that the results would generalize to them. This leads to decisions made that affect these kids, even though there isn't evidence that they would work.
- **The tendency for simplification.** The field that we are in is complicated, and there is severe danger when we try to simplify things too much. We lose out on the richness of our work, and we jeopardize programs that are effective in ways we may not be thinking about.
- **The bias toward short, easily measurable outcomes.** Data usually just reveal short periods in history, as longitudinal studies are time consuming, expensive, and rarely funded. The risk is that we fail to see whole systems and how different elements affect one another. Solutions based on these data, then, may tend to bias the entire sector toward programs that address symptoms of problems vs advocacy, organizing, and other systems-changing work.
- **The focus on "accountability" to place blame.** Data is a vital component of accountability. But accountability, for all its loftiness,

is often about placing blame and punishment. A program that does not have data saying that it "works" may get funding revoked. This creates a pervasive aura of risk-aversion and obfuscation, as nonprofits manipulate evaluation processes and variables to get the results they think funders want to see.

- **The defaulting to white standards.** RVC released an evaluation survey that we translated into different languages. Jondou, our evaluator, reported that some Somali leaders were unhappy with the survey. "This is not a Somali survey," they told him, "this is a generic survey you had translated into Somali. If this were designed for our community, it would be much shorter and to the point." Without realizing it, we had created a survey designed for white respondents and assumed it would work for all communities of color.

Ground Data in Social Justice Ideology

To be effective in our work, we must have a better grounding of data in social justice ideology, which includes a sobering reckoning with capitalism and neoliberalism. As Dr. Nicole Robinson, Founder & President of Milwaukee Evaluation and owner of NNR Evaluation, Planning & Research LLC, says:

> In this new era of rising fascism, data will continue to tell us where to focus our efforts, how to make change and, it will tell us where we are making progress. But the only data that matters in an authoritarian context is data that mirrors, recognizes, and is birthed from pure progressive ideology. This means we are in the era of all new outcomes, all new programs, and all new philanthropy.

She brought up the example of the breakfast program started by the Black Panthers. In 1969, the Black Panthers started feeding 11 school children breakfast at a church. It grew to 135 kids that week. The program spread across the country and by the end of the year, over 20,000 children received free breakfasts.[5] The results from the free breakfasts were astounding. Their hunger taken care of, kids were able to focus and learn better. Grades and test scores improved. Taken in this simple context, the program was greatly successful.

The Panthers, however, grounded their social programs in their ideology of the advancement of Black people. The breakfast programs were vital to helping kids succeed in school, but they were also important in educating kids about Black history, the unjust systems like capitalism that created hunger and poverty in the first place, and resistance to oppression. Over nourishing meals, youth learned about the Black Panther Party's Ten-Point Program, which included demands like freedom for the Black community to determine its destiny; employment for people; economic reparation for slavery; decent housing; and education that teaches accurate history.

Because of the Panthers' "radical views," the U.S. government took aggressive actions to destroy them, murdering several leaders. They sabotaged the breakfast program, including an FBI raid in Chicago where agents smashed and urinated on food that would have been served to children. The party disbanded over the next few years, with the last one, the Seattle chapter, closing in 1977.

While it was destroying the Panthers and their programs, though, the U.S. government also expanded its own free and reduced-priced programs across the United States. Once the free breakfast programs were taken over by the government and by other nonprofits, there were no more outcomes around political education and action, no more Ten-Point Plan.

The divorce of data and outcomes from social justice ideology is pervasive in the sector. We must ground data and research, like all our other work, in social justice. Otherwise, the information we collect, outcomes we achieve, reports we write, are often meaningless, or possibly even harmful, as we delude ourselves into thinking we're successfully addressing injustice, when we may have just been allowing unjust systems to continue.

Rethink Our Concept of Effectiveness

A program officer told me his foundation was thinking of providing general operating funds, but they were concerned about nonprofit effectiveness. "When bread tastes bad, people stop buying it," he said, matching my fondness for a good metaphor. Fair enough. No one likes gross bread. And no funder should have to fund ineffective nonprofits.

But there is a danger of buying into the illusion of objectivity when it comes to data and evaluation. "Effectiveness" is just as subjective as everything else, affected by factors like the race, educational background, and income level of researchers. I grew up in Vietnam, where our bread, a remnant of French colonization, is light and fluffy and neutral tasting, perfect to stuff with fillings for a bánh mì. When I had sourdough bread for the first time, I thought it was terrible; I'm still not overly fond of sourdough to this day, simply because that's not what I grew up eating.

Along those lines, we need to consider who gets to determine what an effective organization is, and how their backgrounds influence their assessment.

White organizations, often led by white men with Ivy League pedigrees, force their preferred concepts on the entire sector. This gives an advantage to white-led nonprofits and white nonprofit leaders, who can much more easily navigate the system they've created. It also punishes organizations led by marginalized communities. To redefine effectiveness so it works for everyone, we need to:

- **Include DEI in the definition.** All organizations, including foundations, to be considered effective, must be able to demonstrate how their work is addressing systemic injustice, inequity, and oppression. They must also ensure the way they go about their work is grounded in these principles. For example, are they paying their staff living wages? Are they using an equity lens in hiring people? Can an organization really be considered effective if its staff, especially its staff of color or who are disabled, are paid so poorly, they qualify for its services?
- **Trust the people most affected by injustice.** The people who must eat the bread every day are the best judges of whether the bread "tastes bad" or not. Let's ask the people who benefit from nonprofits' work if they think programs and services are effective and trust their opinions. We must stop this paternalistic, infantilizing attitude that the people most affected by injustice don't know what's good for them. And we need to respect community members' opinions when they share them in ways that do not fit our formal, quantitative narratives, and frameworks.

- **Have a long-term view.** We are biased toward short-term metrics, which often miss the picture. What if the kids we measure don't show any improvement in the short term, thus the program is considered ineffective, but in the long run they greatly benefit? Or the reverse: What if our programs seem effective right now but may cause great harm to people several years from now? Having a long-term view gives us a better understanding of what works. This prevents overprioritizing programs with short-term impact and unknown and possibly harmful long-term effects.
- **Accept the complex nature of this work.** Nonprofits are not "baking bread." We are dealing with complex issues with multiple confounding variables, yet the concept of effectiveness forces us to isolate our work into clear-cut elements, which means we miss out on the holistic view needed to solve these problems. Problems we're working on have multiple layers, which means we must take the same perspective when determining if we're effective at solving them.
- **Avoid easy proxies.** The complexity of the issues we face combined with the need for instant feedback on effectiveness results in reliance on a variety of useless metrics that have been harmful to our work.
- **Resist defaulting to whiteness.** As mentioned earlier, research often uses white people and communities as the default control variable to compare marginalized people and communities to. For instance, how kids of color do, as compared to white kids. Comparisons may be needed, but it's important to be thoughtful and avoid oversimplifying things. Avoid using whiteness as the standard everyone should strive for.
- **Consider the entire sector.** Let's stop treating an organization's effectiveness as if it's the result of only that org's work. All our work is interconnected. Our community members are not just benefiting from our programs, yet we continue these Nonprofit Hunger Games, with effectiveness as one more weapon to use against one another. We all need to understand, appreciate, and give credit to one another for our results, and funders can help in this by asking nonprofits to credit their partnerships and collaborations when assessing effectiveness.

Use Data to Act, Organize, Mobilize

It's a common sentiment that progressives bring a spreadsheet to a knife fight. It does not have to be this way. We, too, can use data as a tool for action. With the example of Trump's memo to freeze all federal spending, we saw the immediate benefits of nonprofit leaders taking quick and decisive action, based on whatever imperfect data they had at hand. Their courage and quick thinking stopped the horrendous order and probably saved millions of people's lives.

As attacks on our communities ramp up, we cannot operate the same way. Our sector, and progressives in general, have become good at toxic intellectualizing. There's nothing we love more than summits, white papers, theories of change, data, and voting with sticky dots. The problem is the intellectualizing becomes self-reinforcing. Summits beget committees, committees beget white papers, white papers beget summits, and so on.

But we cannot white paper our path to a just society. We cannot achieve an equitable world simply by running programs and services, even if they have amazing outcomes backed by evaluation. Thinking and talking about issues and addressing the ongoing symptoms of injustice are pivotal to our work, but they cannot be our end goal, and our field may have forgotten that. We must simultaneously address the root causes of injustice, and the only way to do that effectively is through organizing. All of us, not just advocacy organizations.

This is not to say that we shouldn't plan or research, or that data and evaluation tools and gatherings are bad, but the pendulum has swung way too far. We need to bring the balance back toward action, including acting significantly faster while embracing failure as important data we need to do our work effectively

Prioritize the Intrinsic Values of Individuals

Our sector's focus on outcomes and metrics and data has had the effect of reducing people to economic units and their worth being determined by what they can do for society. We do this often without realizing it. I've done it myself, for instance, when I wrote about the Curb-Cut Effect, named after the benefits that everyone receives when street curbs are cut to make them more accessible to wheelchair users; thus, the argument goes, helping the most marginalized benefits not just that population, but all of society. Carrie Basas, disability activist and former law professor, adds much-needed context to this view[6]:

> When we frame justice as a situation where those with power will do it if they get something in return, then we make justice access to Whiteness and abled-ness. We must move beyond what is legally "owed" to someone to what we must change to recognize them as our colleagues and neighbors. We can only do that by focusing on racial oppression, the Whiteness of capitalism, and the rhetoric of independence versus our mutual interdependence.

As undocumented immigrants face attacks and deportation, people will often defend them by talking about how prices will increase if we don't have enough people picking produce or working other low-paying jobs. While this is true, it veers toward dehumanizing. On LinkedIn, Isabeau Boody, a small business owner, writes[7]:

> Undocumented people are not valuable because they do jobs others won't. They are valuable because they are people. Limiting the conversation to labor reinforces the idea that a person's worth is tied to productivity—an idea that benefits capital, not people.

While we are focused on outcomes, let's remember the intrinsic values of individuals. Providing seniors with hot meals is worth doing because no one should be hungry. Sheltering homeless individuals is worth doing, because no one should be cold and exposed.

Sure, these activities and other stuff we do in the field will lessen crimes, save society money, and so on, but those effects should be considered awesome bonuses. They should not be the main reason why we do the things we do. We live in community with one another and should do our work with the belief that every individual life has an intrinsic value independent of its value to society.

Our Communities Are the Light

The most vulnerable people and communities face more challenges than ever due to the right-wing movement's ability to grasp and wield data and misinformation with such efficiency and effectiveness. It's up to all of us to use data and evaluation as potent tools in our arsenal to push back the tides of injustice, by grounding these concepts in our values of equity, breaking out of toxic intellectualizing, and acting much faster than we have been. We can start with the guiding belief that our communities are the light and follow their lead.

Discussion Questions

1. What are examples of toxic intellectualizing you've seen in our sector and in your community?
2. Why do you think progressives tend to intellectualize more?
3. How have you seen data being weaponized? What were the results?
4. Should evaluators consider themselves agents of justice, or objective observers?
5. What are other things we need to unlearn when it comes to data and evaluation?
6. How do you or your organization currently define what is successful in this line of work? Does that definition need to be revised?
7. What other lessons about data and research can we learn from right-wing movements?
8. How do we do a better job reminding people of the intrinsic values of individuals?

12

Diversity, Equity, and Inclusion (DEI)

It is not our differences that divide us. It is our inability to recognize, accept, and celebrate those differences.

—Audre Lorde

MY ADOPTED OLDER sister, Mai, was born to a Black father who was a U.S. soldier and a Vietnamese mother. While Amerasians—children born of American soldiers and Vietnamese women—were disliked in general, many facing abandonment by their families and shunning by society, the ones who were Black suffered even more irrational hatred and contempt, thanks to widespread colorism that still sees women go out fully covered even in 100-degree heat to avoid darkening their skin.

Mai's family, facing the shame of harboring an outcast, was neglectful and abusive. It got so bad that my paternal grandmother asked my parents to take her away to live with them. In our small village in the mountains, life was better for my sister, but only slightly. My parents worked early morning to late night, so my sister, a teenager, became a mother figure, taking care of me and my two brothers, bathing and feeding us, and walking us to school each day, weathering the disapproving glares of neighbors.

From my sister's stories, tinged with bittersweet humor, it wasn't easy wrangling the three of us. Phong, my older brother, loved to be contrarian and argued about everything. I had abandonment issues and clung closely to my sister's side, following her everywhere like a shadow. "I couldn't even go to the bathroom without you crying!"

Worst was Bao, my little brother, who was known to be mischievous. Once, she dropped him off at kindergarten, walked home, and found him back at the house. He was marched right back.

She wanted to go to school herself, but since she was Amerasian, she was forbidden from entering the school building. Undeterred, she often stood outside the window with her pen and notebook, learning with all the other kids. "Sometimes it would rain," she said, "and it was so cold standing there."

Through the Amerasian Homecoming Act, she was able to immigrate to the United States, and since we were her adopted family, we were allowed to accompany her. Thanks to my sister and the kindness of Fate, or maybe Karma, we were able to escape poverty. Here, despite more setbacks, Mai has been able to carve out a decent life for herself and raised two successful daughters. She has even managed to find the strength to forgive her biological family in Vietnam and rebuild relationships with them.

Through these childhood experiences, I had an early introduction to systemic injustice and discrimination. This image of my caring, smart, protective sister standing outside the building, drenched by monsoon rain, trying to learn to read and write, the other kids pointing and laughing, while the adults ignored or encouraged the cruelty, is a constant reminder for me of why our sector matters. We work so everyone in our society who, through no fault of their own, has been excluded, can finally come inside where they deserve to be.

This is equity, diversity, inclusion, belonging, and justice, and they are the heart of our sector and our reason for being.

The Attacks on Diversity, Equity, and Inclusion

As I'm writing this, Trump and the Republicans have been in power for only a few weeks, and they have launched brutal and often very effective attacks on diversity, equity, and inclusion (DEI). They have blamed it for planes crashing, used it as a reason to fire people and erase important data and information from government websites, threatened to remove funding from organizations that continue to engage with DEI, and fueled society's fear and disdain of DEI work. This continues the trend that's been building momentum for the past few years, seen in actions such the Fearless Fund being successfully sued by conservative group the American Alliance for Equal Rights (AAER) for working to restore justice by intentionally working to bring more resources to Black women entrepreneurs.[1]

The rush to comply with this blatant violation of free speech has been bewildering, with many corporations such as Amazon, Google, and Meta shutting down the DEI work. Their eagerness to obey these orders may be a sign they were never serious about doing this work in earnest in the first place. These executive orders give corporations an excuse to stop doing something they never wanted to do.

In our sector, while many funders and nonprofits reaffirm their commitment to DEI, many have also capitulated. Some out of valid fear of losing funding or tax-exempt status. Others because they felt DEI has been done so badly it might be better to just not do it at all. And others probably because they also have never understood DEI and felt like they were being dragged along.

Our sector, however, exists because of the prevalence of injustice, which is linked to the lack of DEI. Every issue the leaders before us have tackled decades in the past, from segregation to women's suffrage to voting rights to marriage equality, have been about DEI.

This chapter talks about some overarching philosophies and pitfalls around equity, diversity, and inclusion. There is not much practical advice here, and that is done intentionally, as one of the biggest failures in DEI work is that it is often segregated from other work. For instance, many conferences have various "tracks," with DEI being one of them, forcing people to choose either fundraising or DEI, or leadership or DEI. It should be deeply interwoven

The terminology and acronym may change, but advancing diversity, equity, inclusion, access, justice, belonging, "wokeness," and other concepts has been the main purpose of the work we do. This is the soul of the sector and its primary objective.

into everything we do. Each chapter in this book touches on DEI in one form or another. This chapter makes you think about DEI broadly so that it'll be easier to recognize and understand equity principles when you're reading the other chapters, and when you're doing work in general.

DEI's Existential Crisis

A few years ago, I was speaking at a conference about what equity looks like in everyday practices. After my presentation, a colleague raised her hand. "My nonprofit does not focus on social justice," she said, "We address cancer, which does not discriminate; it affects everyone of all races and class. How are these concepts applicable to my organization?"

This sort of "color-blind" and meritocracy-based mindset has been something our sector and society have been battling. It tapered down a bit as the murder of George Floyd by the police spurred an increase in reflections on systemic racism, though effectiveness has been uneven. For every person who had a light-bulb moment, another person doubled down, rolling their eyes. Cancer does indeed discriminate. According to studies conducted by the Center for Disease Control (CDC), "Compared to members of other racial and ethnic groups, Black and African American people have higher rates of getting and dying from many kinds of cancer" as well as lower overall survival rate[2].

Because of Trump and the Republicans' attacks, DEI is undergoing a sort of existential crisis. But this crisis has long been simmering. DEI has often been used in very counterproductive ways. People, especially people of color, started calling out the ways equity has been done wrong. My colleagues, Erin Okuno and Heidi Schillinger Sohn, created a blog called *Fakequity*, to discuss all the "fake equity" going on, including:

> You host a "multicultural potluck" as a way of "increasing diversity" and then you wonder why no one but people you know show up. When you want "feedback" or "community engagement," you invite people to come to your meeting and you lecture at them for

two hours, use stats and meaningless lingo, and give them comment cards to fill out as a way of gaining feedback and don't follow up.[3]

As DEI continued to expand, we saw more of what my friend James Lovell calls "equity offset," which is like carbon offset, where people and companies can pay money to plant trees or do other things to offset the pollution they contribute to. Carbon offset can be a good thing to do, unless it is used as an excuse to continue doing harmful stuff.

In the same way, equity offset involves taking actions that are aligned with equity but using them as excuses to avoid deeper work and to continue being inequitable. For example:

- Senior staff asking people of marginalized identities to lead DEI committees without providing additional compensation for their time, and often ignoring their recommendations.
- Funders talking about inclusion and requiring their grantees to explain their DEI philosophies and practices, while still mostly funding large, white-led organizations.
- Hiring managers stressing the importance of the diversity of pools of job candidates, while keeping intact their process designed to hire mostly white and male candidates.
- People forming groups to read books and articles about DEI, but not doing anything differently in real life.
- Boards recruiting people of diverse backgrounds, but they're often tokenized and their opinions dismissed, or worse, they uphold the status quo.

The surge of focus on DEI has certainly been effective enough to threaten the right-wing and cause them to bring the hammer down, but that's not the big picture. While lots of good things have resulted from it, it has also been frustrating to many of us who often see DEI work being done to absolve people of guilt. This makes them complacent and helps to maintain capitalism, white supremacy, patriarchy, and other oppressive systems, instead of challenging them. This existential crisis is a necessary one, forcing us to reexamine our framework around equity, and truly achieve it.

Guidelines for DEI and Social Justice

Over the past several years, as our sector has tackled various issues of systemic injustice, I've noticed people often forget basic DEI lessons we should have learned. They often fall into bad habits such as criticizing someone's tone or word choice instead of focusing on the inequity they're trying to bring attention to. Sometimes they allow those who engage in bad faith to have equal air time to argue against those who are trying to advance social justice.

Here are some important reminders for all of us. These are basic but vital principles we need to constantly keep in mind, whether we are talking about major forms of oppression like the prison industrial complex, transphobia, and the genocide of Palestinians, or lesser problems like whether staff should donate to the organizations that employ them:

- **We must have an analysis of the power dynamics.** Power imbalances undergird a lot of systemic injustice. Racism and sexism require a combination of prejudice plus systemic power. It is important when doing DEI and social justice work to understand who has power and resources, and who doesn't.
- **We must center the people and communities most affected by injustice.** Those who suffer most under injustice and oppression must always be the focus of discussions and solutions in addressing these challenges. Otherwise, we drift toward counterproductive habits, such as spending time and energy comforting the privileged.
- **We must prioritize justice over civility.** People often value "civility" and "decorum" more than they do addressing injustice, such as when Beto O'Rourke used profanity in his anger when he discussed kids being gunned down in school, and there was more outrage about his language than about the murdered kids. We need to worry more about injustice than about the word choice and tone people use when calling it out.
- **We must not "both-sides" inequity and injustice.** A colleague, a Black woman, told me she was invited to debate with a white colleague on the topic of whether racism exists. This is called both-siding, and it is done with the idea that diverse ideas and

vigorous discussions are good. They can be, unless those ideas have been repeatedly proven hateful or wrong. We need to stop giving such ideas legitimacy by giving them airtime. There should be no debate, for example, on the existence of racism or on the humanity of trans people.

- **We must use precise terms and concepts and not euphemisms.** For a long time, and even occasionally now, many people in our sector could not say words like "white supremacy" or "anti-Blackness" or even "race." But we can only address systemic injustice when we name things as they are: genocide, fascism, white supremacy, and so on.
- **We must use the active voice when calling out injustice.** This is a lesson we all should learn through the works of leaders like k. kennedy whiters of (un)Redact The Facts.[4] Instead of saying "a Black man dies in traffic stop incident with police," we must say, "police officer kills a Black man during routine traffic stop." This active voice helps with accountability.
- **We must call for justice, not simply a "negative peace."** In his "Letter from a Birmingham Jail,"[5] Dr. King mentioned the white moderate "who prefers a negative peace which is the absence of tension to a positive peace which is the presence of justice." True equity requires more than for the oppressed to no longer raise a ruckus, which itself may be a sign that they have been silenced.
- **We must not water down terms and concepts.** There has been a lot of weaponization of social justice terms and concepts, even among people committed to doing this work. Thoughtlessly deploying terminologies weakens them. For example, many who have criticized Israel for its genocidal actions against Palestine have been called antisemitic. There has been a significant rise in antisemitism globally, but those calling everything they disagree with antisemitic weaken the term, which does not help in the fight against antisemitism.
- **We must not pit one form of violence and oppression against another.** When we talk about missing and murdered Indigenous women, we focus on that issue because it deserves our full attention. When we talk about rising anti-Asian hate crimes, we

focus on that issue because it deserves our full attention. We don't try to divert attention from one issue to another using "whataboutism," since all issues are important.
- **We must not condemn entire communities based on the actions of individuals or groups of individuals.** We learned that white people are treated as individuals, whereas people of color must bear the burden of always reflecting their entire community. For example, when a white man shoots up a school, the media and politicians don't then think this man is typical of all white people.
- **We must not impose conditions when calling for justice.** It doesn't matter if a person is drunk, argumentative, or was once incarcerated, the police are not justified in killing them. What a woman wears does not justify sexual assault. A person or community does not need to be perfect or free of oppression themselves for us to call for their liberation.

Questions to Help You Develop an Equity Mindset

Because there is so much complexity to DEI, especially around equity, it can be difficult to implement consistently. The goal should be to develop an equity mindset that we can apply to every situation. Here are some questions we can use to develop this mindset.

For a concrete example, apply these questions to a long-running debate in the nonprofit sector in the United States about whether nonprofit staff should be asked to donate to the organizations that employ them. Supporters of this practice cite various reasons that seem legitimate on the surface, including the fact that anyone can afford to donate a buck or two, no one is forced to do it if they don't really want to, it shows staff's investment in the organization if 100 percent of employees donate, and if the people who work there don't give financially, how could they ask others to give?

But these reasons ignore equity implications. Let's run this situation through the nine questions that help us develop an equity mindset:

1. **Who are the most marginalized people, and how are they affected?** The default mindset is to assume that everyone is affected equally in a situation. But this is not true. Often, it will

be people of color, LGBTQIA, disabled people, women, neurodivergent, and other marginalized people who will be most affected. When it comes to asking staff to give to a nonprofit, it will be the lowest-paid staff who are and have been most affected, and who are lowest-paid staff? POCs, disabled people, and so on.

2. **How are the voices and opinions of the people most affected by this situation prioritized?** To advance equity, the opinions of the people most affected must be given greater weight. In the case of asking staff to give, since it's people of color and low-income people who are most affected, their opinions should have the most weight, and most of them find this practice inequitable.

3. **What power dynamics are involved? Who holds the most power in this situation?** It is challenging, if not impossible, to have equity when there is a power imbalance. No matter how nice a supervisor is, there are power dynamics involved. Staff cannot feel fully at ease saying no when their supervisor asks them to contribute to the employee giving campaign.

4. **Who developed the relevant systems and processes in the first place?** We need to stop assuming philosophies, systems, and policies just sprang out of thin air, or that they were co-created. Most systems we're trying to undo or make better were created and maintained by white people. Our sector's current fundraising philosophies and practices, including asking staff to give back a portion of their wages as a symbolic gesture of fealty to the organization, have been created and reinforced by white people, and therefore are steeped in white norms.

5. **Who benefits most from things remaining unchanged?** Those who create systems tend to benefit most from them, financially and in other ways. In asking staff to donate, those who would benefit most are likely white fundraisers, who get recognition and praise if there's 100 percent participation.

6. **Who is asking for change, and who is defending against it?** In any argument and discussion, stop and acknowledge the demographics of who is taking which sides. In the conversations about whether staff should be asked to give to their org, the side

that is in favor of asking staff to give tends to be overwhelmingly white. Meanwhile, the side that is against it mostly comprises people of color and white allies. There's also division in terms of socioeconomic status and upbringing as well, with people who have experienced low-income or poverty more likely to be against this practice.

7. **Who created the evidence that supports status quo?** Defenders of inequitable practices often cite evidence such as articles and statistics to support their arguments. But if we dig deeper, we find that most of these pieces are written by white, likely middle- or upper-class people, cisgender people, men, neurotypical people, and so on, who themselves often do not use an equity mindset when they present their arguments.

8. **What does the data say when you disaggregate it?** Data, articles, and reports that are not examined with an equity lens can do significant damage. Due to how polarizing the debate on employee giving is, a white colleague created a survey to ask whether people were in favor of or against the practice. But the survey did not ask people for their race. If it had, it may have revealed stark differences in terms of how people of different races perceived the practice.

9. **How do your identity, upbringing, culture, education, privileges, and biases affect your perspective?** Anaïs Nin said, "We don't see things as they are, we see them as we are." So many people, including me at times, get into supporting or opposing a position without examining how our identity, privileges, how we were raised, and so on affect how we view things. Once we stop and make this assessment, we may be able to see things differently, and hopefully more equitably.

We need to shift our perspective on DEI, seeing it in a systemic and global context and implementing it with this more expansive framework that goes beyond what we've currently been doing.

When we use these questions to analyze the situation, asking employees to donate to the organizations that employ them is an inequitable practice; I say it is unethical. This is just one situation, and a relatively simple one. We have way more complex situations to tend to as we do this work.

Practice using your equity mindset everywhere, not just with work, but in your personal life; use it while watching your favorite shows, while you're going grocery shopping, and so on. If you do this enough, after a while, you may recognize patterns, and it does become faster and more intuitive with time. You may also realize that almost everything is inequitable, since most things are rooted in oppressive systems. But finding and addressing inequity is the main purpose of our work.

DEI as a Precursor to Liberation

"Are you a DEI guy or a liberation guy?" This was a question a friend of mine asked me a few months before she died of suicide. From our many conversations and intellectual arguments, I knew a significant factor that contributed to her death was the injustice she saw constantly in the world, but felt powerless to change.

This dichotomy between DEI and liberation is something I ruminate on a lot, and I think our entire sector needs to reflect on it more. DEI often helps marginalized people and communities survive within existing inequitable structures, whereas liberation works to dismantle those systems altogether to create a just and equitable society. In a liberated society, we probably wouldn't need to do much or any DEI.

The frustration many of us from marginalized communities feel around DEI is because DEI work often supplants liberation work. Liberation would require we confront white supremacy, capitalism, patriarchy, and other systems of oppression that led to colonialization, enslavement, genocide, and other horrific injustices that cause us to not be so diverse, inclusive, and equitable in the first place. Liberation work therefore is way harder and more uncomfortable to do than engage in DEI-related actions like hiring more staff of color, attending trainings on how to be more inclusive of people with neurodiversity, passing a paid family leave policy, and throwing a multicultural potluck. These things, while great to do, can give us a false sense of success and make us complacent, like the equity offset concept I mentioned earlier.

But maybe there doesn't have to be such a dichotomy. When it's done right, DEI allows people to see the systems of oppression more clearly, which is a necessary step toward dismantling them. We need to shift our perspective on DEI, including treating it as a necessary precursor to liberation, seeing it in a systemic and global context, and implementing it with this more expansive framework that goes beyond what we've currently been doing. DEI 201, if you will. An example of what this looks like is in how we think about and act on the current attacks on trans people.

Protecting Trans People and Trans Rights

Over the past few years, the right wing has launched horrific attacks on trans people, ramping up the cruelty and inhumanity on people who just want to exist. We must understand that these attacks on trans people are harbingers of other forms of oppression, and so everyone needs to care about trans people and trans rights. Chris Talbot is an artist, activist, and the creator of the Chrissplains Nonbinary Advocacy to Cisgender People educomics series. They are also the editor of the community-centric fundraising (CCF) content hub. They have a warning for all of us:

> Protecting transgender rights is essential. We need basic human rights like access to healthcare, protection from discrimination and hate crimes, and participation in public life to survive. We need our cisgender siblings to support us now, not delay our rights, or tell us to be patient. Telling us to wait implies we're expendable, and the most vulnerable of us will not survive until this round of fascism has been defeated. But if you won't advocate for us because it's the right thing to do, do it because eventually you'll be next.[6]

This warning is based on history. When Hitler took power in January 1933, one of the first things he did was incite violence and persecution against trans people. On May 6 of that year, Nazi students raided the *Institut für Sexualwissenschaft*, the Institute for Sexology, which had been advocating for gay and transgender people. They publicly burned tens of thousands of books and research papers that night. The Nazi regime then used the names and addresses they found of the Institute's patients to round up trans and gay people and send them to concentration camps, where many were castrated, tortured, and murdered.[7]

DEI as precursor to liberation requires us to be more cognizant of wider patterns and what they mean. Being inclusive and equitable toward trans people is not just, intrinsically, the right thing to do, but it is also a critical line of defense against fascism and helps eventually usher in the dismantling of patriarchy and its oppressive ideas and structures around gender norms. In the same vein, our DEI work with other populations—people of color, immigrants, disabled people, neurodivergent people, older adults, women, nonbinary people, people of different religions, and so on—and our work in calling for the liberation of Palestine, are precursors to dismantling patriarchy, white supremacy, capitalism, and other systems of oppression.

The Dental Hygiene Model for DEI

If you read this chapter so far and are overwhelmed or filled with anxiety about getting things wrong, that's okay. With all the tension in our society regarding race, gender identity, sexual orientation, and so on, along with the attacks on DEI, I see more and more of us walking on eggshells, afraid to make mistakes. But we cannot advance the discussion on injustice, and thus the solutions for it, if we live in fear of having honest conversations with each other, including being able to admit to our mistakes and not feel like we are terrible people.

This is why I am an advocate of Jay Smooth's *dental hygiene* philosophy when it comes to talking about racism, and by extension, other forms of injustice. To paraphrase Smooth, we must stop thinking of prejudice the way we think about our tonsils: We get them removed, and that's it, we don't have to worry about them again.

Learning to not be racist or sexist is more like brushing our teeth, something we must do daily. Says Smooth in his TED Talk called "How I Learned to Stop Worrying and Love Discussing Race":

> We don't assume, I'm a clean person, therefore I do not need to clean my teeth. Being a clean person is something you maintain and work on every day [. . .] And when someone suggests to us that we've got something stuck in our teeth, we don't say, "I have something stuck in my teeth?! But I'm a clean person!"[8]

Fear and anxiety about making mistakes will not lead us to progress in DEI, only honesty and integrity will. The systemic injustice we are trying to address is extremely complex, and we all make mistakes all the time. Undoing racism and other forms of injustice is a practice we must do every day, like brushing our teeth. We must look in the mirror constantly, reflect on our privilege and mistakes regularly, and brush and floss out the racism and other things we get stuck in our pearly whites. That's the only way we will all have the minty fresh breath of social justice.

Equity 201

I did not understand as a kid why my older sister experienced such cruelty and prejudice, why my father was put into a reeducation camp, why my family was poor, why we had to leave Vietnam. What I learned of the Vietnam War in school in the United States had no analysis of the colonization, racism, U.S. imperialism, capitalism, and other factors that fueled the flames of the war. Years of DEI training and reflection allowed me to see how these systems led to the consequences my family and others experienced, and how they continue to further inequity all over the world.

Understanding is the crucial first step toward effective action, which is why those who want to maintain these systems of oppression are so afraid of DEI, and why we must not shy away from it but instead double down. For all its flaws and all the ways it's been implemented wrong, DEI, and especially Equity, is still a powerful framework to guide us in our work. When done right, it leads people to more clearly see the bigger pictures and the overarching systems of injustice behind every issue we're trying to tackle.

Learning to not be racist or sexist is more like brushing our teeth, something we must do daily.

The attacks on DEI reaffirm its importance and force us to examine what's working and what weaknesses exist. This will require us to constantly practice using an equity mindset in all contexts of our work, from boards to fundraising to capacity building and everything else. This allows us to go beyond Equity 101, which is surface level and often rife with *fakequity* and equity offset, and into

Equity 201, which is equity as precursor to liberation, which will be more difficult and even more uncomfortable, but ultimately more likely to bring about a just world.

Discussion Questions

1. How old were you when you first started recognizing that injustice exists?
2. Why do you think there has been such a backlash against DEI?
3. How should our sector respond to the attacks on DEI?
4. What has our sector done well when it comes to DEI work?
5. What are the weaknesses with DEI that we need to address?
6. What are other examples of fakequity or equity offset that you have seen or can think of?
7. Which DEI guidelines resonate with you? Which are the most challenging for you?
8. Which of the questions to help develop an equity mindset resonate most with you? Which ones are most challenging? Can you think of other questions?
9. Attacks on trans people have been shown by history to be a precursor of fascism. How do we ensure people learn from history and not repeat it?
10. When's the last time you had something "stuck in your teeth" when it comes to DEI work? What lessons did you learn?
11. What do you think Equity 201 should include?

13

The Barriers Holding Back Change and What to Do About Them

The secret of our success is that we never, never give up.

—Wilma Mankiller

ONE OF THE greatest joys of my life is being a parent, though I often joke that having a baby is like getting a multi-year government grant: At first, you're like "Yay!" And then you're like, "This is a lot of work" and the requirements change every year, and you can't give it back. It has been endlessly rewarding and amusing watching two tiny, helpless beings who spit up everywhere grow into sassy, hilarious people.

I mention parenting because while it is meaningful and magical, it is often extremely frustrating in lots of different ways. Kids can be oblivious and illogical, like the time my little ones, ages five and three back then, fought over a wood chip at the playground. They can be stubborn and defiant, refusing to eat their vegetables even though you know they need the nutrients. And half of parenting is just trying to seem impressed by your offspring's displays of incremental growth that often come at the expense of other things, like the time my toddler was so proud he planted three kale seedlings, never mind that he had trampled five other ones while doing so.

All of that is very much like our sector. The work is vital, and the people are for the most part wonderful; at the same time, it can be so frustrating trying to get change and progress to happen. Those who want things to be done differently often don't have the power and authority, and those who have power and authority often don't want to rock the boat.

Adults are often more complicated than children. When I pointed out to my kids that they were standing on literally thousands of other woodchips, they immediately stopped fighting. Meanwhile, colleagues have been pointing out the need for our sector to engage in more advocacy, and yet many organizations still don't. Nonprofit leaders and foundation allies have pointed out for years that there's been tons of research on the effectiveness of multi-year general operating dollars (MYGOD), and yet many funders are still skeptical.

None of the stuff I discuss in previous chapters is new or revolutionary, if you think about it. People much smarter than me have been saying similar things for ages. So why has progress been so slow?

With democracy being dismantled, fascism on the rise, and our sector intentionally weakened so we can't be as effective in fighting back, we must figure out how to get people and institutions to change. In this final chapter, I explore some of the reasons holding back change, and what we may need to do to cut through these barriers.

The Wheel of Change

The Wheel of Change is a helpful framework developed by Robert Gass. I learned about it through the Social Transformation Project's Art of Transformational Consulting (ATC) training.[1] To summarize, for meaningful, transformative change to happen, we must consider three elements:

1. **Hearts and minds** are things that are personal to each person, including their hopes, dreams, fears, cultures, religious beliefs, childhood upbringing, unresolved traumas, and so on.
2. **Behavior** includes actions, habits, things we do and don't do. In an organization, it's stuff like meeting frequency, how staff communicate with one another, and so on.

3. **Structures** are external systems, how things are set up, what hierarchies exist, what processes are involved, not just at the organization or foundation, but also relevant elements outside it.

These elements all affect one another. According to the folks behind ATC, "Over 70 percent of organizational change efforts fail. For change to succeed, it must attend to the systemic nature of people, institutions and society." Hearts and minds, behaviors, and structures must all be worked on. Unfortunately, what often happens is that we tend to target these elements in isolation without considering the other ones.

A common pattern is that people go directly into trying to change behaviors or systems without tending to hearts and minds. An example from my own experience was when I went to a Vietnamese elder, a respected community leader who ran a local Vietnamese newspaper, to ask him to sign a letter of support endorsing a grant proposal I was submitting. I went to his office, presented my arguments, and got reprimanded and accused of using the community to grift money to support my excessive salary and lavish lifestyle. His words stung; I left demoralized.

Talking to more experienced leaders, I learned I had approached it completely wrong. I was so focused on the behavior (getting the letter signed) that I had ignored cultural customs, which are a part of people's hearts and minds. With further advice, I came back, this time bearing a basket of tangerines, and apologized. I didn't talk about the letter of support but instead became genuinely curious about the elder's life both in Vietnam and in the United States. I also shared about my own family. I left without the letter (I would get it later), but with a crucial personal endorsement that would be handy for years to come.

The people we work with and serve are multifaceted individuals and it's important to treat them as such. In our rush to get things done, it's easy to see those standing in the way of change as just obstinate people who are resistant for no reason. Sometimes we, with our own hearts and minds, may ascribe motivations and qualities to them that may not be true, such as they want to sabotage the mission. Slow down and take some time to understand, empathize, and connect on a human level when possible. Behavioral and systems change usually doesn't happen successfully without hearts and mind work being done.

Immunity to Change

Immunity to change is a concept created by Harvard professors Robert Kegan and Lisa Lahey, introduced in their 2009 book *Immunity to Change: How to Overcome It and Unlock the Potential in Yourself and Your Organization.* They posit that people want to change, but they often have unconscious hidden agendas they may not be aware of that then create competing commitments that prevent change from happening. These hidden agendas are often buried deep, and just the process for surfacing them can take significant effort, requiring deep reflection. In their article titled "The Real Reason People Won't Change" in the *Harvard Business Review*, they state:

> [The process] asks people to call into question beliefs they've long held close, perhaps since childhood. And it requires people to admit to painful, even embarrassing, feelings that they would not ordinarily disclose to others or even to themselves. Indeed, some people will opt not to disrupt their immunity to change, choosing instead to continue their fruitless struggle against their competing commitments.[2]

The team at my former organization RVC and I went through such a process, though with lower stakes, focused on our own individual issues, such as trouble sticking to an exercise routine or committing to a relationship. We worked to uncover hidden competing commitments and the big assumptions behind them.

I chose to examine why I was so resistant to writing a book. I had wanted to write this book for years, but always had valid excuses, the main ones being my role as the parent of small children and having a demanding job as an executive director, which left little time or energy. When I was no longer an ED and had a lot more free time, I came up with other seemingly reasonable excuses. When I had no more excuses, I still dragged my feet.

Through the exercises and reflection questions, which you can find in their article mentioned earlier, we each learned something about ourselves. I uncovered I feared failure and being considered a fraud. Writing an informal blog was one thing, since no one takes blog posts too seriously. A book, on the other hand, is a Very Serious Project, with citations and interviews and a table of contents. If I wrote a book and it sucked, people would realize I had no idea what I'd been talking about, and my career would be over, and with it, my ability to feed my children.

These beliefs were based on some unconscious assumptions I didn't know I carried. For instance, the assumption that if this book is terrible, it would end my career. Maybe it would, but likely nobody would care.

Immunity to change is pervasive in our personal and professional lives. In our sector, this may explain why many people and organizations refuse to do things differently, despite claiming to want to. Program officers who are hesitant to support multi-year general operating funds, for example, may have an unconscious agenda of protecting their jobs, because giving general operating funds over several years means a much more hands-off approach, and if so, would there even be enough work for foundation staff to do? This may be based on the assumption that they can't switch to doing much more meaningful work if they weren't micromanaging nonprofits.

Surfacing unconscious agendas and assumptions preventing change can be effective, even transformational, but it's way easier to do that oneself than to get other people, especially those with positional power, to do it. It does help to shape strategies to understand that people are often guided by things they may not even be aware of. Still, it's frustrating if they're standing in the way of progress.

Strategies to Effect Change

I get asked this question a lot: "How can I make change as a younger professional when I don't have positional power?" Here's some advice I found to be useful, not just for younger professionals, but for anyone trying to shake things up:

- **Stick around.** One of the lessons from grad school that stuck with me was from my professor of a course on community organizing. He said, "If you want change to happen, be willing to stick with a community at least five years." Five years is not always feasible with the urgency of our work, but the point is that people and systems often need time to change, and you need time to move the pieces into place.

- **Create allies both inside and outside your organization.** Spend time really getting to know folks. You may feel like these coffees and meetings, especially if they have no overt agenda, are a waste of time, but they are critical to developing a strong network that you can rely on for guidance and support. Read Mark Granovetter's paper "The Strength of Weak Ties,"[3] which refer to the seemingly insignificant but vital bonds you build between colleagues, neighbors, and acquaintances. Strengthen your relationship with the people at your organization, while simultaneously developing relationships with people outside your org.
- **Use external voices to deliver the same messages.** Because of what I call *outsider efficacy bias*, people who are external to an organization or community tend to be taken more seriously. Figure out who among your allies might be able to say what you've been saying. Perhaps a consultant. There's no law that says you can't just have a colleague come in and pretend to be a pro bono consultant. Remember the elder I mentioned earlier who wouldn't sign the letter of support for the grant proposal I was writing? Building a personal connection with him was a first step. The second step was convincing another elder to persuade him to sign it.
- **Examine if imposter syndrome is holding you back.** A few months ago, a younger colleague asked me if I knew someone who would be good for the ED position at her org. I asked her, "Have you considered applying?" She looked surprised. "Wow, I never thought about myself in the position." Often, I meet people who have vision and drive to change things, but who do not think they are qualified to be in charge. This is especially true for women and people of color. You can try to convince those who have power and authority to change things, but sometimes, you may need to aim for that power and authority and change things yourself.
- **Learn to have courageous conversations.** Courageous conversations[4] and radical candor[5] are good tools/frameworks to practice. You can get your points across better while preventing the various forms of resistance that often accompany difficult conversations. It is hard at first, especially since few of us are trained

in discussing difficult topics, so we tend to default to less effective means of communication, such as triangulation, where you talk to other people about the issue instead of the person you should be talking to. The more you practice these skills to have direct, honest conversations, the easier it gets.

- **Have people think it's their idea.** Yeah, this is a little Machiavellian, but it's a strategy to consider. People are more likely to implement an idea if they think they're the ones who came up with it. There are ways to go about this, such as talking around an idea but not directly about it, underselling an idea, and using other psychological techniques.[6] Those with huge egos are particularly vulnerable to this, as it allows them to claim credit for the ideas. Just make sure you use this strategy for good and not evil.
- **Organize and speak as a collective.** It's much harder to dismiss people and organizations when they band together to deliver the same message. This is how a lot of change happens in society. Get a bunch of nonprofits to sign an open letter to a funder about increasing their funds and cutting down on reporting and other requirements during these tumultuous times. Have several staff attend the board meeting, share their perspectives on paid family leave or other relevant issues, and ask the board to pass the appropriate policies. Do it thoughtfully so people don't feel like they're being ganged up on.
- **Use public shaming.** Sometimes, the only way to motivate people in power to change is through calling them out publicly. When other tactics—such as giving feedback in private—have failed, using social media to name and shame is something to consider. Crappy Funding Practices (CFP), for example, has a submission form you can fill out to anonymously report funders who engage in timewasting, unreasonable, or even harmful behavior. The CFP team of volunteers calls out the funder on LinkedIn. A few funders, such as the Internet Society Foundation, have been gracious in accepting the feedback and changing their processes.
- **Consider walking away.** I know, this isn't always practical, but sometimes, after you've put enough energy into trying to make a

difference at one place and going nowhere. It may just be better to leave and find a place where you may be more effective. Organizations have various life stages, cycles, and leaders. Maybe you couldn't create the change you want to see now, but perhaps you laid the groundwork that allows someone else to do so in the future.

Burning Bridges

This sector tends to attract kind, compassionate people, but those qualities often come bundled with a tendency for conflict avoidance. Plus, we are trained to avoid upsetting people with money and power for fear they could take away their support. But sometimes, ruffling feathers or even tanking a relationship is what's needed to push for equity and justice.

History is filled with cases of leaders needing to burn bridges with colleagues, organizations, and movements for the greater good. Alice Paul, for example, a key leader in the fight for the rights of women to vote, broke away from the National American Woman Suffrage Association (NAWSA) after they disagreed with her more "militant" tactics in favor of more incremental state-by-state campaign.[7]

In more recent history, we see courageous examples of bridge burning like Colin Kaepernick, who upset the NFL, his sponsors, and former supporters by kneeling during the national anthem to protest police brutality; his career tanked but there's no argument his actions sparked conversations and movements against racial injustice.

Meanwhile, millions of people around the world have been alienated by their colleagues, friends, neighbors, and even family members for speaking up against the genocide of Palestinians, committed by Israel and funded by U.S. tax dollars. I estimate about a quarter of my readers and social media followers immediately left, many sending "I'm disappointed in you" messages along the way.

Before I started speaking up on Palestine though, I'd burned my fair share of bridges with foundations, fundraising experts (one of whom labeled as "dangerous" my views on the importance of asking donors to reflect on things that contributed to their wealth like slavery, stolen Indigenous land, and tax avoidance), and other colleagues who don't agree with some of my tactics, such as naming and shaming foundations through Crappy Funding Practices. Some of the losses of these relationships I'm OK with, but others I'm still mourning.

Sometimes, to advance a just and equitable world, we must be willing to give up a few relationships we care about. It is especially important that those of us who have more privilege—white, male, cisgender, able-bodied, neurotypical, and so on—take on more of the burden and consequences of burning bridges. Throughout history, those things have often fallen on women of color, trans people, and others who are already the most marginalized in society.

Severing the relationships we care about may be painful, but as colleague Aubrey Alvarez quoted from a novelty flask, "May the bridges we burn light the way."

Brussels Sprouts of Equity

One time, in my quest to get my two- and five-year-olds to eat more vegetables, I deep-fried some Brussels sprouts, sprinkled Maldon, and drizzled them with balsamic glaze. The kids did not like the dish, especially the balsamic glaze, and to this day they still bring it up: "Daddy, remember that nasty sauce you made us try one day? It tasted like a giant threw up a cat and the cat threw up a rat and the rat threw up that sauce."

A lot of our work is like trying to feed the Brussels sprouts of equity to toddlers in power. But sometimes, *we* are the toddlers in power and don't realize it. It's frustrating that no matter what we do or how many times we try, people don't want to change, so ineffective systems and policies remain in place.

But what may feel futile is part of the process. But research shows it takes 8–15 exposures to a food before kids develop a liking for it. Most parents give up after a few tries. For the past several years, for instance, I've been ranting about overhead. I think it is ridiculous that we still must talk about it and that some foundations are still fixated on it. Endless studies have shown how effective general operating funds are. And the hyperfocus on making sure nonprofits have low overhead rates disproportionately affects organizations led by and serving marginalized communities. I had been saying these things repeatedly, not sure if it was making any difference at all. Then one day in 2022, I was reading this article,[8] and got to this paragraph:

> Oak Foundation [. . .] invited nonprofit thought leader Vu Le to address an in-person event with staff and trustees. "We all had a moment of truth," recalled Program Officer Medina Haeri, "Vu Le used the analogy of baking a cake—if you want a fully baked cake, you can't only pay for the ingredients. You also have to pay for electricity, the bake staff, and all the other costs beyond ingredients. That was a light bulb moment."

Before that conference, which was in 2016, Oak had a rule of funding only 15 percent overhead; now they provide multi-year core support grants. I had been so jetlagged during that trip, I barely remember what I said. It took several years, and I'm sure there were many other variables along the way that moved the foundation forward, but it was nice to get some evidence that change does happen.

Keep Fightin' the Good Fight

A significant part of our profession feels like beating our heads against a wall. Do not despair, thinking that what you are doing has no effect. You may think that bringing up an important equity consideration at a meeting or retreat, or passing along an article, or bringing in a local consultant, and so on, and then nothing changing means you failed. But maybe you didn't.

Our work, especially the work around equity, is not simple or direct or easy. It often feels pointless, and it's tempting to give up after trying three to five times. But don't. You may have to try some new strategies, such as finding someone with formal power who has already bought into what you're trying to do and get them to deliver a serving to their peers.

All of this, of course, comes with a caveat. Some of us, especially those from marginalized communities, are very tired of force-feeding equity, diversity, inclusion, and justice to people who have power and influence, but are still very resistant to change. Those of you who are white and male allies and others with more privilege, you may have to jump in because a lot of times, your privilege may allow you to be able to deliver the same messages better than others can.

Still, the point is a lot of change comes from persistent effort over a long period of time. It comes with frustration and exhaustion and a fair amount of cussing. Sometimes you may have to rest and have others take over. But don't give up or feel like what you're doing isn't making a difference. You may be one serving away from a breakthrough, and if not, you may have done the critical step of having pushed an individual, organization, or movement one step closer toward it.

We Bend the Arc

I know this work is not easy, especially over the past few years. We have been assured repeatedly by various leaders that the arc of the moral universe bends toward justice. Lately, it seems like it's been bending the opposite way, toward cruelty and chaos, and our communities have been stuck in the middle.

On a walk around my neighborhood this weekend, I saw rows of beautiful daffodils, plums, and cherry blossoms getting ready to bloom. Poets often write about flowers "bursting" out of the ground, out of branches, triumphantly, full of life and color. But flowers don't burst, not really. They spend months storing up energy, and then wait patiently, enduring the cold and the hard soil, constantly watching for signs—the rise in temperature, the softening of the Earth. What we see as "bursts" are the culmination of hard, relentless, unseen movements—tiny growth one day at a time.

As you end this chapter, and this book, I want to remind you of the power we have as a sector, and that you have as an individual. Power that has lain dormant like tulip bulbs storing up energy.

No, this work is not easy, but that's why we are needed. It's been demoralizing to see the state of the world, but I do believe, like Arundhati Roy says, that "a better world is on her way." And we are a vital force for ushering in that world. To do that well, we need to reclaim our vision, own our power, and let go of the things that no longer serve us, our communities, and the world. We must have the audacity to take bold and courageous actions.

It is a long road ahead. Please take care of yourself. Get plenty of rest. Spend time with people you love and who love you, because love is resistance. Connect with your neighbors, because community is resistance. Do things you enjoy, because joy is resistance.

I am grateful to you and others who take actions every day to make the world better. I will be there beside you. Let us continue the fight. I believe in us and our sector. The arc of the moral universe bends toward justice—because we are the ones who bend it.

Discussion Questions

1. Considering your work as well as everything you've read in this book, what's a change you think you, your organization, or the sector needs to prioritize to be more effective?
2. What would be the basic steps for getting that done?
3. What are some of the potential barriers preventing it from happening?
4. What elements of the Wheel of Change (hearts and minds, behaviors, and systems) might be driving these challenges? How are these elements affecting one another?
5. Who might be the biggest roadblock? What unconscious agendas and assumptions might explain their immunity to change?
6. What about you? Do you think you may have some immunity to change that may be affecting your ability to work in collaboration with others?
7. Which of the strategies for effecting change have you seen work successfully? Which ones have you seen fail? What other strategies can you think of for getting people to change their opinions or behaviors?
8. Which, if any, might be helpful for your situation?
9. Are there bridges you may need to burn? Are there some you may need to rebuild?
10. How will you sustain yourself in this work when it may take years to see the results, if you ever see them at all?

A

Principles of Community-Centric Fundraising

HERE ARE THE main principles of community-centric fundraising (CCF). As this is a movement, the principles may change and evolve, and not everyone will agree with all the examples listed of what they look like in action. Use this as a starting point as you explore CCF. Go to communitycentricfundraising.org for the latest information and lessons learned and to build community with other CCF practitioners.

Principle 1: We Ground Fundraising in Race, Equity, and Social Justice

These elements must be centered in everything related to raising funds. They must inform and guide every decision and action taken by fundraisers.

- Provide fundraising professionals with regular training in undoing racism and other equity topics.
- Create opportunities for donors to engage in conversations about race and examine the source of their wealth.
- Call out when donors are being racist, ableist, sexist, transphobic, and so on.
- Hire and invest in fundraisers who come from marginalized communities.
- Address disparity in pay and responsibilities on fundraising teams.

Principle 2: We Prioritize the Collective Community over Individual Missions

Nonprofit missions are interrelated, and the community is best served if we see ourselves as part of a larger ecosystem working collectively to build a just society.

- Avoid actions that benefit one's nonprofit at the cost to other nonprofits. For instance, do not boast about your organization's low overhead rate because that furthers the belief that overhead is bad, which affects all nonprofits.
- When forced to choose, prioritize what's best for the entire community over what's best for one's own organizations.
- Decline funding opportunities so that other organizations that do critical work in the community have a better chance if that best serves the community.
- Check annually to see if your mission is still relevant and responsive to community needs.
- Adjust, merge, or shut down if your nonprofit's presence negatively affects the community.

Principle 3: We Are Generous and Mutually Supportive of Other Missions

Nonprofits see and treat one another not as competitors, but as critical partners with the common mission of strengthening the community.

- Share resources, such as funding opportunities, relevant data, tools, and advice.
- Introduce one another to existing and potential donors.
- Give credit to one another publicly, during events and in publications such as annual reports.
- Help other organizations during important campaigns, such as when they're trying to get certain bills passed.
- Avoid applying for grants, and decline funding if your organization has sufficient funds.

Principle 4: We Value and Appreciate Equally All Elements That Strengthen Community

We respect, appreciate, recognize, and build relationships with our donors equally, no matter their level of giving. And we use the same approach with and have the same appreciation of others in the sector, including staff, board members, volunteers, and clients.

- Compensate staff fairly, invest in their growth, and appreciate them as much as you appreciate donors.
- Appreciate board members for their contributions and invest in their growth as leaders.
- Treat volunteers with respect and gratitude.
- See clients not just as recipients of your services, but also as vital contributors to the work.
- Recognize all donors of every level equally.
- Avoid terms like "major donors."
- Avoid giving special recognition and treatment to those who give more financially.
- End all employee giving campaigns, where employees are asked to donate a portion of their earnings back to the organizations that employ them. This prioritizes money as the most important contribution.

Principle 5: We Value Time Equally as Money

Time is the only resource we cannot make more of, and thus the donation of time (from volunteers and from staff who work unpaid hours) must be valued as much as the donation of money.

- Understand that, especially for many marginalized community members who may not have the financial means to contribute to an organization, the gift of time is significant and should be treated as such.
- Treat donors of time the way you treat donors of money.

- Send handwritten thank-you notes and make thank-you calls to volunteers, clients, and even staff for all the extra hours they donate to the organization.
- Recognize and acknowledge when team members put in a lot more time than they are getting paid for, and provide compensation.

Principle 6: We Respect Our Donors' Integrity and Treat Donors as Partners

Have honest, respectful conversations, including strong disagreements as needed, with your donors. Do not hide challenging truths from donors, but instead treat them as adults who are capable of handling difficult conversations and feedback.

- Create opportunities for donors to further their understanding of the complexity of nonprofit work.
- Respectfully and firmly push back when donors do or say things that may be detrimental to the work or to the community you are serving.
- Be honest and transparent with your donors about the resources that it takes to comply with their wishes and to maintain relationships with them, and push back when that becomes excessive.
- End relationships with donors if their presence or demands come at the expense of your clients and community.

Principle 7: We Foster a Sense of Belonging in Our Fundraising Work; We Avoid Treating Anyone as an "Other"

Strive to ensure everyone feels a sense of belonging, whether they are donor, volunteers, staff, or clients, and authentically partner with community members when asking them to be involved in fundraising efforts.

- Obtain informed consent from community members when asking them to share their stories for fundraising purposes.
- Be thoughtful about what images you use on your websites, brochures, and social media in order to avoid poverty porn.

- Use "we" language that includes the donor as part of the community doing this work.
- Have reasonably priced tickets to events so people of all income levels can participate.
- Seat clients, volunteers, staff, and donors together, instead of having donors in the front of the room and clients and volunteers in the back.
- Ensure all events, whether in-person or virtual, are accessible to people who use wheelchairs, who are deaf or hard of hearing, or who are blind or have low vision.

Principle 8: We Encourage Everyone to Believe We All Benefit from This Work

Some call it "enlightened self-interest." It is important to get donors to see they and their families benefit from their donations, that they are not donating only for others' benefits.

- Help donors examine their role in the work and what they have to gain in creating a just and equitable world.
- Audit communications and remove language that conditions donors to believe they are heroes and saviors.
- Use language that includes donors as part of the community that benefits from the work, such as "with everyone's support, we create a strong and vibrant community that works for us all."

Principle 9: We Treat the Work as Holistic, Not a Collection of Isolated Segments

We need to stop simplifying our work and breaking it into misleading parts, and instead get everyone to see and understand how the entire sector operates.

- Report holistically on how donors' contributions have helped. Do not segment out by which donors paid for what. For instance, do NOT say, "Your $100 bought school supplies for 10 kids." Instead say something like, "Your donation, combined with funding from grants and other donors, along with support from

volunteers and staff helped provide over 800 kids with school supplies this year."
- Encourage funders and donors to understand and support core mission support, also known as overhead or indirect expenses.
- Accurately report how high your core support expenses are.
- Avoid saying things like, "We got a funder/donor to underwrite this event, so 100 percent of your donations go to programs and services."

Principle 10: We Recognize That Healing and Liberation Requires a Commitment to Economic Justice

This involves fundraisers and donors grappling with and addressing the root causes of inequity, including the destructive effects of capitalism and how we may be complicit in furthering them through our practices.

- Support progressive policies such as universal basic income, free healthcare and higher education, raising minimum wage, tenants' rights, and so on.
- Work toward changing tax policies so wealthy individuals and corporations pay their fair share.
- Educate funders and donors on worker exploitation, environmental degradation, colonialism, and other inequities that lead to the existence of philanthropy in the first place.

B

White Moderation Checklist

Here are a few ways White Moderation shows up in nonprofit and philanthropy. Go through the list by yourself, and then discuss with your team how many of them you or your organization participate in and how often. This list is not comprehensive. In what other ways do you think White Moderation shows up?

1. Calling for unity and for people to get along instead of focusing on white supremacy and other causes of inequity
2. Steering away from publicly condemning white supremacy, racism, fascism, and so on because that might affect funding
3. Prioritizing the feelings of white donors and avoiding anything that could make them uncomfortable
4. Encouraging people to be more "civil" or to use a "respectful tone" when having conversations about race and other challenging subjects
5. Avoiding anything that may be too "political"
6. Being more worried about organizational reputation or upsetting team dynamics than about inequity and injustice
7. Using white-people-determined standards such as academic writing, formal credentials, "articulate" speech, and "professional" personal appearance to judge people and organizations' intelligence and effectiveness, which often rewards white men and white-led orgs
8. Avoiding talking about race white supremacy and instead talking only about class and other factors contributing to injustice

9. Spending significant time and money to "find" solutions when marginalized communities have already proposed solutions multiple times
10. Helping marginalized people and organizations survive and compete in inequitable systems instead of working with them to dismantle those systems
11. Allowing racist, sexist, white supremacist, and other hateful views to have airtime for the sake of "diversity of thoughts/perspectives" or "equal time"
12. Dismissing people's actions to advance social justice if they're not done through the "right" and "proper" channels
13. Spending more energy comforting the privileged when their privilege is challenged and they're upset than addressing the injustice suffered by marginalized people and communities
14. Prioritizing costs over equity, for example, going with the cheapest vendors/contractors than intentionally hiring women- and BIPOC-owned businesses
15. Playing devil's advocate when activists and organizers bring up solutions that may actually lead to radical changes
16. Saying marginalized people and communities complain too much and that they don't offer enough solutions
17. Acting on the belief that the potentially equitable ends justify the inequitable means you may use to get there, for example not, paying interns or not providing disabled people fair wages
18. Believing in radical changes in theory but thinking people should be pragmatic and incremental in their approach

In foundations, White Moderation additionally manifests in:

- Refusing to increase funding given out each year beyond the bare legal minimum 5 percent of endowments, believing it's more important to hoard resources for the future than to spend out more to effectively address current injustice

- Striving to create "objective" processes for grants and so on, believing that would ensure those with the most merit would be selected
- Making major decisions, such as grant selections, on the timeline of and what's convenient for wealthy foundation trustees
- Funding research, white papers, and other intellectual projects in lieu of strategies proposed by marginalized communities
- Avoiding funding advocacy and systems change work

Notes

Chapter 1

1. Independent Sector, "Impact of America's Nonprofit Sector," 2024, https://independentsector.org/wp-content/uploads/2024/04/is-sector-impact-2024.pdf.
2. Johns Hopkins Center for Civil Society Studies, "2020 Nonprofit Employment Report," *Nonprofit Economic Bulletin* No. 48, June 2020, https://baypath.s3.amazonaws.com/files/resources/2020-nonprofit-employment-report-final-6-2020.pdf.
3. LendThrive, "Overhead Costs for Small Businesses: Calculate & Reduce," May 30, 2022, https://lendthrive.com/blog/overhead-costs-for-small-businesses.
4. Allison Carney Consulting, "Bizsplaining: Mansplaining for Nonprofits," February 25, 2016, https://allisoncarney.com/2016/02/25/bizsplaining-mansplaining-for-nonprofits/.
5. U.S. Bureau of Labor Statistics, "Business Employment Dynamics: Establish Age and Survival Data," https://www.bls.gov/bdm/bdmage.htm.
6. Arundhati Roy, "No Propaganda on Earth Can Hide the Wound That Is Palestine: Arundhati Roy's PEN Pinter Prize Acceptance Speech," The Wire, October 11, 2024, https://thewire.in/rights/palestine-israel-apartheid-arundhati-roy-pen-pinter-prize.
7. Venkatesh Rao, "The Gramsci Gap," Contraptions, January 10, 2025, https://contraptions.venkateshrao.com/p/the-gramsci-gap.

Chapter 2

1. KMBC News 9, "This is How Much America's 10 Largest Cities Spend on Police, Other Services," KMBC.com, June 12, 2020, https://www.kmbc.com/article/us-police-department-budget-10-cities/32850512.
2. Center on Juvenile & Criminal Justice, "More Law Enforcement Spending Accompanies Worse, Not Improved Crime-solving," October 21, 2024, https://www.cjcj.org/reports-publications/report/more-law-enforcement-spending-accompanies-worse-not-improved-crime-solving.
3. University of Illinois Chicago School of Public Health Law Enforcement Epidemiology Project, "U.S. Data on Police Shootings and Violence," https://policeepi.uic.edu/u-s-data-on-police-shootings-and-violence/.
4. Martin Luther King, Jr. "Letter from a Birmingham Jail," April 16, 1962, https://www.africa.upenn.edu/Articles_Gen/Letter_Birmingham.html.
5. The Onion, "Nonprofit Fights Poverty With Poverty," July 28, 2006, https://theonion.com/nonprofit-fights-poverty-with-poverty-1819568577/.
6. Phil Buchanan, "Who Runs the Big Foundations? A Look at the Leadership of the Largest 100 Foundations," The Center for Effective Philanthropy, https://cep.org/who-runs-the-big-foundations-a-look-at-the-leadership-of-the-largest-100-foundations/.
7. Andrea Arenas, "Philanthropy's Golden Handcuffs: The Illusion of Liberation and the Complex Balance Between Self-Preservation and Complacency Among Foundation Workers," Community-Centric Fundraising, August 7, 2023, https://communitycentricfundraising.org/2023/08/07/philanthropys-golden-handcuffs-the-illusion-of-liberation-and-the-complex-balance-between-self-preservation-and-complacency-among-foundation-workers/.
8. Claire Reilly, "Juicero is Still the Greatest Example of Silicon Valley Stupidity," CNET, September 1, 2018, https://www.cnet.com/culture/juicero-is-still-the-greatest-example-of-silicon-valley-stupidity/.
9. Ellen Huet and Olivia Zaleski, "Do You Need a $400 Juicer?" Bloomberg, April 19, 2017, https://www.bloomberg.com/news/features/2017-04-19/silicon-valley-s-400-juicer-may-be-feeling-the-squeeze.
10. Devin Coldewey, "Juicero May be the Absurd Avatar of Silicon Valley Hubris, Buy Boy Is It Well-engineered," TechCrunch, April 24, 2017, https://techcrunch.com/2017/04/24/juicero-may-be-the-absurd-avatar-of-silicon-valley-hubris-but-boy-is-it-well-engineered/.
11. Eviana Hartman, "Introducing the Completely Mess-Proof Juicer That Will Change Your Life," *Vogue Magazine*, March 31, 2016, https://www.vogue.com/article/juicero-cold-pressed-juice-home-juicer-no-mess

Chapter 3

1. Vivien Trinh, "Focusing on Fundraising Goals Is Harmful—Let's Measure Love Instead," Community-Centric Fundraising, April 10, 2021, https://communitycentricfundraising.org/2021/04/16/focusing-on-fundraising-goals-is-harmful-lets-measure-love-instead/.
2. Classy, "6 Fundraising Psychology Hacks You Need to Know," March 30, 2018, https://medium.com/classy-blog/6-fundraising-psychology-hacks-you-need-to-know-5debb7da5ef4.
3. Paul Bloom, "Think Empathy Makes the World a Better Place? Think Again. . ." February 18, 2017, https://www.theguardian.com/commentisfree/2017/feb/19/think-empathy-makes-world-better-place-think-again.
4. Emily Burack, "Austrian Heiress Marlene Engelhorn Is Giving Away Her $27 Million Fortune," *Town & Country Magazine*, January 11, 2024, https://www.townandcountrymag.com/society/money-and-power/a46351899/marlene-engelhorn-heiress-giving-away-fortune/.
5. Andrea Miller, "How Companies like Amazon, Nike, and FedEx Avoid Paying Federal Taxes," CNBC, April 14, 2022, https://www.cnbc.com/2022/04/14/how-companies-like-amazon-nike-and-fedex-avoid-paying-federal-taxes-.html.
6. Casey Newton, "Amazon is Finally Realizing it Has a Labor Problem," The Verge, April 16, 2021, https://www.theverge.com/2021/4/16/22386992/amazon-is-finally-realizing-it-has-a-labor-problem.
7. Detroit Justice Center, "Detroit Justice Venter Welcomes $2 Million from Yield Giving Open Call," March 20, 2024, https://detroitjustice.org/detroit-justice-center-welcomes-2-million-donation-from-yield-giving-open-call/.
8. CompassPoint, "Underdeveloped: A National Study of Challenges Facing Nonprofit Fundraising," https://www.compasspoint.org/underdeveloped.

Chapter 4

1. Ontario Nonprofit Network, "ONN Governance Framework," https://theonn.ca/wp-content/uploads/2021/05/ONN_Governance-Framework_2021_final.pdf.
2. Erin Kang, "Governance as Shared Leadership for Nonprofits," Ontario Nonprofit Network, January 27, 2023, https://theonn.ca/2023/01/governance-as-shared-leadership-for-nonprofits/.

244 Notes

3. Ananda Valenzuela, "New Framework for Governance Duties: Loving Accountability and Abundant Resourcing," *Nonprofit Quarterly*, February 11, 2025, https://nonprofitquarterly.org/a-new-framework-for-governance-duties-loving-accountability-and-abundant-resourcing/.
4. Em Ironstar, Personal Communications, February 10, 2025.
5. Amy Fontinelle, "How Much Board of Directors Members Get Paid and What They Do," *Investopedia*, September 24, 2024, https://www.investopedia.com/articles/wealth-management/040416/retired-execs-what-do-corporate-boards-pay.asp.
6. Philanthropy News Digest, "New Report Looks at Foundation Trustee Compensation," September 3, 2003, https://philanthropynewsdigest.org/news/new-report-looks-at-foundation-trustee-compensation.
7. Wikipedia, "Robert's Rules of Order," https://en.wikipedia.org/wiki/Robert%27s_Rules_of_Order.
8. Erin Kang
9. Doing Better Work Together, "How Enspiral Developed Culture and Processes for Distributed Governance," YouTube, November 30, 2022, https://www.youtube.com/watch?app=desktop&v=zR4lkWj4xaQ.
10. https://vanessalebourdais.medium.com/evolutionary-governance-part-i-principles-772e18345881
11. Vanessa LeBourdais, "Evolutionary Governance; Part I: Principles," Medium, September 16, 2020, https://vanessalebourdais.medium.com/evolutionary-governance-part-ii-practices-92ddf7604449.
12. Natale Bamdad and Mark Leach, "Experimenting Towards Liberated Governance," December 9, 2021, Change Elemental, https://changeelemental.org/resources/liberated-governance/.
13. Living Justice Press, "What Do We Mean by 'Circle?'" https://livingjusticepress.org/what-do-we-mean-by-circle/.
14. Sociocracy for All, Homepage, https://www.sociocracyforall.org/.
15. Yodit Mesfin Johnson, Personal Communication, February 7, 2025.
16. Facilitators Academy, *The Mindful Meetings Guide*," https://tinyurl.com/e9jzaht5.

Chapter 5

1. RVC, "Let's Change How We Define Perfect," May 14, 2018, https://rvcseattle.org/2018/05/14/lets-change-define-perfect/.
2. Building Movement, "The Push and Pull: Declining Interest in Nonprofit Leadership," 2024, https://buildingmovement.org/wp-content/uploads/2024/01/BMP_The-Push-and-Pull-Report_Final.pdf.

3. RVC, "The Executive Director Jobs Is Impossible," February 21, 2018, https://rvcseattle.org/2018/02/21/executive-director-job-impossible/.
4. Robert K. Greenleaf, "The Servant as Leader," *Servant Leadership*, 1977, http://www.ediguys.net/Robert_K_Greenleaf_The_Servant_as_Leader.pdf.
5. Vu Le, "The Best Leaders May Be Those Who 'Give Up'," *Stanford Social Innovation Review*, June 26, 2018, https://ssir.org/articles/entry/the_best_leaders_may_be_those_who_give_up.
6. Aja Couchois Duncan, Susan Misra, and Vincent Pan, "Cultivating Leaderful Ecosystems," *Nonprofit Quarterly*, April 21, 2017, https://nonprofitquarterly.org/cultivating-leaderful-ecosystems/.
7. Building Movement, "The Push and Pull: Declining Interest in Nonprofit Leadership," 2024, https://buildingmovement.org/wp-content/uploads/2024/01/BMP_The-Push-and-Pull-Report_Final.pdf.
8. Strela Cervas, *Nonprofit Leadership Models*, Asian Pacific Environmental Network, 2021, https://apen4ej.org/wp-content/uploads/2022/03/APEN-Report-Nonprofit-Leadership-Models.pdf.
9. Caroline McAndrews, Frances Kunreuther, and Shifra Bronznick, "Structuring Leadership," 2011, https://buildingmovement.org/wp-content/uploads/2019/08/Structuring-Leadership-Alternative-Models-for-Distributing-Power-and-Decision-Making-in-Nonprofit-Organizations.pdf.
10. Sustainable Economies Law Center, "Workplace Democracy in Nonprofit Organizations," June 3, 2015, https://www.theselc.org/workplace_democracy_in_nonprofit_organizations.
11. Sustainable Economies Law Center, "Resources for Worker Self-Directed Nonprofits," https://www.theselc.org/wsdn_resources.
12. Jo Freeman (aka Joreen), "The Tyranny of Structurelessness," https://www.jofreeman.com/joreen/tyranny.htm.
13. Simon Mont, "Autopsy of a Failed Holacracy: Lessons in Justice, Equity, and Self-Management," *Nonprofit Quarterly*, January 9, 2017, https://nonprofitquarterly.org/autopsy-failed-holacracy-lessons-justice-equity-self-management/.
14. Reinventing Organizations Wiki, https://reinventingorganizationswiki.com/en/.

Chapter 6

1. Kenneth Rainin Foundation, "Reexamining Capacity Building," 2024, https://krfoundation.org/wp-content/uploads/2024/08/KennethRaininFoundation_Reexamining-Capacity-Building_web.pdf.

2. National Committee for Responsive Philanthropy, "*Moving a Public Policy Agenda: The Strategic Philanthropy of Conservative Foundations,*" July 1997, https://ncrp.org/wp-content/uploads/2016/11/Moving-a-Public-Policy-Agenda.pdf.
3. Cina Lawson and Rory Stewart, "A Global Cash-Transfer Fund Could End Extreme Poverty," GiveDirectly, February 28, 2024, https://www.givedirectly.org/a-global-cash-transfer-fund-could-end-extreme-poverty/.
4. Jeanne Bell, Richard Moyers, and Timothy Wolfred, "Daring to Lead 2006," CompassPoint Nonprofit Services and the Meyer Foundation, https://www.compasspoint.org/sites/default/files/documents/194_daringtolead06final.pdf.
5. April Nishimura, et al., "Transformational Capacity Building," *Stanford Social Innovation Review*, Fall 2020, https://rvcseattle.org/wp-content/uploads/2020/10/Fall2020-Feature-Nishimura-Capacity-Building_1.pdf.
6. Hildy Gottlieb, "Building Movements, Not Organizations," *Stanford Social Innovation Review*, July 28, 2015, https://ssir.org/articles/entry/building_movements_not_organizations.
7. Thaddeus Squire, "Four Ways the Nonprofit Sector Can Tell the Trump Administration to F**ck Off," The Undersector, February 8, 2025, https://thaddeussquire.substack.com/p/four-ways-the-nonprofit-sector-can.

Chapter 7

1. Lews Faulk, Mirae Kim, and Heather MacIndoe, "The Retreat of Influence," https://independentsector.org/wp-content/uploads/2023/07/PENS-Advocacy-Report.pdf.
2. Quorum, "Tough Months Ahead for Nonprofit Public Affairs Teams," September 5, 2024, https://www.quorum.us/blog/survey-tough-months-ahead-for-nonprofit-public-affairs-teams/.
3. Kevin Dean, "An Open Letter to National Foundations and Nonprofit Organizations," Nonprofit Network, February 11, 2025, https://tnnonprofits.org/an-open-letter-to-national-foundations-and-nonprofit-organizations/.
4. Jan Masaoka, "Aspirin and Democracy," *Stanford Social Innovation Review*, June 21, 2018, https://ssir.org/articles/entry/aspirin_and_democracy.
5. Jasleen Singh and Sara Carter, "States Have Added Nearly 100 Restrictive Laws Since SCOTUS Gutted the Voting Rights Act 10 Years Ago," Brennan Center for Justice, June 23, 2023, https://www.brennancenter.org/our-work/analysis-opinion/states-have-added-nearly-100-restrictive-laws-scotus-gutted-voting-rights.

6. Matthew Haag, "Mitch McConnell Calls Push to Make Election Day a Holiday a Democratic 'Power Grab'," *The New York Times*, January 31, 2019, https://www.nytimes.com/2019/01/31/us/politics/election-day-holiday-mcconnell.html.
7. Jim Collins, "*Good to Great.*" HarperCollins, 2001.
8. Nonprofit Vote, "Nonprofit Power: Building an Inclusive Democracy," 2024, https://www.nonprofitvote.org/wp-content/uploads/2024/03/2024-Nonprofit-Power-digital-edition.pdf.
9. Viet Rainbow of Orange County, "Our Story," https://www.vietroc.org/history.
10. Jasmine Banks, Email Communication on February 17, 2025.
11. University of Washington Center for Studies in Demography & Ecology, "Expanding Participation in Municipal Elections: Assessing the Impact of Seattle's Democracy Voucher Program," https://www.seattle.gov/documents/Departments/EthicsElections/DemocracyVoucher/Biennial%20Reports/UW_Seattle_Voucher_Final.pdf.
12. Shannon Grimes, "Six Reasons Seattleites Should Be Proud of Their Democracy Vouchers," Sightline Institute, May 27, 2025, https://www.sightline.org/2025/05/27/six-reasons-seattleites-should-be-proud-of-their-democracy-vouchers/.

Chapter 8

1. Vanessa Daniel, "Philanthropists Bench Women of Color, the M.V.P.s of Social Change," *The New York Times*, November 19, 2019, https://www.nytimes.com/2019/11/19/opinion/philanthropy-black-women.html.
2. Edgar Villanueva, *Decolonizing Wealth: Indigenous Wisdom to Heal Divides and Restore Balance* (Berrett-Koehler Publishers, Inc.,), 2018.
3. Malkia Devich Cyril, et al., "*Mismatched,*" Philanthropic Racial Equity, September 2021, https://racialequity.org/wp-content/uploads/2021/10/PRE_Mismatched_PR_141.pdf.
4. Susan Taylor Batten and Nat Chioke Williams, "The Case for Funding Black-Led Social Change," ABFE and the Hill-Snowdon Foundation, 2017, https://www.abfe.org/system/files/documents/2024-08/BSCFN-Case-Statement.pdf.
5. Native Americans in Philanthropy, "Native Americans are 2.9% of U.S. Population But Receive 0.4% of Philanthropic Dollars," November 17, 2020, https://nativephilanthropy.org/blog/2020/11/17/native-americans-are-2-of-u-s-population-but-receive-0-4-of-philanthropic-dollars.

248   NOTES

6. Trust-Based Philanthropy Project, "What Is TBP?," https://www.trustbasedphilanthropy.org/.
7. Pia Infante, "The Future of Philanthropy Is Trust-Based," *Stanford Social Innovation Review*, Spring 2024, https://ssir.org/pdf/Spring_24_Suppl_Building_a_Multiracial_Democracy.pdf.
8. National Committee for Responsive Philanthropy, "Moving a Public Policy Agenda: The Strategic Philanthropy of Conservative Foundations," July 1997, https://ncrp.org/wp-content/uploads/2016/11/Moving-a-Public-Policy-Agenda.pdf.
9. Hal Harvey, "Why I Regret Pushing Philanthropy," *Chronicle of Philanthropy*, April 4, 2016, https://gwpa.org/sites/default/files/resources/Chronicle%20-%20Why%20I%20Regret%20Pushing%20Strategic%20Philanthropy.pdf.
10. Andrew Perez, Andy Kroll, and Justin Elliott, "How a Secretive Billionaire Handed His Fortune to the Architect of the Right-Wing Takeover of the Courts," ProPublica, August 22, 2022, https://www.propublica.org/article/dark-money-leonard-leo-barre-seid.
11. Julia Mueller, "Who is Barre Seid, the Billionaire Who Donated Rector $1.6 Billion to Conservative Group?" The Hill, August 23, 2022, https://thehill.com/homenews/campaign/3612396-who-is-barre-seid-the-billionaire-who-donated-record-1-6-billion-to-conservative-group/.
12. Candid, "Center for American Progress," https://app.candid.org/profile/7303672.
13. Candid, "Institute for Policy Studies," https://app.candid.org/profile/7747870.
14. Candid, "The Heritage Foundation," https://app.candid.org/profile/7207066.
15. Rajasvini Bhansali, "Philanthropy Must Safeguard Our Right to Protest, a Key Pathway to Progress," Inside Philanthropy, June 27, 2024, https://www.insidephilanthropy.com/home/2024-6-27-philanthropy-must-safeguard-our-right-to-protest-a-key-pathway-to-progress.
16. Hannah Finnie, et al., "Building Tomorrow: The Need For Sustained Investment in America's Progressive Youth," Generation Progress and Young People For, April 2017, https://genprogress.org/wp-content/uploads/2017/04/04200346/Youth-Infrastructure-Paper-FINAL.pdf.
17. Elizabeth Bibi, "Human Rights Campaign Calls Out New York Times for Publishing Transphobic Column One Day After an Open Letter Condemning its Anti-Transgender Coverage," Human Rights Campaign, February 16, 2023, https://www.hrc.org/press-releases/human-rights-campaign-calls-out-new-york-times-for-publishing-transphobic-

column-one-day-after-an-open-letter-condemning-its-anti-transgender-coverage.
18. Brigitte Alepin, "The Growing Tax Threat from Private Charity Foundations," *Policy Options*, December 5, 2024, https://policyoptions.irpp.org/magazines/december-2024/private-charity-foundations/.
19. Foundation Advocate, "2024 Gains," https://www.foundationadvocate.com/2024-gains/.
20. Dimple Abichandani, "*A New Era of Philanthropy*" Penguin Random House, 2025, page 24.
21. Michelle Morales, "Increasing Our Payout for Longterm Grantmaking," Woods Funds Chicago, https://t.e2ma.net/message/lorigj/5n080q3n.
22. Dan Parks, "General Operating Support Is Vital to Advancing Equity, Strengthening Nonprofits, Say Leaders," *Chronicle of Philanthropy*, April 12, 2022, https://www.philanthropy.com/article/general-operating-support-is-vital-to-advancing-equity-strengthening-nonprofits-say-leaders?sra=tru.
23. National Committee for Responsive Philanthropy, "Moving a Public Policy Agenda: The Strategic Philanthropy of Conservative Foundations," July 1997, https://ncrp.org/wp-content/uploads/2016/11/Moving-a-Public-Policy-Agenda.pdf.
24. Peak Grantmaking, "Project Streamline," https://www.peakgrantmaking.org/principles-for-peak-grantmaking/project-streamline/.
25. Iara Duarte Peng, "The Origin and Impact of the JustFund Common Application (Part 1)," Just Fund, https://justfund.us/the-origin-and-impact-of-the-justfund-common-application/.

Chapter 9

1. Aysa Gray, "The Bias of 'Professionalism' Standards," *Stanford Social Innovation Review*, June 4, 2019, https://ssir.org/articles/entry/the_bias_of_professionalism_standards.
2. Alice Wong, *Year of the Tiger: An Activist's Life* (Penguin Random House), 2022, pages 227–228
3. Bill Leonard, "Study Suggests Bias Against 'Black' Names On Resumes, February 1, 2003, Society for Human Resource Management (SHRM), https://www.shrm.org/topics-tools/news/hr-magazine/study-suggests-bias-black-names-resumes#:~:text=The%20results%20are%20a%20bit,men%20and%20women%20were%20contacted.

4. Patrick Kline, Evan K. Rose, and Christopher R. Walters, "A Discrimination Report Card," The University of Chicago Becker Friedman Institute for Economics," April 8, 2024, https://bfi.uchicago.edu/insight/research-summary/a-discrimination-report-card/.
5. The Muse Editors, "Achieving Gender Equity at Work and in the Hiring Process is Still a Work in Progress," The Muse, March 26, 2024, https://www.themuse.com/advice/womens-workplace-experience-report.
6. ABA Commission on Disability Rights, "Implicit Biases & People with Disabilities," American Bar Association, https://www.americanbar.org/groups/diversity/disabilityrights/resources/implicit_bias/.
7. Heather Barbour Fenty, "20 Helpful Examples of Gender Coded Words in Job Ads," Ongig, July 21, 2021, https://blog.ongig.com/diversity-and-inclusion/list-of-gender-coded-words/.
8. Erika Andersen, "Is 'Cultural Fit' Just A New Way To Discriminate," Forbes, March 17, 2015, https://www.forbes.com/sites/erikaandersen/2015/03/17/is-cultural-fit-just-a-new-way-to-discriminate/#73497d193923.
9. National Women's Law Center, "Pay Range Transparency Is Critical for Driving Pay Equity," March 2024, https://nwlc.org/wp-content/uploads/2024/03/Pay-Range-Transparency-2024v2.pdf.
10. Christina Marfice, "Pay Transparency Laws: A State-by-state Guide [Updated 2025]," Rippling Blog, May 26, 2024, https://www.rippling.com/blog/pay-transparency-laws-state-by-state-guide.
11. HR Dive, "Salary History Bans," April 30, 2025, https://www.hrdive.com/news/salary-history-ban-states-list/516662/.
12. Ryan Golden and Kathryn Moody, "Resource Actions: Would You Pay a Candidate for Time Spent Interviewing?" HR Dive, October 2, 2020, https://www.hrdive.com/news/resource-actions-pay-candidate-time-interviewing/586357/.
13. DRG Talent Consulting Experts, "Emerging Trend: Compensating Candidates for Interviews and/or Skills Assessments," September 5, 2023, https://drgtalent.com/emerging-trend-compensating-candidates-for-interviews-and-or-skills-assessments.
14. NCSL, "Racial and Ethnic Disparities in the Criminal Justice System," May 24, 2022, https://www.ncsl.org/civil-and-criminal-justice/racial-and-ethnic-disparities-in-the-criminal-justice-system.
15. Center for American Progress, "America's Broken Criminal Legal System Contributes to Wealth Inequality," December 13, 2022, https://www.americanprogress.org/article/americas-broken-criminal-legal-system-contributes-to-wealth-inequality/.

Chapter 10

1. Beth Kanter and Aliza Sherman, "*The Happy, Healthy Nonprofit: Strategies for Impact Without Burnout*," Wiley, 2017, https://happyhealthynonprofit.wordpress.com/.
2. Judy Lubin, et al., "Talent Justice Report: Investing in Equity in the Nonprofit Workforce," https://fundthepeople.org/toolkit/wp-content/uploads/2019/05/Talent-Justice-Report.pdf.
3. The Durfee Foundation, https://durfee.org/.
4. David Burkus, "Research Shows That Organizations Benefit When Employees Take Sabbaticals," *Harvard Business Review*, August 10, 2017, https://hbr.org/2017/08/research-shows-that-organizations-benefit-when-employees-take-sabbaticals.
5. Dave Roos, "The 5-Day Work Week: How We Got Here," History.com, August 26, 2024, https://www.history.com/news/five-day-work-week-labor-movement.
6. Isaiah Thompson, "The Growing Movement for a Four-Day Workweek," *Nonprofit Quarterly*, February 13, 2024, https://nonprofitquarterly.org/the-growing-movement-for-a-four-day-workweek/.
7. Adam Jespersen, "MNA Pilots a Four Day Work Week," MNA, June 30, 2022, https://mtnonprofit.org/mna-resources/mna-pilots-a-four-day-work-week/.
8. Common Future, "Four-Day Workweek," https://commonfuture.co/four-day-workweek.
9. Jim Rendon, "Why Workers at Growing Number of Nonprofits are Unionizing," Associated Press, January 31, 2023, https://apnews.com/article/labor-unions-southern-poverty-law-center-business-race-and-ethnicity-7fd961c88c614db47db63ffcd80e084e.
10. Mental Health America, "Quick Facts: Quick Mental Health Facts and Statistics," https://mhanational.org/quick-facts/.
11. Kevin Dean, CEO of the Tennessee Nonprofit Network, https://tnnonprofits.org/employees-with-mental-health-diagnoses-can-beassets-not-liabilities/.

Chapter 11

1. Staff Writer, "How Colonialists Used Phrenology, A Pseudoscience, To Justify Racism & Slavery," *Madras Courier*, January 4, 2024, https://madrascourier.com/insight/how-colonialists-used-phrenology-a-pseudoscience-to-justify-racism-slavery/.

252   Notes

2. Shasha Seakamela, "Black Hair – Bridging a 'Code of Conduct'," Fair Planet, September 20, 2016, https://www.fairplanet.org/story/black-hair-bridging-a-code-of-conduct/.
3. Jondou Chen, Personal Communication, July 15, 2014.
4. Rochelle Gutiérrez, "A 'Gap-Gazing' Fetish in Mathematics Education? Problematizing Research on the Achievement Gap," *Journal for Research in Mathematics Education* 39(4), July 2008, https://www.jstor.org/stable/40539302?seq=1&cid=pdf-reference#page_scan_tab_contents.
5. Taylor Pellizzari, "The Radical History of the Free Breakfast Program," Solid Ground, September 14, 2020, https://www.solid-ground.org/the-radical-history-of-the-free-breakfast-program/.
6. Fakequity, "The Problem with Curb Cuts," March 4, 2024, https://fakequity.com/2021/03/04/the-problem-with-curb-cuts/.
7. Isabeau Boody, "LinkedIn Post," January 28, 2025, https://www.linkedin.com/posts/isabeauboody_i-love-that-people-are-trying-to-be-supportive-activity-7290419283761778688-DYLk?utm_source=share&utm_medium=member_ios.

Chapter 12

1. Jonathan Franklin, "A Venture Capital Grant Program for Black Women Officially Ends After Court Ruling," NPR, September 11, 2024, https://www.npr.org/2024/09/11/nx-s1-5108729/fearless-fund-atlanta-grant-program-shut-down-lawsuit.
2. Centers for Disease Control, "Cancer and African American People," February 13, 2025, https://www.cdc.gov/cancer/health-equity/african-american.html.
3. Erin and the Fakequity Team, "Welcome to the Fakequity Blog," Fakequity, https://fakequity.com/welcome-to-the-fakequity-blog/.
4. (un)Redact the Facts, "(*un*)Redact the Facts of (*hi*)Story to Tell a Full(*er*) Story for Racial Equity + Healing," https://www.unredacthefacts.com/.
5. Martin Luther King, Jr., "Letter from Birmingham Jail," August 1963, https://www.csuchico.edu/iege/_assets/documents/susi-letter-from-birmingham-jail.pdf.
6. Personal Communication, March 2, 2025.
7. Laure Marhoefer, "Historians are Learning More About How the Nazis Targeted Trans People," The Conversation, June 6, 2023, https://theconversation.com/historians-are-learning-more-about-how-the-nazis-targeted-trans-people-205622.
8. Jay Smooth's TED Talk called "How I Learned to Stop Worrying and Love Discussing Race," https://www.youtube.com/watch?v=MbdxeFcQtaU.

Chapter 13

1. Art of Tools Consulting, "Wheel of Change Planning Template," Change Elemental, 2022, https://atctools.org/toolkit_tool/wheel-of-change-planning-template/.
2. Robert Kegan and Lisa Lahey, "The Real Reason People Won't Change," *Harvard Business Review*, November 2001, https://hbr.org/2001/11/the-real-reason-people-wont-change.
3. Melissa De Witte, "50 Years on, Mark Granovetter's 'The Strength of Weak Ties' is Stronger than Ever," *Stanford Report*, July 24, 2023, https://news.stanford.edu/stories/2023/07/strength-weak-ties.
4. Courageous Conversations, https://courageousconversation.com/.
5. Radical Candor, https://www.radicalcandor.com/.
6. Adam Dachis, "How to Plant Ideas in Someone's Mind," Life Hacker, October 22, 2014, https://lifehacker.com/how-to-plant-ideas-in-someones-mind-5715912.
7. Allison Lange, "National Woman's Party and Militant Methods," National Women's History Museum, Fall 2015, https://www.crusadeforthevote.org/nwp-militant.
8. Katie Smith, et al., "Five Accelerators of Equitable Grantmaking and How to Harness Them," *Stanford Social Innovation Review*, April 27, 2022, https://ssir.org/articles/entry/five_accelerators_of_equitable_grantmaking_and_how_to_harness_them.

Acknowledgements

I AM GRATEFUL to everyone who made this book possible, starting with the team at Wiley. I was lucky to get to work with Brian Neill, Kezia Endsley, Gabriela Mancuso, Debbie Schindlar, Christina Verigan, Philo Antonie, and Ashley Edwards. Brian, thank you for convincing me to write this book and for your patience as I sent you emails with ridiculous ideas throughout the writing process. Kezia, your editorial skills and diplomacy kept me on track and kept this book below three billion words. Gabriela, Debbie, Christina, Philo, and Ashley, thank you for all your support around cover design, copyediting, marketing, indexing, production, bulks sales, and all the things I don't see but know are important.

I am deeply appreciative of my family. Marquita Prinzing, the best co-parent anyone could ask for, who was pivotal especially during times when I faced deadlines. My babies Việt and Kiệt, your hilarious antics and witty comments kept my spirit up and reminded me why the work of this sector is so important. My mom, Liên Ngô; dad Lợi Lê; siblings, Mai, Bảo, and Linda; and nieces, Lina and Laura, I'm grateful for your encouragement, even when you had no idea what I do, and you still don't. Martha Prinzing, Marquis Jenkins, and Rashad Jenkins, thank you for taking care of the kids on some weekends to give me time to write.

256 Acknowledgements

This is where it gets tricky, as I think about all my friends and colleagues who provided morale support, reality checks, quotes, resources, and dark chocolate, which were all pivotal to this project. There are so many amazing people, and I'm afraid that with my absentmindedness, I will miss some names. If that happens, please forgive me. Stacy Nguyễn, you've been a rock for me and nonprofitAF.com throughout the past decade or so, even if you yell at me, like, a lot. Ananda Valenzuela, I learn so much from you, not just about this work but also about living a more authentic and joyful life. Ben Reuler, Amy Liu, and James Lovell, hanging out with you helped keep me from going over the edge during some rough days. Mỹ-Nga Lê, you brought food all the time and helped me plant hundreds of bulbs, which this year were an especially helpful symbol of hope and persistence. Mari Kim, thank you for the encouragement and chocolates and wild ideas. Kevin Dean, you inspire me with how you show up even when things are hard. Erica Barnhart, I appreciate our lunch and conversations about sometimes very tough topics. Pia Infante and Vini Bhansali, you are hilarious and unapologetically yourselves, which allows me to do the same. Mỹ Tâm Nguyễn, for some reason you always show up in a car while I'm walking along the road, one time giving me half the food you got from a temple; you remind me what community looks like. Judy Pigott, I love our deep, thought-provoking conversations and jokes. Seth Ehrlich, thank you for always checking in on me all the time. Steve Pearson, thanks for checking in and for inviting me to visit, which I promise to do one day. Rashad Morris, I'm grateful for our laughter and deep conversations. Byron Au Yong, for constantly reminding me of the power of art and music. Vanessa Lebourdais, your hilarious adventures never fail to perk me up when I'm down. Tree Willard, I love our irreverent conversations and laughter. Julie Pham, you remind me to always be curious and always move forward. Glenda Pacha, the dad jokes you email regularly keep me from losing it. Vi Nguyễn, Kris Archie, Alejandra Lopez Bravo, and Eugene Kung, my crew from Vancouver BC, thank you for always being so welcoming when I need an escape from the United States.

To everyone I quoted or whose work I referenced in this book, who are too numerous to name here (my apologies), thank you for bringing so much of your brilliance. I hope I was able to capture at least a fraction of your vital work.

And to all the readers of my blog and all my Patreon supporters, my sincerest gratitude for sticking by me and my ramblings and antics, especially over the past couple of very challenging years. Your dedication to making our world better and your spirit, joyfulness, and sense of humor keep me going.

About the Author

Vu Le (pronounced "voo lay") is a writer, speaker, and former nonprofit executive director known for his incisive and humorous take on nonprofit and philanthropy. Through his blog NonprofitAF.com, he tackles issues of funding dynamics, fundraising, equity, and the importance of the Oxford comma. Vu is the former Executive Director of RVC, a nonprofit in Seattle that promotes social justice by developing leaders of color, strengthening organizations led by communities of color, and fostering collaboration among diverse communities. His passion to make the world better, combined with a low score on the Law School Admission Test, drove him into the field of nonprofit work, where he learned that we should take the work seriously, but not ourselves. He is a founder of the Community-Centric Fundraising movement and Crappy Funding Practices. He received the inaugural Pablo Eisenberg Memorial Prize for Philanthropy Criticism by the National Committee for Responsive Philanthropy and was recognized as of the Nonprofit Times Power and Influence Top 50 in 2019. When he's not speaking, writing, and vexing people in power, he spends time in Seattle with his two kids, Viet and Kiet.

Index

A
Abichandani, Dimple, 152
Abundance, 34, 88
Accountability, 74, 79, 116, 139, 196–197, 211
Achebe, Chinua, 135
ACLU, 113, 130
Advice process, 95
Affordable Care Act, 13
Against Empathy (Bloom), 49
Agents of justice, 52, 60, 194–195
Alicdan, Raul, 95
Alinksy, Saul, 122
Alternative structures, 98, 105, 115–116, 182
Alvarez, Aubrey, 229
Amerasian Homecoming Act, 206
American Alliance for Equal Rights (AAER), 207
American Enterprise Institute, 143, 148
AmeriCorps, 3, 158

Anti-Blackness, 178, 211
Anti-discrimination statements, 178
Apartheid, 192
Arenas, Andrea, 37, 55
Art of Transformational Consulting (ATC) training, 222–223
Asian Pacific Environmental Network, 89
Assumption of generalizability, 196
Asymmetric requirement of gratitude (ARG), 161
Audacity of ambition, 40–41
Audits, 163, 178, 237

B
Bakke, Dennis W., 95
Banks, Jasmine, 131
Barnhart, Erica, 175
Barrett, Amy Coney, 143, 146
Barron, Deborah, 114
Bhansali, Rajasvini, 149

Biases, 18, 162–163, 168, 170–171, 178, 180, 196, 200, 214, 226
Bizsplaining, 16–17, 36
Black Future Co-op Fund (BFCF), 138
Black Lives Matter, 65
Black Panthers, 197–198
The Blaze, 144
Bloom, Paul, 49
Bloomberg, Michael, 149
Board diversity, 71–72
Board engagement, 65
Board giving, 72
Board leads, 75
Boards, 67–72. *See also* Governance
Boeing, 170
Boody, Isabeau, 202
Bradley Foundation, 146
Breitbart News, 144, 151
brown, adrienne maree, 42
Brown, Michael Jr., 54
Bui doi, 101
Building Movement Project, 84, 92
Burnout, 109, 174–175, 184

C
Calibration, 80
Caminar Latino, 90–91
Candid, 139
Capacity builders, 102–103
Capacity building irony, 102–106
Capacity-building strategies, 5, 103–107, 110–115, 117, 218
Carmona, Leslie, 55
Carney, Allison, 17
Cato Institute, 143, 148
Center for American Progress (CAP), 148

Center for Cultural Innovation (CCI), 149–150
Center for Effective Philanthropy, 36
Change Elemental, 77–78
Charismatic leaders, 86
Charles Koch Foundation, 146
Charters, 155
Chauvin, Derek, 27
Check in process, 80, 154, 178
Check out process, 80
Check points, 80
Chen, Erika, 55
Chen, Jondou Chase, 192, 197
Choose 180, 180–181
Chrissplains Nonbinary Advocacy to Cisgender People series, 216
Circle process, 78–79
Citizens United, 127, 146
Civil Rights Act, 13, 127
Claremont Institute, 144, 148
Clark, Robert Sterling, 154
Clean Air Act, 13
Clean Water Act, 13
Clyne, Sarah, 107
CNN, 151
Co-directorships, 89–90
Coates, Ta-Nehisi Paul, 150
Collective communities, 56, 234
Collins, Jim, 127
Color-blind mindset, 208
Common Future, 184
Community-alliance model, 108–110
Community boards, 63–64, 75–77
Community-Centric Fundraising (CCF), 37, 55–59, 114, 216, 233–238

Community-Centric Fundraising Global Council, 54
Community Partners, 110
CompassPoint, 59, 109
Compensation, 72, 111, 174, 178, 180–181, 209, 236
Concentration of influence, 31
Confederated Salish and Kootenai Tribes, 139
Copeland, Robert, 63
#CopsOffCampus, 131
Copy City, 149
Coral, Racquel, 165
Courageous conversations, 226
Covington, Sally, 105, 140–141, 143, 153
Crappy Funding Practices (CFP), 227
Creating the Future, 32, 38, 115
Criminal justice system, 149, 167–168
Cultural fit, 164, 187
Cultural narratives, 144, 146, 151
Curb-Cut Effect, 201–202

D
The Daily Caller, 144
The Daily Wire, 144
Daniel, Vanessa, 137
Dark money, 145–146
Data disaggregation, 194, 214
Dean, Kevin, 121, 186
Decision-making models, 74–75, 79, 95–96
Decolonizing Wealth (Villanueva), 138
Delusion of validity, 196
Democracy Forward, 191
Democracy vouchers, 132–133
Dental hygiene model, 217–218

Detroit Justice Center (DJC), 53
Digital natives, 180
Disability justice, 122, 125. *See also* Justice
Distributed Leadership, 92–93, 95–96
Diversity, Equity, and Inclusion (DEI), 22, 52, 144, 177–178, 199, 205–219
Donor circles, 140
#DonorLove, 50
DonorsTrust, 146
DreamRider Productions, 77
D'Souza, Rachel, 54
Due diligence, 33–34, 190
Duncan, Aja Couchois, 88
Dunning-Kruger effect, 35
Durfee Foundation, 182–183
Dust of life, 101

E
East African Community Services (EACS), 83–84
Effectiveness, 3, 34, 137, 198–201
Empathy, 3, 48–50, 60, 77
Enlightened self-interest, 57, 237
Enspiral, 75
EquaSpace, 107
Equitable hiring practices, 164–170
Equity-based compensation, 180–181
Equity mindset, 212–215, 218
Equity offset, 209, 215, 218
Evaluators, 194–195, 197
Evolutionary governance, 77

F
Fair Labor Standards Act, 183
Fakequity, 208, 218

Fascist Extremist Assholes' Reign (FEAR), 18
Fearless Fund, 207
Federalist Society, 143, 146–148
First Mile Circle, 114, 147
Fiscal sponsorship, 63, 104–105, 108, 110–111, 116
501 Commons, 17
501(c) organizations, 108, 113
501(c)(3) organizations, 113–114, 121, 130, 134, 140, 147
501(c)(4) organizations, 114, 121–125, 134, 147, 153
Fix Democracy First, 132
Flathead Reservation Native Americans in Philanthropy, 139
Florida Rights Restoration Coalition, 149
Floyd, George, 27, 40, 54, 59, 208
Formerly incarcerated people, 149, 167–168
Forward Through Ferguson (FTF), 54
Four-day workweek (4DW), 183–185, 187
Fox News, 125–126, 144, 151
Free markets, 30, 143, 145
Freedom Together Foundation, 152
Freeman, Jo, 93
Fund the People's Talent Justice Report, 181

G
Gap-gazing, 194
Gass, Robert, 222
Generation Progress, 150
GETTR, 144
GLADD, 130
Gladiator Consulting, 54

Golden handcuffs, 37
Good to Great (Collins), 127
Goode, Sean, 180
Gorsuch, Neal, 143, 146
Gottlieb, Hildy, 32, 39, 115
Governance, 66–67, 71, 74–75, 77–79. *See also* Boards
Gramsci, Antonio, 22
Granovetter, Mark, 226
Gratitude, 46, 50, 159–161, 170
Greenleaf, Robert, 86
Gutierrez, Rochelle, 194

H
Haas Jr. Fund, 59
Haeri, Medina, 230
Hannah-Jones, Nikole, 150
Hare, Carly, 139
Harris, C. Nathan, 47
Headwaters Foundation, 139
Hedgehog concept, 127, 129
Heritage Foundation, 125, 143–144, 148
Heroic leaders, 86
Herrera, Jaqueline, 91
Hitler, Adolph, 216
Hong, James, 47, 55, 65
Hoover Institution, 148
Hose-to-water ratio, 14–15
Howard Gilman Foundation, 141
Huerta, Dolores, 119

I
Ignite NPS, 67
Illusion of objectivity, 196, 199
Impact Grant Program, 104
Implicit bias, 163, 171. *See also* Biases
Imposter syndrome, 236

Incrementalism, 31–32, 38–39, 41, 240
Independent Sector, 120
Individual missions, 56, 88, 159, 234
Infante, Pia, 140
Inferiority complex, 18, 36–37
Informal networks, 115–116
Inner wellbeing, 113
Institut für Sexualwissenschaft, 216
Institute for Policy Studies (IPS), 148
International nongovernmental organizations (INGOs), 101
Internet Society Foundation, 227
Intrinsic values, 191, 201–202

J
Johns Hopkins Center for Civil Society Studies, 13
Johnson, Yodit Mesfin, 79
Joy at Work (Bakke), 95
Judicial Watch, 148
Juicero, 40–41
JustFund Common Application, 154
Justice, 20, 28, 30, 39–41, 45, 48–53, 60, 67–69, 87–88, 122, 189–203

K
Kaepernick, Colin, 228
Kandelia, see Vietnamese Friendship Association (VFA)
Kang, Erin, 74
Kanter, Beth, 174
Kavanaugh, Brett, 143, 146
Kegan, Robert, 224
Kenneth Rainin Foundation, 104
Keynes, John Maynard, 183
Kim, Angie, 149–150
King, Martin Luther Jr., 27, 28, 211

Koch brothers, 130–131
Ktisis Capital, 132

L
Lahey, Lisa, 224
Laloux, Frederic, 95
Law Enforcement Epidemiology Project, 27–28
Leaderful sectors, 87–88
Leadership Institute, 148
Learned helplessness, 65, 120, 133, 181
LeBourdais, Vanessa, 77
Leo, Leonard, 146–147
LGBTQIA+ community, 48, 129–130, 158, 179, 193, 213
Liberation, 215–217, 219, 238
Liberatory governance, 77–78
Limbaugh, Rush, 144
Limited liability corporations (LLCs), 105, 113, 116, 140, 155
Linking, 79
Living Justice Press (LJP), 78
Lobbying, 39, 113, 120–122, 133, 148–149
Long, Nancy, 17
Lopez, Ana Rebecca, 55
Lord of the Rings (Tolkien), 19–20, 73
Lorde, Audre, 205
Lovell, James, 147, 209
Loving accountability, 69–70

M
Madan, Pragya, 181
Mankiller, Wilma, 221
Martyrdom, 34
Masaoka, Jan, 122

Maslach, Christina, 195
Mental Health, 11, 27, 55, 107, 130, 167, 185–186
Mercer Family Foundation, 146
Meritocracy-based mindset, 208
Meyer Foundation, 109
Microaggressions, 178
Milwaukee Evaluation, 197
Mindful meetings, 80
Minimally viable boards (MVBs), 75, 76
Minnesota Council of Nonprofits, 185
Misra, Susan, 88
Mission Creep, 127–129
Moen, Patricia, 91
Mondros, Jacqueline B., 122
Money mobilization, 140
Mont, Simon, 94
Montana Nonprofit Association, 184
Morales, Michelle, 152
Multi-entity structures, 113–114, 117, 134
Multi-year general operating dollars (MYGOD), 15, 105, 113, 153, 222
Multicultural potlucks, 208, 215
Muñoz-Howard, Estevan, 132–133
Muri, Michelle, 55
Muse and Recruitment Marketing, 163
Musk, Elon, 126
Mussolini, Benito, 22
Mutual aid networks, 140, 155
Mutual support, 54, 56, 60, 68, 107, 109, 234
Mycelium, 102–103

N
National American Woman Suffrage Association (NAWSA), 228
National Bail Out, 40
National Committee for Responsive Committee, 140
National Council of Nonprofits, 191
National Network of Fiscal Sponsors, 110
Neoliberalism, 30–31, 38, 40, 151, 197
Neurodiversity, 179–180, 215
Never Too Late (NTL), 75
New Era for Philanthropy (Abichandani), 152
New Hampshire Supreme Court, 131
New Left Accelerator (NLA), 114
The New York Times, 137, 151
Nin, Anaïs, 214
Nishimura, April, 112
Njuguna, Jennifer, 184
NNR Evaluation, Planning & Research LLC, 197
Nonprofit Enterprise at Work (NEW), 79
Nonprofit Hunger Games, 4, 46, 112, 159, 200
Nonprofit Power report, 129
Nonprofit rut, 26–27, 32
Nonprofit VOTE, 129
Nonprofit workers' unions, 185
Notaro, Heidi, 90–91

O
Oak Foundation, 230
Obama, Michelle, 157
Okuno, Erin, 208
The Onion, 34, 151

Ontario Nonprofit Network, 67, 74
Oregon Food Bank (OFB), 47–48
Organizing for Power and Empowerment (Mondros and Wilson), 122
O'Rourke, Beto, 210
Outsider efficacy bias, 226. *See also* Biases

P
Pan, Vincent, 88
Paris Climate Accord, 13
Parker, Nancy A., 53
Parler, 144
Paul, Alice, 228
Pay ratios, 182
PEAK Grantmaking, 154
PEN Pinter Prize, 21–22
Pencil test, 192
Personal integrity paradox, 35
Philanthropic Initiative for Racial Equity (PRE), 138
Pinocchio, 104–105
Planned Parenthood, 113
Plaque and sack technique, 66
Pocket Manual of Rules of Order for Deliberative Assemblies (Robert), 72
Political action committees (PACs), 113, 125, 134, 147, 155. *See also* Super PACs
Power dynamics, 77, 92, 93, 210, 213
Power generation, 112
Power imbalance, 44, 85–86, 210, 213
PragerU, 144
Pragya Madan Coaching & Consulting LLC, 181

Pride in scarcity and sacrifice (PISS), 34
Privatization, 30
Privilege, 46, 49, 68, 122, 167, 178, 210, 214, 218, 229–231
Professionalism, 161–162, 177, 187
Professor Watchlist, 144
Progress Alliance of Washington, 113–114
Progress Alliance (PA) of Washington, 147
Progressive Theory of Change, 125–127
Project 2025, 143
Project Streamline, 154
Proxies, 151–162, 167, 200

Q
Quorum, 121

R
Racial bias, 163, 168, 178. *See also* Biases
Radical candor, 226
Rainier Valley Corps, *see* Rooted in Vibrant Communities (RVC)
Rao, Venkatesh, 22
Reagan, Ronald, 143
Reimagining Governance, 67, 74
Reinventing Organizations (Laloux), 95
Religious beliefs, 179, 222
Religious organizations, 116–117, 155
Retailification of nonprofit work, 45
Return on investments (ROI), 31
Reuler, Ben, 40, 59
Righteous anger, 5, 20–21
Risk aversion, 31–32, 197

Robert, Henry Martyn, 72–73
Robert Sterling Clark Foundation (RSCF), 135–136
Robert's Rules of Order, 65–66, 73, 80
Robinson, Nicole, 197
Roosevelt, Franklin D., 183
Rooted in Vibrant Communities (RVC), 5, 63, 76, 83, 93–98, 110–113, 135, 148, 192
Roy, Arundhati, 9, 21, 231
Rule of One-Thirds, 65
Rules for Radicals (Alinsky), 122

S
S-Corps, 113
Sabbaticals, 98, 113, 182–183, 187
Sampath, Roshni, 98, 112
Sanderson, Andrea Caupain, 138
Scaife Foundation, 146
Scalia, Antonin, 143
Scarcity, 34, 88, 152–153, 181
Schure, Aviva Zukerman, 75
Scott, Mackenzie, 53
Seattle City Council, 132
Seattle Ethics and Elections Commission (SEEC), 132
Seattle Works, 40, 59
Seid, Barre, 146
Self-interest, 37–38, 40, 57, 237
Servant leaders, 86
Shared spaces, 106–107
Sharma, Regina M., 53
Sheikh, Anbar Mahar, 112
Sherman, Aliza, 174
Shimizu, Christina, 55
Shiny object syndrome, 137

Short-term metrics, 142, 200
Sierra Club, 113
Smith, James. A., 140
Smith, Linda Tuhiwai, 189
Smooth, Jay, 217
Snowflake application, 137
Social Impact Commons, 116
Social justice, 56, 68, 78, 131, 155, 186, 197–198, 208, 210–212, 218, 233, 240. *See also* Justice
Social Justice Fund, 49
Social Transformation Project, 222
Sociocracy, 73, 79
SociocracyForAll.org, 79
Sohn, Heidi Schillinger, 208
Solidaire Network, 149
Southern Poverty Law Center, 185
Spin offs, 105, 110
Squire, Thaddeus, 115–116
SSIR, 140
Stanford Social Innovation Review, 87, 112, 162
Star Trek model, 108–110
State of Government Affairs Survey, 121
Stone, Lisa M., 160
Strategic philanthropy, 105, 140, 142–145
Super PACs, 145, 147. *See also* Political action committees (PACs)
Susan B. Anthony Pro-Life America, 145
Sustainability, 15–16, 70, 91
Sustainable Economy Law Center (SELC), 93–94
Swell Collective, 80

Synergistic paradigm action matrix (SPAM), 16
Systemic change, 31
Systemic issues, 31, 37, 109
Systems change, 112, 121, 124

T
Talbot, Chris, 216
Talent Hunger Games, 159
Talking pieces, 78
Tax codes, 52, 145
Tax Me Now, 52
Taylor, Sonya Renee, 173
Tendency for simplification, 196
Tennessee Nonprofit Network, 121, 186
Thomas, Clarence, 143
Tides, 110
Tolkien, J.R.R., 19k
Toxic Intellectualizing, 32–34, 38, 40, 106, 142, 190–192, 201, 203
Toxic productivity, 175–176
Trans people, 22, 123, 144, 211, 216–217, 229
Trinh, Vivien, 47
Trump, Donald, 18, 87, 103, 107, 121, 146, 191, 201, 206, 208
Trust-based philanthropy, 139–140, 155
Trusted Advisory Council, 75
Truth Social, 144
TSNE, 110
Turning Point USA, 144, 148, 150
Tutu, Desmond, 20
Twitter, 126, 144, 165
Tyranny of structurelessness, 93

U
Unconscious agendas, 225
Unconscious bias, 162–163, 170, 178. *See also* Biases
Undocumented people, 202
United States Supreme Court, 70, 124, 127, 143, 145–147
UnKoch My Campus, 130–132
Unpaid work, 166
(un)Redact The Facts, 211
Unrig the Game (Daniel), 137
USAID, 19
USDA, 19

V
Valenzuela, Ananda, 69, 85, 92, 95–96, 98, 112
Values misalignment, 71
Vietnamese Friendship Association (VFA), 3, 5, 9–10, 72, 110, 147
Vietnamese Rainbow of Orange County (VROC), 129–130
Villanueva, Edgar, 138
Villarosa, Lori, 138
Voting rights, 126–128, 145, 149, 207
Voting Rights Act, 13

W
Waifs of War (WOW), 101
Wala, Rehana Lane, 55
Washington Examiner, 144
The Washington Post, 151
Washington Public Campaigns, 132
Watts, Sean, 55
Weaponized data, 192–194

Westminster City Council, 130
Wheel of Change
    framework, 222–223
White moderation, 6, 28–30, 38, 40, 77, 106, 131, 211
White moderation checklist, 239–241
White standards, 197
White supremacy, 6, 19, 22, 30, 45, 51, 54, 60, 68, 77, 209, 211, 215, 217, 239
whiters, k. kennedy, 211
Wilson, Scott M., 122
Wokeness, 144, 207
Wong, Alice, 162
Woods Fund Chicago
    (WFC), 152–153
Work/life balance, 183
Worker self-directed nonprofits
    (WSDNs), 92–94
Workers' Self-Directed Nonprofit
    model I, 184

Y

Year of the Tiger (Wong), 162
Yeats, W. B., 25, 35
YouTube, 144, 150